Praise for *Diamonds, Deals, and Divine Guidance*:

"Bobby's interlacing journey through baseball, the business world, and his growing religiosity is a captivating read for all audiences. With marvelous fluidity and abundant use of metaphors, he draws parallels and unearths keen insights from life's abrupt low moments. In relatable, everyday words, Bobby's story offers inspiring examples of our need to contextualize setbacks, maintain hope amid adversity, and search for a lodestar to allow ourselves to persevere when despair seems more apt. I felt heartened by Bobby's beautiful personal account—as will all who read it—to draw from it in times we may otherwise feel resigned. I hope being guided by Bobby's seven precepts will bring me the peace that penning these reflections undoubtedly brought him."

—**Neeraj Mital**, Senior Managing Director at Evercore Partners

"Sports, the business world, and spiritual matters relate to each other, and *Diamonds, Deals, and Divine Guidance* showcases these connections through the true story of one man's journey. From seeking worldly approval to discovering life's true purpose, Bobby's story is compelling. Despite self-imposed inadequacies, he achieved success and found a deeper desire to meaningfully impact the lives of others. Seven principles, derived from his experiences, are now available to you and offer a powerful framework for influence. With humor and insight, numerous examples illustrate how trust in God, rather than in his own abilities, broke the self-doubt and fear that once held him captive. Dive into this must-read for inspiration and practical wisdom."

—**Joyce L. Campbell**, National Board Certified, Licensed Professional Counselor and Author of *Dare to Say No: Stop Saying Yes When You Really Mean No*

"*Diamonds, Deals, and Divine Guidance* is an enlightening journey where the realms of sports, careers, and spirituality intertwine seamlessly. In this captivating narrative, Bobby Kocol invites you into his world, divulging the highs and lows of his personal voyage. With a growing faith as his compass, he imparts invaluable insights, knowledge, and wisdom gleaned from every challenge and triumph. Brace yourself for a transformative experience that promises to leave an indelible mark on you—one that will I.M.P.A.C.T your endeavors and the essence of your existence."

—**Michael McLay**, Vice-President of Worldwide Sales at Storage Technology

"When Bobby Kocol played college baseball, it was obvious to me that he had an extra gear—a persistence and drive few athletes possess. His determination on the field laid the foundation for his success beyond the diamond. His book, *Diamonds, Deals, and Divine Guidance*, encouraged my faith and revealed how persistence, strength of character, and a resilient faith can take us on a journey beyond our dreams. This book will challenge, encourage, and inspire readers through Bobby's story and the biblical principles he grasps so very well."

—**Keith Madison**, Head Baseball Coach at the University of Kentucky and American Baseball Coaches Association Hall of Famer

"Bobby touches all the bases with his transparent 'put it all out there' journey through his life, encompassing family, personal, and professional aspects with clarity and depth. He scores the winning run with his spiritual insight and invaluable advice on how to handle life's inevitable peaks and valleys. Reading this inspiring and practical toolkit will leave you fulfilled and empowered for eternal success."

—**Scott Galloway**, Executive Managing Director, JLL Capital Markets, and College World Series teammate

"Transforming a company's culture proves challenging, particularly when strategic goals remain more aspirational than achievable. As my partner, Bobby was instrumental in steering that change, and his story is one of exceptional leadership."

—**Pat Martin**, Former Chief Executive Officer

"Bobby invites the reader to learn how to grow under the weight of the 'dawgpile,' to find purpose and divine guidance when life is difficult. He does a tremendous job of providing guidance on how to find hope in the disappointments of life, how to experience joy when life 'pitches' you curve balls, and how to navigate the 'slumps' of life. This book offers some incredible and practical answers and is a great resource for group studies. I highly recommend reading this book; you will find yourself swept up in the amazing personal and interesting stories that Bobby shares."

—**Bill Orsborn**, Senior Minister at Mountainview Christian Church

"This book grabbed me right from the start and didn't let go. Its thought-provoking message will challenge anyone who reads it, offering a compelling set of values to live by, irrespective of one's profession or beliefs."

—**Ernie Rosseau**, National Junior College Baseball Hall of Fame inductee

DIAMONDS, DEALS, AND DIVINE GUIDANCE

Diamonds, Deals, and Divine Guidance

Discovering Peace and Purpose
through Lasting Impacts

BOBBY KOCOL

LUMINARE PRESS
WWW.LUMINAREPRESS.COM

DIAMONDS, DEALS, AND DIVINE GUIDANCE:
Discovering Peace and Purpose through Lasting Impacts
Copyright © 2024 by Bobby Kocol

Some names have been changed to protect the privacy of individuals.

Scripture references are quoted from the New International Version (NIV) unless noted otherwise.

All rights reserved. This book or any portion thereof may not be reproduced or used in any manner whatsoever without the express written permission of the publisher, except for the use of brief quotations in a book review.

Printed in the United States of America

Luminare Press
442 Charnelton St.
Eugene, OR 97401
www.luminarepress.com

LCCN: 2024903398
ISBN: 979-8-88679-501-1

*To my wife, Lindy, the love of my life and my best friend.
You have been with me through every twist and turn—
as my pillar of strength and source of inspiration.*

Contents

Foreword | xi

THE JOURNEY

1. Bottom of the "Dawgpile" | 5
2. Another Day, Another At-Bat | 27
3. Looking for Signs | 43
4. Turning Points | 65

THE I.M.P.A.C.T.S.

5. **I**dentification—Determine Who You Are | 89
6. **M**otivation—What Moves You? | 107
7. **P**reparation—Master the Fundamentals | 123
8. **A**ccountability—Measure and Own It | 139
9. **C**ompassion—Be There When Needed | 157
10. **T**rust—Use Your Instincts | 177
11. **S**peech – Speak Softly and Embrace Silence | 197

THE FINISH

12. Influencing and Encouraging Others | 219
13. The Finish Line | 233

Acknowledgments | 249
About the Author | 251
Endnotes | 253

Foreword

My encounter with *Diamonds, Deals, and Divine Guidance* was truly an honor and a transformative experience. It has guided me through a journey filled with valuable lessons and profound reflections that have touched every aspect of my soul. Whether you are an athlete who thrives on competition, a businessperson closing deals, a devout believer praying in silence, or a dedicated parent and spouse, this book has something to offer you.

As I turned each page, I found myself walking alongside Bobby on an extraordinary path. This path is not just about reaching the pinnacle of success; it's about stumbling, falling, and rising again. This book is more than just a collection of words on paper—it is a mirror that reflects what it truly means to be human, especially for me as a man.

Reflecting on my own life—changing experiences as an athlete, struggles as a business owner, personal tragedies, and battles with faith—I have found this book to be a guiding light for those in search of help and direction. It teaches us how to find blessings in our struggles through the power of vulnerability and faith.

While there are many impactful quotes, chapters, and lessons in this book, the most important takeaway for me is the reassuring whisper that echoes through every page: You are not alone. Feelings of inadequacy and exhaustion may make you feel isolated, as if you are the only one carrying burdens too heavy to bear. However, this book reminds us that the shared nature of our struggles is a vital step toward finding the strength to move forward.

Understanding that others have grappled with self-doubt, defeat, and a lack of motivation serves as a powerful reminder that you are not a lone warrior. In this connection lies a wellspring of empathy, support, and inspiration. *Diamonds, Deals, and Divine Guidance* will help you find solace in your vulnerabilities and realize that perseverance, no matter how small, is a universal human endeavor.

This book can light a flicker of hope in the darkness, reminding you that with faith, you can find the strength and peace you seek. It is a reminder that you are not alone on this journey and that there is always a source of support and inspiration to guide you through even the toughest times.

—Joshua Vickers, D.C.

I feel like I'm living out a purpose that was set for me.
I can't control the hand I was dealt. Every day you wake up
is a gift. Make it impactful. Pour into others just like
they have poured into you.

—Justin Carpenter, my son-in-law, three-and-a-half years
after being diagnosed with ALS.

Many are the plans in a person's heart,
but it is the Lord's purpose that prevails.

—Proverbs 19:21

THE JOURNEY

Bottom of the "Dawgpile"

*A life is not important except in the impact
it has on other lives.*

—Jackie Robinson

Who decides if you are good enough? And when is good enough ever good enough?

If the questions above capture your attention, chances are you have felt unsure of yourself recently or at some other time in the past. Take comfort in knowing you are not alone. Everyone experiences uncertainty and doubt during their lifetime.

I had reason to believe I was destined for success. An accomplished Division I collegiate athlete. A National Collegiate Athletic Association (NCAA) Academic All-American. A corporate executive of a multibillion-dollar company. Access to global banks, investment firms, and Fortune 500 leaders. Those following me deemed me successful.

I didn't share the same view, however, since my goals were plagued with failures. I was trapped beneath the crushing weight of self-doubt, and with each setback, haunting questions beleaguered me.

Resiliency became my battle cry. I was certain my efforts and stubborn attitude would win, eliminating any lack of confidence.

However, my internal conflicts persisted for decades. The disappointments, heart-wrenching events, shortfalls, and shattered dreams kept the self-doubts alive.

I fought the battle of uncertainty, unsure of the reasons that were driving me and doubtful I could reach established goals. I felt determined but needed a compass to navigate these stormy waters. I appeared successful in the eyes of many—teammates, classmates, friends, colleagues, and spiritual people. But I struggled to validate this belief in my mind until I understood the lasting impacts of specific values and the importance of using them to serve and influence others.

These learned values taught me to appreciate the race I was running and propelled me to the finish line I longed to reach. Even better, they equipped me with the tools I needed to help others do the same. These principles helped me determine the parameters of what is good enough and the true meaning of winning. They can empower you to succeed in a similar way if you practice and make them part of your life.

June 1979

Lingering questions accompanied a robotic pace. My eyes widened, the dark browns locking in on two devices: a clock on the wall, with its precise ticks coming every two steps, and a deskbound phone that, in silence, spoke volumes. A dial tone confirmed that the phone worked. Minutes later, another sound check. A loud clank echoed a growing angst. The cadence of my steps accelerated, and if the linoleum floor had been carpeted, it surely would have been rutted by now. Anxious and annoyed, I waited for breaking news connected to my past and tied to my future.

The phone should have rung by now.

Armed with a college degree, I had returned home. Time for celebration and personal reflection had been placed on the back burner, replaced with tension that permeated the living room where family and friends gathered—all with hopeful expectations of good news to come.

A musty hallway led to a closet-sized bedroom once shared by four boys. At its entrance hung a picture of the youngest. Wearing baggy baseball pants and an oversized hat, the young toddler posed beside his brothers, twirling a big-barreled Wiffle ball bat with molded hand grips. The three-year-old boy was me. I grew up in this house, where *it* all started.

The *it* was a passion for baseball that had started early and deepened every year as I progressed from Little League to the more competitive Babe Ruth leagues and then into high school and college. When I couldn't find other kids for pickup games, I would create a way to mimic game time alone—bouncing a scuffed ball off the outside house walls peppered with dirt rings and running around makeshift base paths simulating doubles and triples. A daily allotment of swings, blasting fallen palm-tree acorns off the rooftops across the street, helped develop hand-eye coordination. I would swing until dusk, only stopping when my mother shouted "Enough!" or if I rattled one off the neighbor's window, fearing it broken.

An assortment of family pictures cluttered the walls. My Farrah Fawcett swimsuit poster didn't make the cut. Mom allowed it for a few years but never liked it. The photos stirred memories of living in the shadows of my three brothers, all successful in sports into their early collegiate years. It's no wonder the boys' practices and games dictated our family activities.

The only attention my sister received came when she got a bedroom to herself, a reward for putting up with all our shenanigans. I'm glad she did, despite the cramped one-hundred-square-foot bedroom we boys had to squeeze into, which included my penthouse view from the top of a bunk bed. With no air-conditioning, we wore the humidity. Our only reprieve came when our dad allowed us to open the unscreened windows when mosquitos were dormant.

Our parents treated us well, though we had little. Dad coached my older brothers until their baseball days ended, which limited his involvement with me throughout my athletic development. My father rarely engaged in direct discussions of competition between my brothers and me. But his frequent innuendos like "you didn't have three doubles like your brother today" stoked the ashes.

Whether this contributed to any perfectionistic tendencies remains a mystery, though it seems likely. I started setting lofty standards early in my life, looking for people I deemed successful, comparing myself with and trying to emulate them, attempting to be who others thought I should be rather than making the determination myself. Indiscreetly, I played the role of an impostor.

A snapshot of our family having dinner with legendary Detroit Tiger pitcher Mickey Lolich brought back memories of his inspiring story. He was born right-handed but learned to throw left-handed after a childhood accident. At age two, he rode his tricycle into a parked motorcycle that fell on him. He broke his left collarbone and wore a cast for four months. Rehabilitation efforts strengthened his left arm and helped him develop into a left-handed thrower.[1]

He didn't look like a sculpted athlete but was portly like my father. His trademark was playing the game with passion and heart. A few years later, he earned the Most Valuable Player award in the 1968 World Series, pitching and winning three complete games against the highly favored St. Louis Cardinals.

The Detroit News stated, "Lolich could always be counted on to finish what he started."[2] A good line for a baseball player, and a great attribute to embrace regardless of life's direction.

There was no better way to get my juices flowing than to listen to a big leaguer talk about playing in the major leagues. His ability to switch pitching arms convinced me to expand my horizons about what was achievable in baseball. It hooked me early and inspired me to work hard, to be the first on the field and the last to leave, to not stop until I was finished—traits I've carried with me to this day.

By the time I graduated from high school, my siblings had moved on. Baseball was all I cared about at that time, and by then I looked the part too. Callused hands from innumerable swings of the bat. Increased arm strength through never-ending heaves from the warning track to home plate. Broadened shoulders from incessant weightlifting. Success at every level and awards received year after year.

I wasn't great at any of the five tools scouts evaluate when looking at prospects (hitting for average, hitting for power, great speed, excellent fielding, and significant arm strength), but I was good enough in all of them to turn some heads. The stars had aligned for something unique. It seemed all the arduous work would pay off.

I left the room thinking dreams do come true.

Still, no phone call.

MY NAME CROSSED THE WIRES IN THE MAJOR LEAGUE BASEBALL draft two years earlier. It seemed bizarre then that the Chicago White Sox had selected me a third time. The local newspaper made a big deal that I had already turned them down twice, rejecting a decent chunk of change for a fourth-round pick—more than half of my father's annual salary. It didn't compare to what my high school friend and summer league all-star teammate Clint Hurdle fetched from the Kansas City Royals six months earlier in the 1976 summer baseball draft.

Then again, I wasn't a six-foot-three-inch quarterback, baseball phenom, or *Sports Illustrated* cover boy. But the money was enough and could have helped a blue-collar family like ours should a need arise—like paying for a college education if my baseball career ended prematurely.

The *Florida Today* headline read, "White Sox Persist in Trying to Sign Titan Centerfielder."[3] Why would they do so and for a third time? They must have seen something I didn't see in myself.

After all, what athlete wouldn't want to sign a professional baseball contract? What father wouldn't want the chance to live his unfulfilled dreams vicariously through his child? Especially a kid with so much promise?

Turning pro at that time seemed logical to those who knew me and followed my success. But I held onto a different view, and so the contract went unsigned. In the earlier drafts, I had convinced myself of my unreadiness, that I wasn't good enough to play professional baseball. There were too many others with better skills and greater potential. My inner thoughts kept telling me I couldn't compete professionally, that I was out of my league. If I couldn't believe in myself, it's no wonder I couldn't take this big step.

The question remained: Why not sign a professional baseball contract? I carried the label of a star athlete who was physically strong, formidable to opponents, and with a great baseball IQ. Yet something kept holding me back. It had nothing to do with baseball or money and everything to do with me. The exact cause loomed unknown. And if I couldn't figure it out, when would I?

Mentally, I lived in a place where thoughts of inadequacy surrounded me. I was self-doubting and risk-averse, always hesitant to take on a new challenge because the fear of failing painted a devastating picture that was too real to imagine. I was spiraling down a pathway of skepticism and had no clue what kept holding me back. Most kids would play minor league baseball without a signing bonus, but not me. Something prevented me from moving forward. With two more years of college eligibility remaining, I kicked this proverbial decision-to-go-pro can down the road.

A full scholarship to play baseball at Mississippi State University of the up-and-coming Southeastern Conference gave me a reason to do so. Playing Division I baseball provided another opportunity for me to compete at a higher level and more time to prove my worth, though I still didn't know who needed the proof.

The same pattern of baseball success continued in my junior season. Our nationally ranked 1978 team came loaded with experience and talent. My roommate Russell Aldrich, Del Bender, Jack Lazorko, Howie McCann, Donny Robinson, and my good friend, the late Buddy "Love" Maher. All would play at some level professionally after we reached the championship game of the regional finals, falling one win short of making it to the College World Series (CWS) in Omaha.

Our run that year came with a price. We faced a significant overhaul for the next season with all the senior departures, including our entire starting-pitching rotation. Our chances of playing in the CWS that next season were slim since we were only returning three starters from the previous season. And it wasn't a matter of simply recruiting a few replacements; we needed to rebuild the team. We had too many unknowns with limited experience at that level. The players' transfer portal didn't exist then either, so we didn't have the luxury of a quick fix. The pundits predicted a changing of the guard to more experienced competitors in our conference. At best, a middle-of-the-pack finish awaited us, they said. On paper, we just weren't good enough.

My aspirations for our 1979 team mirrored public opinion enough to get engaged to Lindy, my high school sweetheart whom I dated for five years. With the unlikelihood of reaching the playoffs in the coming year, setting a wedding date for May 26th after our regular season concluded seemed logical. At least, it did to me.

And it left plenty of time for wedding preparations. It never crossed my mind what the future might unveil. What would I do after college? No idea. Where would we live? No clue. How would I make a living beyond baseball? I was still trying to figure that out. To say I was naïve about our future is a significant understatement. I was blinded by love and unaware of its importance with what lay ahead. The date was etched in stone.

The postseason wedding plans made more sense a few months later. I spent the summer in Hyannis on Cape Cod, home to a premier summer baseball league for collegiate players. In a game against the Orleans Cardinals, a fly ball in my direction bent foul toward the grandstand fence. My attempt at a one-legged sliding catch to avoid running into the fence was neither graceful nor effective. My left leg got tangled in the turf, and a pop in my knee preceded an awkward tumbling.

Days later, my summer season ended prematurely. Surgery removed loose bone fragments that had floated undetected around my knee for years. Nolan Ryan encountered a similar diagnosis, had bone chips removed around his elbow, and followed his surgery with a Hall-of-Fame career. My surgery appeared successful, pending validation after six weeks in a hard cast.

During rehab, I immersed myself in the self-help book *Psycho-Cybernetics* by Maxwell Maltz (Simon & Schuster, 1960). His research suggested that the mental images we create of ourselves and a positive self-image lead to success. Often, we look down on ourselves because we perceive others as having a different view of us, and we allow their ideas to permeate our minds and influence our thoughts. Visualizing positive occurrences can shape the mind and enhance the chances of success. I quickly realized this approach could give me an edge, and the sooner the better.

After the cast was removed, my leg remained fully extended and locked. I was unable to bend it at the knee, no matter how hard I pushed. X-rays revealed the need for a second surgery. The medical rationale read, "To prevent further deterioration of the articular cartilage, additional bone debris requires removal to allow for smoother rotational mobility." They removed inch-long corkscrew pieces of bone fragments as though whittled away from a piece of wood.

Another round of rehab replaced the fall baseball activities leading up to my final collegiate season. With only two returning starters now, it didn't look promising. But on the bright side, my wedding date scheduled for the following year looked much more secure.

Head trainer Strat Karatassos and his rehab crew pushed me to physical limits I had never experienced. I rehabilitated quickly, enough to restore 80 percent capacity and thus get me ready enough for a return to the diamond.

Only one thing surpassed the importance of trotting out to the outfield in the top of the first inning and playing in the season opener of my last year of college ball—seeing the impact on my teammates, who had cautiously watched and encouraged me through rehab. Their hopes for the upcoming season, which didn't match those in press clippings, impacted me beyond what I could do for them. Those guys greatly inspired me.

The rehab demands ultimately paid dividends. I had come a long way. Not only was I ready to play, but I was good enough to do so. Game on!

RAIN DESCENDED UPON DUDY NOBLE FIELD THE NIGHT BEFORE opening day, but heavy tarps protected the infield until the clouds sealed. Overcast conditions wouldn't cancel the first game or its festivities, most notably the ones in the Left Field Lounge student section, where BBQ and beer were the staple products.

However, damp outfield grounds might be problematic for someone nursing a two-time surgically repaired knee. The lineup card showed my name in the number-three slot but crossed out and replaced with that of another team member. For precautionary reasons, the coaches made a game-time decision to bench me.

Anger got the best of me as I flung folding chairs across the locker room. So much for my leadership skills. Opening day would have to wait for me. Mangled folding chairs displayed my disappointment, but a 5–0 opening-day victory appeased me.

Starlit skies foretold dry grounds the next day. Empty campus streets indicated students filled the dormitories, either sleeping or watching Johnny Carson on late-night television. Humphrey Coliseum's floodlights shined a dim beam on the adjacent baseball field. It was late evening, and nothing seemed out of the ordinary, with one exception: me—standing in the batter's box at home plate, "imagining" my first at-bat in tomorrow's game, pitch by pitch.

Ball one. I stepped out of the box, looked toward the invisible third-base coach Mark Johnson for the hit-away signal, and then stepped back into the box.

Next, the umpire called strike one—no need for a second look at the coach.

Ball two set up an excellent pitch to hit. I imagined the fastball coming into my hitting zone. I visualized bat-to-ball contact, just like in my boyhood when I practiced with palm tree acorns. Smack! In baseball terms, it's called a rope. In Bulldawg terms, it's called a "six," which is the highest numerical value assigned for hitting a baseball in the production rating system.

The ball raced toward left field, diminishing in size by the millisecond. A home run!

I looked back toward the stadium, void of spectators. (Duh, it was midnight.) With nobody in sight, my fear of embarrassment eased. I followed through with my midnight escapade, trotting around the bases before pouncing on home plate.

Crazy? Certainly! What could be crazier? Doing it a second time, including the trot around the bases.

But the absolute craziest thing? In my first official at-bat of the season, I jogged around the bases, having hit a home run, just as I imagined I would the night before. I even saw remnants of my sneaker footprints in the base paths. Thank you, Mr. Maltz!

The sportswriters' doubts about this group of no-names with untested talents seemed logical, at least until the season started. When it did, we won, again and again. Halfway through the season, we had posted a 29–3 record and were ranked fourth in the nation. The unlikely odds of MSU winning our division and the SEC championship had changed.

I never imagined the May 26th wedding date set a year earlier would be sandwiched between winning the regional tournament and playing in the College World Series. Lindy and I celebrated our honeymoon during the national championship tournament in Omaha, Nebraska. Omaha! In June! Let that sink in. It took decades to repay her for that less-than-romantic honeymoon adventure. But she became an MSU Bulldawg fan for life!

HAVING COME FULL CIRCLE, THE DREAM OF SIGNING A PROFESsional baseball contract, which I put on hold three times, remained alive. Back home, this night carried a new outlook. There was no need to convince me the time was right to turn pro, though no other options existed. The stars had aligned again. I had just returned from the CWS, where I competed for a national championship. Along with the exposure from such an event, I received the kinds of accolades regularly awarded to the best players in college baseball: team captain, Most Valuable Player, and Academic All-American.

A highly supportive collegiate fan base expressed hope that I would make it to "The Show," and a handful of scouts evaluated me thoroughly and expressed interest in me for the upcoming draft. Agents wooed me with promises of being able to secure me a lucrative contract. Everything pointed to a storybook finish as the local sports hero from the small town of Cocoa, Florida, made his way to the big leagues.

So, naturally, I paced, waiting with bated breath for the phone call, wondering which team would select me for the summer baseball draft. Ready to sign a professional baseball contract, I felt convinced I was good enough to compete at the highest level. Little did I know this was the beginning of my dream's end. Why?

Because the phone never rang!

When the draft ended, my shoulders slumped, my lungs emptied, and my chin wedged into my chest. Words evaded me. What had just happened? Or not happened? Could there have been a mistake? Would a call come the next day? Or later in the week?

Nope.

No call ever came, nor were any explanations given. No fourth-time selection in the baseball draft. Instead, the previous three drafts had turned out to be my proverbial three strikes, and now I was out.

The silent night stunned me but didn't stop me. I had no plans to give up. Have you ever heard of a walk-on? This refers to someone who simply shows up for a tryout. In my case, I showed up at the Minnesota Twins' complex. My hopes were rekindled after a promising audition, where I accumulated impressive stats and received encouraging support from former all-star outfielder and talent evaluator coach Tony Oliva.

I was extremely confident because I was performing at a higher level than anyone in camp. I had every reason to believe an offer was forthcoming, with an assignment somewhere in the minor leagues. But this lift to my spirits was short-lived. A month later, the manager in charge approached me in an empty locker room and informed me, "We don't need you anymore."

Those devastating words stuck with me for a long time. Was I just a pawn in the way of a better choice or a better prospect? Subsequent tryout opportunities with other baseball organizations didn't materialize. Months later, a letter written by a scout from the Toronto Blue Jays revealed their past interest in signing me, with a potential assignment to Triple-A ball, one step from the big leagues. But they decided not to do so for organizational diversity, financial reasons, and the shadow cast over me because of my knee surgeries.

Wasn't I good enough? Whatever the reason or reasons, I knew the end had come. I was finished.

For years, I could neither forgive nor watch the game of baseball.

THIS STORY—A BOYHOOD DREAM TO PLAY MAJOR LEAGUE BASEball—may seem trivial since hundreds of thousands of kids have the same dream. But for me, it was a significant loss. My dream was shattered. Losing baseball crushed me.

Some believed playing at the highest level was a stretch for me, that I had been a good college player but wasn't a genuine pro prospect. They said I should join the throngs of the ordinary, get over it and move on. Others would tell me it was just a game, with sincere attempts to console. They would advocate that my whole life was ahead of me and none of this stuff mattered. It wasn't a big deal. Again, get over it and move on.

Those comments were challenging to process, but ones I mentally validated. I began fixating on my inability to live up to the expectations of others and myself, and soon discovered I had a fear of failing. I struggled to reconcile my efforts and resiliency with that fear.

Breaking up with baseball was, of course, hard to do. But little did I know that this first-time disappointment would begin to shape my life and start a learning curve filled with even greater untimely setbacks and devastating losses. I didn't consider this the beginning of more to come. Nor did I foresee future unfulfilled dreams, unsuccessful attempts at glory, extreme views by critics, and beatdowns by naysayers. I did, however, need a new light cast on the mental reprogramming required to conquer the only relevant point in those dialogues: learning to let go of a dream and press forward after a loss, to get over it, and move on.

My elementary years at St. Mary's Catholic School didn't foster any authentic inner spiritual movement. I made no claims of being a saint, but I wasn't a devil either—at least not to every parent or nun who knew me. I experienced moments of youthful exuberance, even though strict behavioral discipline was the order of the day. The threat of a wooden-ruler knuckle-hammering loomed large should any missteps occur.

On one occasion, the teacher assigned my best friend, Glenn Fayer, and me to retrieve preordered lunches from the cafeteria.

We nonchalantly grabbed the handle of the Styrofoam box, loaded with steamed hot dogs in soft buns. Along the way, disaster struck when the handle broke, and forty franks emptied onto the tilted sidewalk, rolling down a hill. We swiftly picked them up, wiping them under the armpits of our shirts to remove any debris, before placing them back in their broken buns, neatly stacked. When one student mentioned his hot dog tasted a bit sandy, we thought our cover was blown. We avoided detention but continued to fear new witnesses would surface.

For eight years, episodes like this contributed to learned behaviors, fear of the ruler, and the repercussions for a missed assignment or shameful conduct. I also developed a healthy trepidation of a note being sent home to my parents where a cat-o'-nine-tails dangled on my parents' bedroom doorknob. I didn't encounter those tails often, but the fear of them lingered. At least until one unnamed brother took scissors to them. And a punishment he couldn't "sit on" to think about for weeks.

I reluctantly memorized some Bible verses, not for the sake of any soul-searching but for eligibility to receive sacramental benefits. If spirituality had stood as my top priority as a kid, the story of Jericho might have inspired me. The obstacles facing the Israelites, victories followed by new challenges, and faith in things that didn't make sense were all remarkable. Their will to keep moving forward would have both lessened any disappointment burdening me and instilled hope for the future.

Joshua, a skillful military leader serving as Moses's second-in-command, took over the reins as the new leader after Moses died. A Promised Land waited for anyone willing to fight for it. His first task required taking thousands of fighting men across the Jordan River. The instructions seemed simple: be strong, courageous, unintimidated. And why wouldn't they follow such exhortations? God had already assured Joshua He would be with him wherever he went, so there was no reason for the Israelites to feel fear or doubt of any kind.

So, Joshua brought the whole clan to the edge of the Jordan, a river at flood-stage levels, an obstacle God's miraculous power could help them overcome. The only impediment at that point would be their faith, or lack thereof, especially when it was required for matters that defied logic and appeared impossible.

The first test belonged to the priests carrying the ark of the covenant. They had to believe that, through God's power, they could halt the river's current by dipping their toes into the river. This simple act gave them a passageway over rocky beds to dry ground. When the kings in power and all the people saw the miracle unfold, their hearts melted with fear. The plan worked. Stars began to align. Their dreams of the Promised Land seemed possible.

But that wasn't all. Joshua and the others would have to fight for the promised land. Another obstacle lay before them and was ready to extinguish any hope of them reaching their dreamland. They had crossed a river, but that was no big deal. They now stood at the bottom of Jericho, with its thick, daunting walls surrounding a heavily armored city, looming over them.

Walls incapable of being breached by them and their toylike tools or weapons. Nobody came into that place, and nobody came out. They prepared for enemies' arrivals, and, indeed, they had been waiting, ready to rumble! Conquering Jericho made crossing the Jordan River seem trivial. Rather than simply passing one test and moving forward, the challenges for Joshua and the Israelites accumulated and became more complex.

Nobody is immune to complications showing up on their doorstep. We often face speed bumps. And while it is true these minor annoyances slow us down, they can also allow us time to think, reflect, and even change course if necessary. If we ignore too many of them, we end up paying for a realignment at the local auto repair shop. They are a nuisance but not the end of the world.

But then, bigger challenges show up. Roadblocks with higher hurdles to clear. Struggles that are more difficult to endure or maneuver through. The unbearable disappointments. A vanishing dream. The frustration from an unmet goal, a failed exam, a slowly developing career, or a struggling business.

It might be worrying about a dire financial situation, a bad medical report, or a persistent addiction. The emptiness after allowing a relationship to sour or the sorrow from the death of someone you loved. The emotional harm to children from parents who chose to live inappropriately. A self-imposed guilt from not living up to expectations. The feeling that you are not good enough, not needed, or not wanted anymore, whether by others or by God.

We all face significant challenges like Joshua's walls. They may not include taking down a wall the size of Jericho or fighting a Goliath-like beast as David did, but they exist, preventing us from moving forward and reaching our goals. They give and take—they give us burdens to bear, fear, doubt, worry, anger, depression, and more, and in return, they drain us of our enthusiasm, crush our confidence, and strip us of our will to win. Huge, insurmountable, and intimidating, life is filled with such setbacks and barriers. These are our walls of Jericho, and we must confront and conquer them, even though it appears impossible.

But how?

Fortunately, God has a knack for giving out great game plans, free of charge, and all it requires is an open and compliant heart searching for truth.

Joshua's plan had a clear pathway to victory: conquer Jericho, its kings, and their armies. He was told to take his men and march around the city one time for six straight days. The seven priests were also to carry their trumpets in front of the ark.

However, Joshua and his army were to make a slight adjustment on the seventh day—using the same routine, God ordered them to march around the city seven times. After this, the priests were ordered to blow their trumpets loudly, and, while this was happening, everyone was to shout and scream as if their lives depended on it! Because they did. If they did this, God said, the city's walls would collapse. No cannonballs, bullets, or bombs would be fired or detonated; they didn't exist anyway. No fires or floods (did that years ago with Noah). The walls would come down, and Joshua and his army would be free to go in and clean house. The city was theirs for the taking. This was their metaphorical AND literal wall. But God told Joshua that they could conquer it and that this plan would succeed; they just had to make it happen.

Imagine the reactions Joshua received as he tried to explain this plan to his soldiers.

Really?

Are you serious?

Is this the best plan you have?

These bulky, unshaven guys were eager to fight a real battle, wanting to take matters into their own hands. You know, a testosterone-flying fight to the end. You can't help but think they figured Joshua was crazy for suggesting such a strategy. But their ideas didn't matter. The battle plan God wanted Joshua to deploy was quite simple, and it wouldn't result in a long, drawn-out war. It would work.

Joshua's story ended well. His faithful fighters bought into God's plan. When the trumpets sounded and people shouted with all their might, the wall collapsed, removing the obstacle. They charged in. They conquered. They took the city. Their dream was back on track.

WHAT ABOUT YOUR WALLS OF JERICHO? DO YOU GO NOSE-TO-nose with them with a glare? Do you become motionless, unable, or unwilling to take them on any longer? Do you ignore or avoid them while looking for alternative ways or workarounds? Breaking down walls begins with a change of mind and heart that prompts a willingness to change your course of action, even if it seems odd and cumbersome.

The dreadful thoughts of not being good enough imprisoned me at a young age. Without the mental keys to unlock any doors,

I couldn't escape, frozen as I was from a fear of failing. I held onto a deeply embedded sense of being unable to live up to the expectations of my parents, siblings, friends, teammates, and the Chicago White Sox. I could not break out, much less move forward. I had neither an answer nor a how-to strategy. By the time I was finally ready to play professional baseball, it was too late. I needed to deal with the loss and move forward.

Disappointments tend to multiply like waves, becoming plentiful and sizable, especially during stormy seasons. Each wave surges ashore, bringing with it new pain or discouragement. The temporary relief of having worked through one disappointment gets overshadowed by the trepidation of what might come next. If we aren't battling an issue currently, we will be soon.

I never experienced a shattered dream until my hopes for a career in baseball ended, and I had a limited spiritual foundation to fall back on. Time and additional hardship would prove to be part of my curriculum—a lifelong education.

We listen to stories of prominent people like Hollywood actors, TV commentators, leading executives, and professional athletes who use elevated platforms to divulge their success in overcoming obstacles. Their hardship stories are inspiring. But it doesn't mean their suffering is any more significant than yours or mine, the young man who didn't become a professional baseball player.

I am as common as any person in the eyes of the secular world. Maybe you are too. But the misery you endure makes you unique and special. You get to overcome adversity your way and determine what it means to be good enough.

Baseball fans enjoy a special event when a team wins a championship. It's called the "dawgpile" (I spell it in line with my alma mater). The night we won the regional tournament on our home field in Starkville, Mississippi, over ten thousand raucous fans enjoyed a classic. When we secured the final out, total mayhem broke out. Every player on the field sprinted toward the pitcher's mound, where catcher John McDonald hoisted pitcher Kenny Kurtz in the air. All arms pointed to the skies. Gloves became frisbees. Airborne bodies collided in a massive pile. Full mugs of beer showered students in the Left Field Lounge. A second wave of players from the dugout—coaches, ball boys, and bat girls—arrived with the same intent of jumping on top.

This celebratory spectacle looked like a blast to the Mississippi State fans. But if you happen to be deep down in the dawgpile, it's scary. An uneasiness grows for the early arrivers as breathing becomes difficult under the deadweight of muscled athletes. What starts as euphoria about winning a championship quickly becomes dreadful. The lengthy seconds spent at the bottom of the pile can be the longest time of your life, with each additional body catapulting itself atop the growing pile, squeezing out all remnants of breathable air. Push-ups to create space are not an option. Panic sets in for the claustrophobic.

Not soon enough, the pile stops growing and exuberant bodies begin to pull away. Finally, airflow resumes. The bottom-dwellers reappear, their body parts no longer implanted in the turf, free to breathe and continue celebrating a well-earned victory. In our case, an unexpected trip to the College World Series.

The dawgpile is a microcosm for a life full of enduring struggles. We work hard to achieve our goals, and our success brings elation. But eventually, we incur a setback. Discouragement ensues—sometimes panic—when a horrible or demanding situation rears its ugly head. We search for ways to get relief, hoping to restore joy. We feel buried under the weight of a bad financial situation, pressure from a lost job, the death of a loved one, or a personal disappointment. At our lowest point, the happiness we once had seems distant.

Eventually, however, we experience relief from the weight brought on by previous problems because the passage of time dilutes the pain or suffering, or it diverts our attention to something more pleasant and hopeful. Joy returns, and we are at peace until the next time.

When I lost baseball for good, I might as well have been at the bottom of a dawgpile. Baseball gave me a sense of worth, and ultimately, it put me in a good place where I felt complete. I didn't appreciate its significance until it was no longer with me.

When my parents placed the Wiffle ball bat next to me in the crib, it didn't suggest who I should be. But it was me until the moment it couldn't be. I could no longer hold on to that dream and had to let it go.

What did I know at the age of twenty-two? If I could find value in myself through that loss, I could find it again through another avenue. All athletes dream of a second chance at some point, so when they get one, they seek to finish what they started. A new direction would replace what I once had. I wanted and needed that.

Losses in life are inevitable. They insist we reflect, learn, and change. The adjustments help us grow and find new value and meaning in life, with greater urgency and appreciation for what we love. These adjustments also help us conclude we are good enough.

For decades, new acquaintances asked, "Why didn't you sign a contract? What barrier did you face? Why didn't a talented can't-miss prospect get one more chance?"

At that point, I hadn't failed at anything significant. The Chicago White Sox had taken a chance by drafting me, but it hadn't worked out. It happens every year with baseball prospects. Scouts sign baseball prospects based on their abilities but often have difficulty determining their confidence levels. In the end, some work out, but most—like me—don't. That's baseball. And that's life. Sometimes it's just that simple.

My journey isn't a message specific to baseball, business, or the Bible but, rather, a combination of how each of these things impacted my life. It's my learning curve, with its wins and losses, good and troubled times, prosperity and scarcity, joy and heartbreak, and pressure and peace. It's the blueprint I wish I could have had earlier. I can only speak about what I went through to get to where I am today, sharing unique lessons learned that can be helpful to you and highlighting mistakes I made so that you might avoid them. Lord knows you will create your own. But some of your experiences may prove similar. Perhaps, we can learn from each other.

Each of us drafts a story every time we make a choice when we are down but not yet out. Your story is unique and yours to live through and learn from as you navigate life. Let's rekindle the joys you once pursued. Let's find the release from any dawgpile currently burying you—the dawgpile of disappointment over a plan gone wrong, a goal not met, an effort bearing no fruit, or a dream not lived.

My journey started with a desire to please others, to give them what they wanted, assuming it was the best way to influence them. I discovered influencing others is more effective when I'm serving them. It's the best way to impact their lives while having peace in my own. It's the means to prepare them for the incessant walls of difficulty they will encounter, to share what I learned and how I changed, so they can determine their direction, to help them recognize their finish line and know what it takes to cross it. I hope this book can do the same for you.

The end of baseball didn't leave me in a good place. But while I may have been down, I was not out.

2

Another Day, Another At-Bat

Often we look so long at the closed door that we do not see the one that has been opened for us.

—Helen Keller

The abrupt end to a two-decade dream didn't end the world, but it did prompt some questions. Top of the list: "What now?" With no clear answer, I began running an obscure race, without any idea of where its finish line lay.

As I ran, one sports lesson stuck with me: "Hesitation will kill you"—an adage most coaches use when discussing instincts. Do you take an extra base on a miscue in the outfield, or do you stay put? Throw into coverage, or take a sack on a third-down play? Launch a lower-probability three-pointer to win a game, or pass to a teammate under the rim for a sure basket, forcing overtime? Quick decisions usually decide which team wins and loses a game.

Hesitation and second-guessing cost me an opportunity, one I would never get back. When I mulled over options, even crafting new alternatives, I justified my hesitation as using good judgment.

It's the same idea behind the Russian proverb: "Measure seven times, cut once" If you plan to act, especially with something you cannot change, you better do it right.

It seemed logical to approach my choice this way. Yet persistent overthinking or the presence of time constraints rendered this principle useless. I couldn't overcome my hesitation then, and it haunted me not knowing what could have happened if I had signed a pro contract, so I vowed never to let that happen again.

Yet as baseball faded away, its valuable insights started to take center stage in my life. Baseball is an odd sport in that you can fail seven out of ten times as a hitter and be considered an incredibly skilled player.

Billy Stein, who lived next door when I was a teenager, played fourteen seasons in the major leagues. He returned home in the offseason and once told me, "Even when you hit a baseball perfectly, you'll likely line out to the shortstop."

This high failure rate requires hitters to have a short memory, which is why coaches and teammates remind each other that tomorrow brings another day, with another at-bat. This principle goes beyond sports, though. Bad days will undoubtedly occur for all of us, regardless of our yeoman efforts to do things well. We must acknowledge that failures, disappointments, or vanishing dreams will be a part of our journey, but realize we'll get another chance with new opportunities and experiences.

It was time for me to move forward, so I jumped at the first job offer and its whopping $13,000 annual salary. Hours later, however, I withdrew my commitment like a college athlete in the transfer portal as a second offer, from General Motors, bumped my annual starting salary by another $5,000.

I followed the money, unaware of the culture shock I was about to experience when moving to the friendly town of Laurel, Mississippi. It was located near two cities, appropriately named Soso and Whynot. The irony of the latter made sense to me. Lindy and I stayed one year before packing our bags and returning to Florida. We left with two memories: Laurel's friendly people and the impacts of Hardy Eubanks.

Hardy was the preacher at a church Lindy wanted to attend

because it had similar doctrines to what she had learned during childhood. The peculiar thing, though, was that, besides preaching, Hardy also made announcements, recited prayers, led the singing, served communion, gathered the collection, offered the invitation, thanked everyone for coming, and reminded them to return for the evening service and a repeat of the morning service.

I joined Hardy as the only two males in attendance. Three other women attended services regularly, adding up to a robust six members. I didn't count, though, because I wasn't a member of the church or considered one of the saved, so I couldn't help with the worship-service duties. It didn't matter because I still wasn't making religion a priority at that time. But sometime later I came to view Lindy's dedication and Hardy's example as unique and incredibly impactful. Little Laurel, Mississippi, introduced me to something special. And it wasn't just the people.

Before reaching thirty years of age, we celebrated the birth of our daughters, Brooke and Jamie. Lindy left her good-paying job to stay home with the girls. We had $17 in our bank accounts and used the little credit we had to purchase baby formula and diapers. We didn't think about being poor but knew we needed a better plan.

It was then that I fancied a new idea. A new plan. Another big dream.

Greatness resides in everyone, including you.

I've had many opportunities to speak to diverse audiences. Each time has been a privilege and an honor. I've spoken to students, athletes, and investors, and yes, I've even spoken at religious assemblies. I once told a group of college students that greatness was in that auditorium. I couldn't pinpoint if it was a single individual or several, an idea that would be created soon, or an event likely to occur. But I emphasized greatness existed at that moment or would come soon from someone or something in that audience.

This simple proclamation intrigued the audience, as evidenced by their focused eyes and upright posture.

Many people lay claim to being the greatest. Boxing fans remember Muhammad Ali articulating how he floated like a butterfly and stung like a bee. He teased opponents, saying they couldn't hit what they couldn't see. He bragged of being "doubly great" because he could pick the round he would knock out his opponent. Whether boastful or confident, his abundant championship belts supported his claim.

Others may not boast like Ali but are considered the greatest by their peers or self-proclaimed experts. Healthy debates advance the case for nominating the greatest president, inventor, author, executive, or athlete, among others. Every profession has its most remarkable person, and the nominee's record supports their consideration as best in their field. The only variables are the opinions expressed by the so-called experts.

Away from the limelight, unknown people deserve the same recognition of greatness for reasons not easily quantifiable. Their work is tiresome, their deeds unrecognized, and their tasks deemed unimportant. I'm speaking of mothers, teachers, nurses, police officers, firefighters, volunteers, the military, and their families. Their sacrifices are often taken for granted.

Who gets to decide who is the greatest? And by what criteria do they make such a claim? How does someone become great or do something so incredible? How is greatness unleashed within you? What barriers prevent you from being or becoming the greatest? Why is greatness a good thing?

I never considered greatness to be necessary, although I wanted to do good things. Though my first job wasn't as lucrative as I had hoped, even with a business degree, I received a priceless education playing sports. I learned about character-building, discipline development, preparation principles, and teamwork, to name a few things—traits learned through the experiences of living, not taught by a textbook. They provided tremendous benefits as my aspirations shifted to a new venture: starting my own business!

My plan was to hang a shingle with my name on it attached to a building, accumulate a large clientele, and let the big bucks roll in. I had a gift for numbers and could spout answers to any arithmetic equation in seconds. Before I entered Little League, I could calculate baseball batting averages in my head with only the occasional help of a slide rule (google it if you are under fifty). What better way to use my skill with numbers than to indulge in personal and corporate taxes, financial planning, business law, and strategies? And make some good bank doing so.

Only one hurdle stood between me and my new business. State certification requires passing the Certified Public Accountant (CPA) examination—a five-section, three-day-long written test covering a plethora of financial terms, theories, rules of practice, and business law applications. I thought it was no big deal. I could do this. More education, more training. Plenty of courses that specialized in helping participants pass the examination littered the trade magazines. The marketing pitches made passing the examination sound easy. One sponsor proclaimed that 80 percent of their enrollees passed the state-run test on their first attempt. I liked the odds.

This time, I signed the contract without pause and paid the hefty fees, despite the distant location where the course was held. Full-time employment filled my week. The review sessions consumed weekends. After rising at four o'clock every Saturday morning, I faced an east-to-west-coast drive of Florida that took three hours. The rigorous review sessions lasted ten hours, leaving the lengthy return home and nine o'clock arrival. This became my routine for twenty straight weeks, driving a Vega GT that consumed a quart of oil with every tank of gas.

Driving at dawn in Florida's low-lying areas can be dangerous after dense fog settles overnight. When entering a patch, the general rule is to reduce speed but never stop. Roll down the windows to listen for other vehicles and, if possible, pull over. Some drivers screech to a complete stop, but too many maintain their speed, thinking the fogged roads will lift with the distance traveled in a few seconds.

After all the training, I never doubted I would pass the examination. But I also never thought I would face a "hesitation will kill you" moment either.

At sixty miles per hour, a dense patch instantly made the front of the hood disappear. Instincts kicked in, and I tapped the brakes. The thought of another vehicle planted in the trunk flashed in my mind. I navigated slowly, peering all the while at the white passing lane lines on the two-way road. Drainage ditches steeply bordering both roadsides instantly erased any inklings of pulling over. Seconds later, an eighteen-wheeler appeared, jackknifed, and lying across the road. My drum-beating heart raced with my shifting eyes until a thin passage brought to sight an escape route around the truck's trailer. Fifty yards later, the sun shone.

Every drive that followed brought apprehension if I encountered even the slightest sign of fog. But if I could survive the drive, I thought, then I could tackle the test. The last review session and final drive elicited a sense of eagerness for the examination. I believed that course had given me an edge. Along with essential knowledge, it provided historical data on the frequency and subjects of questions asked, with probabilities of when they would appear on a given exam. Like studying tendencies in sports, where scouting reports provide information on the type of pitch to throw in a certain count, where to position players for certain hitters, and what player matchups work best with specific opponents, I used these tendencies to dictate how I organized and spent my time and efforts as I waded through the vast amount of material.

As the course suggested, I dialed in on the high probability and predicted topics. The training simplified memorization techniques, provided meaningful acronyms to gain extra points, and raised my confidence. It prepared me to go where I hadn't gone before. My new business waited, ready for takeoff.

Test day soon arrived and, with it, only one problem: the probabilities and predictions didn't match up with questions I received that hadn't appeared on examinations for decades. The topics looked foreign, like the small print on a warning label. I struggled with the test all three days. Occasionally, my mind drifted to the risks of driving in the dense fog. I lost focus and memory recall. It was a grind, but I finished.

After that, all that remained was to await the outcome. Email and texting didn't exist then, so the results would come via the US Postal Service three months later. A single index card enclosed in an envelope said it all. The Department of Professional Regulation for the State of Florida's Office of Examination Services bluntly stated the outcome.

Robert S. Kocol, you have **FAILED.**

Why I kept this card is beyond reason! But as reality set in, I once again found myself crushed. Twenty weeks of preparation proved to be all for naught. Twenty weekends wasted. Risky driving conditions encountered unnecessarily. Huge fees invested for two feet of notes and information that were now worthless to me. An 80 percent probability of passing upon completion of this well-renowned course? Pointless. And to top it all off, I spent each day for three months living with the angst of waiting for an answer only to find out I had failed!

An albatross from the past reemerged at that point, one I had yet to conquer: *I'm still not good enough.*

Ever ask yourself why you didn't see something coming? Your chin slumps, knuckles pound the temples, and you whisper to yourself, "How could I miss the obvious?" Happens all the time, or at least to me it does.

For example, your child's behavior changes shortly after they bring home a new friend whose parents don't share the same values as you. An expected promotion is nixed after a colleague takes credit for a project done chiefly by you. A negative Google review gets published about your business by a disgruntled customer with bad intentions. Maybe a relationship or marriage is damaged because neither party is willing to compromise. Perhaps your health suffers following prolonged periods of physical inactivity and nutritional neglect. Or anxiety reaches new limits because you have overcommitted to many activities you couldn't turn down. The list goes on.

I wrestled with this during the baseball draft days, and now I had unsuccessfully dallied with plans to start a business. In each case, clues popped up along the way, and I didn't see them. At the time, I didn't recognize what I was doing or why. I had remained uncertain, still trying to fill a void. Afterward, however, I kept saying to myself, "I should have seen this coming."

A passion for goals is usually apparent. It's in your DNA, what you were called to do, your destiny. You prepare, overload with information, and take all measures to cross your self-imposed finish line. You are convinced this feat is necessary because of its significance. It drives you daily. You figure it's your time. All you need is an opportunity and the chance to excel.

But time passes. Life's distractions take over. Setbacks occur. And the effort that consumed your entire being for a lengthy period doesn't materialize as you hoped. Your inner thoughts whisper, "This will not work for you. It's not your time. Your plan is nonsense, and your dream unrealistic. It's not meant to be." It poses questions, and the more this goes on, the more you wonder if there is anyone you can talk to who will listen.

THINK OF A GOD MOMENT YOU HAVE EXPERIENCED. PERHAPS it occurred during a rough patch in your life, or when something or someone was inadvertently inserted into your situation. Maybe it happened when an idea popped up, a solution became apparent, an accident was averted, a sickness disappeared, or a friend consoled you with the right words. It was in those moments when escape from hardship, or disappointment was bearable, or whatever crisis you were in got solved satisfactorily, you thought God was with you and had his hand in the outcome.

Sometimes you come to that conclusion quickly; other times, it takes years. As I grumbled over my testing failures, my thoughts gravitated toward understanding my purpose in life. It was, at that time, I recalled some obscure thoughts from an incident almost ten years earlier.

February 1976

Opening day for baseball at Brevard Junior College couldn't come soon enough. I was eager to step back onto the diamond. With the White Sox having recently drafted me and the mounting pressure to sign a pro contract, expectations were soaring. The high hopes of my family, friends, teammates, and recruiters, as well as my own, put an immense weight on my shoulders. It felt like I was carrying the dreams of an entire community, and I was on the brink of exploding.

Unfortunately, the season was a massive letdown when it finally did arrive. I had developed a pattern of being a slow starter but usually found ways to bounce back and be more productive deeper into the season. This time was different. Mired in a multiweek slump, I couldn't find a way to shake it.

I returned home from another dismal game, hitless in four at-bats with a couple of strikeouts. My lack of production with runners in scoring position had contributed to another team loss. Pressure grew as the slump persisted. I was the team captain, and letting the team down increased my frustration. I struggled, thinking the White Sox wasted their draft pick.

The night was thick and still, the eerie silence occasionally interrupted by trilling crickets and buzzing mosquitos. Time pushed its way into the next day. The houselights slept except for the front-door light, waiting for my return home.

I noticed the twelve-foot rooftop I had jumped off ten years prior. The neighborhood kids dared me, so to impress them, I leaped. I remembered my knee popping when it hit the turf, but I didn't tell the kids it hurt or let my parents know. The incident remained hidden at the time, but eventually, it would be linked to the need for multiple surgeries.

A stone concrete bench, strategically placed, sat in front of my mother's semicircular flower garden. Massive ten-foot evergreen bushes gnarled together supplied privacy from anyone who drove or walked the streets of LeGay and Cherbourg. The parcel would never grace the cover of *Better Homes and Gardens*, but still, it displayed cleverly positioned flowers around a three-and-a-half-foot-tall statue of Mary, the mother of Jesus.

As devout Catholics, Mom and Dad participated in most church activities. I grew up going to a Catholic church, and at nineteen years old, that made me one. I'm not sure what it meant, though, other than the strict requirement to attend church every Sunday morning and to become proficient at slogging through the repetition of a weekly mass. Any faith I had in God was by association, coming from my parents' beliefs rather than my initiative. I did little to search for and understand God, but I still suspected he might be real.

Lindy would tell me later that she knew I believed in God and hoped I would understand it one day. One thing was sure: the way she lived and treated people intrigued me. Deep down, I wanted what she had, even though I wasn't living like it.

As I sat motionless on the bench, my mind fixated on my dream of playing professional baseball, the White Sox drafting me, and the contract offer, before pivoting cruelly to my batting average, which was less than my weight (175 pounds). Failure was winning the night. Tears moistened the soil. Randomly, I began to pray. No, that wasn't quite right; I started negotiations with God.

"Why is this happening?" I asked aloud. "Why now? Do you plan to turn this around? When will you show me something? Are you listening? Are you for real?"

And then.

"Excuse me, sir."

Startled, I jerked around to face a young boy, no more than eight or nine years old.

"Would you be interested in subscribing to the newspaper?" he asked, extending one toward me with others hanging in a bag under his arm.

The back of my hand wiped tears away as if nothing were wrong. I was nineteen years old, wearing a baseball uniform in the dark, talking to a stone statue. What a nerd! My first reaction? Act cool without drawing attention to any peculiar behavior I had just been engaging in. And camouflage the sobbing.

"No, thanks," I muttered. "We already get one."

"Okay, thanks," he said as he walked around the evergreen trees, disappearing into the night.

Oblivious to the interruption, I returned to my muddled thinking, self-pity, and occasional praying. A moment later, it hit me.

Wait a minute. Why is an eight-year-old kid selling newspaper subscriptions at midnight?

I scurried around the evergreens to find nothing but dark, vacant streets.

THIS MIDNIGHT EXPERIENCE RESURFACED AS I STARED AT THE failed test results. Sitting there questioning God, the sudden appearance of the boy, my embarrassment, and peering around the bushes after realizing something unusual had occurred. Something beyond my understanding had happened that evening, and now, after another disappointment, I wondered why I remembered it.

I didn't think of the incident as any God moment because I wasn't sure what that meant. Besides, all I gave God were my leftovers, the scraps of time left after all the career development, goal achievement, money-making, and parenting requirements.

I had a tinge of curiosity over the timing of two difficult letdowns separated by nearly a decade and wondered if it had something to do with overcoming failures.

IN THE BOOK OF ACTS, KING HEROD INTENDED TO PERSECUTE anyone associated with the church. He killed James, the brother of John, with a sword. The Jews approved of his tactics, and this emboldened him. Peter became his new target. They imprisoned Peter until Herod could orchestrate a public trial after Passover. Four squads, a total of sixteen soldiers, guarded Peter closely. Throughout his imprisonment, the church prayed for Peter. The night before the trial, additional security strengthened the watch. They bound Peter in two chains, forced him to sleep between two soldiers, and posted other guards at his cell's entrance. There would be no escape that evening. Impossible.

Many can relate to this scenario when burdened with failure, discouraged by defeat, stressed from hopeless circumstances, or saddened by a loss. We think there is no way out and no way to recover, so the only thing left to do is give in and give up.

In these times, remember to pray and wait for your God moments, because behind the scenes, God is working his plan for you. He is with you in your darkest moments. He never leaves you, even though it seems like it. When there doesn't appear to be any evidence supporting that backup plan, rest assured it's there. And it's coming for you.

In Peter's dire case, an angel suddenly appeared, bringing light to his cell. The angel didn't lightly touch his shoulder to gently wake him, as if the plan were to sneak him out of captivity. No, this angel was serious when striking Peter. The Greek word *patasso* is translated as giving a blow with the hand, fist, or a weapon.[4] It is also used to describe Moses killing the Egyptian who mistreated his Israelite brother.[5] Without question, the angel's blow startled Peter.

It's easy to question the angel's aggressiveness. That's one heck of a wake-up call. But aren't those necessary sometimes? When misfortune or heavy burdens drop on us, bringing in their counterparts of self-pity, sadness, and seclusion, a good smack might be what we need. To shake us, to help us understand that life goes on, and to remind us that God is in control and continues working full-time on more significant plans for us. Depression and addiction become coping mechanisms needing medical attention if not dealt with swiftly. But procrastination or (worse yet) giving up aren't good reasons to stall the healing process and the attempt to move on.

The angel told Peter to get up quickly. Surprisingly, the chains fell from his wrists. No longer constrained, he put on his cloak and was told to follow the angel. Still stinging from the angel's blow, he thought this vision was a dream. He remained between two guards, with others positioned at the entrance of his cell. There was no time for Peter to ask questions, to be idle, or wait for an explanation concerning a plan for which he had provided zero input. No time to decipher if this was the right way or the best way.

Instead, his senses returned. He looked at the current situation and saw a door of opportunity to escape. He trusted someone other than himself—the angel sent by God, and, by extension, he placed his trust in God.

Following the angel, Peter stepped over the first set of guards. He was still okay. He passed by the second set of guards at the gate of his cell. Still not caught. When outside, he approached an iron gate that led to the city. Good grief! Another obstacle. Did the guards have a set of keys to this thing? Indeed, there was no going back and risking the chance of recapture. Besides, the guards were likely in pursuit already. Before panic set in, the gate randomly opened. How did this happen? Was this a trick, a setup? Were the guards waiting on the other side, ready to pounce on Peter for an attempted escape?

Together, they walked through the gate and down the street, and suddenly, the angel left him. Peter was alone, but he came to his full senses and understood. Without a doubt, God had sent the angel to help him escape Herod's grip. It was God's plan from the beginning, put together at a time when Peter lay handcuffed in prison, with little hope, waiting for the unknown consequences of his trial.

At each of these critical escape points, Peter could have asked for an explanation of the escape plan, though that seemed unlikely considering the heat of the moment. No sense in asking for advice because none would be given. Just because we seek guidance or help doesn't mean we will get it in our desired time frame. We may never get it. God doesn't always answer our questions, nor give us what we want, much less on our timeline or even in the manner we would like to receive such things (God is full of surprises after all!). It is in these moments when our trust in him is absolutely essential.

Too often, when facing extreme hardship or reoccurring problems, we become so engrossed with the situation that we don't end up seeing the solution that is right in front of us. We see a door of opportunity closed but have a blind spot to the one that is being opened. Peter could have seen the loosened chains, focused on the guards surrounding him, and decided to go back to sleep because the idea of escape didn't register. Instead, he saw the open door and took the chance to be free, unaware of what lurked ahead, and with no guarantee of his safety and security.

Often our attempts to solve problems don't pan out. Despite making an effort to change, the problem persists, and our efforts don't seem to matter. Or when we avoid people or issues, they return. Or when we adjust to a situation, different issues emerge. When these sorts of things happen, *keep trying*. Persevere. Sometimes a new door will only appear at the very end once you have used all your energy. Keep pushing yourself. Trust that God will be there to open new doors when you have done everything you possibly can. His plans are designed to be the best for you so you can achieve your greatness and he can receive all glory.

Diamonds, Deals, and Divine Guidance

Though I didn't have angels slapping me around to shake me after falling short of the mark in my pursuits, the memory of a little paperboy lingered. A subsequent review of the fine print in the course contract revealed an additional claim: those repeating the course before reexamination had a 95 percent chance of passing, and no additional fees were required. Who would be crazy enough to go through all that again? The drive, the threat of fog-saturated roads, and weekend living lost forever? I knew one person who might.

Me!

After twenty more cross-state drives and ten-hour classes consuming every Saturday, I returned to the examination site, determined to be one of the 95 percent and hoping the odds were in my favor.

Three months later, with high hopes, I lifted the single index card enough to get to the same line. The message stayed the same—I had failed again. Head down, knees on the ground. I repeated a single word, "Why?"

I scrolled down the test card a moment later and noticed some caveats. The news wasn't all bad. I passed three of the four parts, meaning only one of them required retesting.

Six months and a third attempt later, and two years after this ordeal began, the last index card included bold congratulations. I had finally passed.

An unforgettable story with a successful conclusion? The fruits of hard labor soon to come? Time to start a business and live the dream?

Not exactly!

By the time I passed the examination, my interests had changed. I no longer fancied the idea of owning a business. I had moved on, climbing the corporate ladder as part of my backup plan. (Always have a backup plan). I would not use the license I earned to start a business, and I wondered if it would ever be helpful, much less pay off the investment incurred. Only time would tell.

How could I go from the difficulty of moving on after baseball to the ease of doing so after passing the examination? One ambition was taken away, but the next one was given away. Why was the door of one opportunity closed *on* me, yet the other closed *by* me? What changed? What did I learn?

I pursued opportunities because I thought they were suitable for me to fulfill my ambitions and desire to achieve personal success. Each time, however, my aspirations collided with adversity. As it turned out, some of the best-made plans—including my own—fell flat. As much as I wanted or thought I deserved specific outcomes, they didn't materialize. Maybe the timing wasn't right, or perhaps it simply wasn't meant to be. Regardless, my plans tumbled like clothes in a dryer, spinning in circles, waiting for the final buzzer of accomplishment.

At the time, I wrestled with something but was unclear about what I was wrestling with. I contemplated the need to work harder, prepare more diligently, or wait patiently for the right time. Then again, maybe God had a different direction for me. Maybe God was bringing me along, helping me learn and understand something important, that my plans weren't like his plans.

If only I could grasp the significance of what Jeremiah wrote: "For I know the plans I have for you," declares the Lord, "plans to prosper you and not to harm you, plans to give you hope and a future. Then you will call on me and come and pray to me, and I will listen to you. You will seek me and find me when you seek me with all your heart."[6]

I needed to trust and follow God.

With scars from failures and missed opportunities adding up, the finish line remained distant and unrecognizable. Other days loomed on the horizon, and other at-bats would happen soon enough. But as to the when and where or even how the at-bats would turn out, I remained completely in the dark.

Looking for Signs

Our deepest fear is not that we are inadequate; our deepest fear is that we are powerful beyond measure.

—Marianne Williamson

If missing the opportunity to play professional baseball or owning a business taught me anything, tackling feelings of inadequacy stood front and center. Why these thoughts persisted, where they came from, and from whom remained a mystery. Their quarrel with me and my need to succeed became a mental winner-take-all confrontation.

In his article "Why Persuasion Is Personal: The Neuroscience of Influence," Andrew Luttrell states, "Compelling, persuasive messages tend to be the ones that get people to connect the ideas to something about themselves."[7]

He explains that a region of the brain, the ventromedial prefrontal cortex, is tied to evaluating the world around us and plays an essential part in persuasion. Brain-scanning technologies show that advertising messages are more persuasive when people connect these ideas to some aspect of themselves. This self-centered thinking, based on our emotional preferences, makes persuasion personal.

The bottom line? We persuade ourselves.

As I navigated through several attempts to succeed, the results were mixed. I experienced similar fluctuations playing baseball, where you are either in or out of a hitting slump at any given time. The only variable was their length. Some lasted a few games, others a few weeks. As a contact hitter, I was fortunate most of mine were not lengthy or persistent.

Coaches isolated any mechanical issues in my swing but often concluded the answer resided between my ears. They stressed the importance of mentally anchoring myself on flat ground to eliminate peaks and valleys. The first step in fighting these mind battles was anticipating and expecting them, thus eliminating the element of surprise.

As it was with baseball, this skill is helpful in any search for answers.

I often returned to previous setbacks, hoping to uncover why I struggled with the mental battles. Times of progression were almost always followed immediately by regression, and whenever I experienced stagnation, I fixated on the fact that I was going nowhere. Some interests faded, expired with time, or got lost in distractions, and I immersed myself in numerous could've, should've, would've, and might've scenarios. I kept working hard and became comfortable settling with the results, concluding it wasn't meant to be. I simply accepted unrealized dreams, unmet goals, or missed opportunities whenever they occurred.

Until I realized a critical sequence to creating self-worth—*think, believe, and know.* Thinking something can happen precedes believing it can happen. Believing something will happen leads to knowing it will happen. I needed to persuade myself of this if I had any hopes of crossing a finish line.

Early success in high school and junior college, being an athlete in a baseball family, and the persistent interest from the Chicago White Sox all signaled potential existed. I had every reason to think I could play professionally. A successful collegiate career at Mississippi State, participating in the College World Series as a top-five team in the country, and a productive stint with the Minnesota Twins boosted my outlook.

Add to that the attention given by the press, scouts, competitors, and people with baseball knowledge, and I had enough evidence to believe I could advance to the next level. By the time I believed I was ready, however, the opportunity had already passed. I never reached the point of convincing myself that I knew I could succeed.

When I took best-in-class preparatory courses designed to ease the examination process, was given tips on areas of concentration, and read the claims of a high probability of achievement, I believed success was a foregone conclusion. My belief pushed me to retake the examination, and partial success nudged me to try a third time. But when I completed the requirements, time had passed, and my interests had changed. Again, I never went far enough to know I could succeed in owning my own business.

Both setbacks taught me I couldn't think or believe my way to success. I assumed success would follow if I followed a process, learned, and worked hard. But it didn't. I needed to be convinced and know I was destined to succeed. That last step remained a challenge and solving it would bring closure.

A commonly used practice to solve problems or reach goals is to start at the end. How this concept directs a particular line of thinking is the topic of numerous books.

Entrepreneurs start with their endgame, whether launching a product to global markets or creating sufficient value should they want to sell their company. They can formulate business plans to achieve their goal with a defined endgame in place. They'll determine the required skills, the timeline to market their product, the necessary investments and amounts borrowed, the number of new customers needed to drive sales targets, and the support systems required to enable a profitable business.

The endgame is their goal. It's their finish line. They are willing to take the risk for the potential rewards. There is no holding back once the endgame, or finish line, is in sight.

Interviews with near-death patients reveal interesting thoughts about their regrets when facing their last days. The common themes are spending too little time with family, wasting time developing careers, and building financial stability. In his late eighties, my father said he had a simple life, spent too much time living in a rut, and wished he hadn't been afraid to try new things.

We generally live predictable lives. We work forty to fifty hours weekly, complete weekend chores, raise our children, grocery shop, and pay bills. Limited thinking dominates discussions, like what little can be done with what we have. Conversations about potential, the amazing things we can do with the little we have, take a back seat because someone insinuates we are incapable of achieving anything noteworthy or our ideas are nonsensical. With these seeds planted in our minds, the persuasion cycle begins. The issue becomes: Who owns the power of persuasion?

Bronnie Ware, a nurse who counseled dying people for over a decade, concluded that the most common regret she recorded was, "I wish I'd had the courage to live a life true to myself, not the life others expected of me. When people realize their life is almost over and look back clearly on them, it is easy how many dreams have gone unfulfilled. Most people had not honored half of their dreams and died knowing it was due to choices they had made or not made. Health brings a freedom very few realize until they no longer have it."[8]

Life should include risks, trying new things, exploring, and going out on a limb with a crazy idea. Differentiating yourself by doing what others refuse to do can reduce regretful thinking. It highlights the difference between those who watch things happen and those who make things happen.

My success with sports and the early years of my business career gave me a warped sense of security. I was able to string together a few productive years, rising in stature with each promotion and financially with minor pecuniary gains. Setbacks brought me back to earth, but I always found a way to turn them into something better. I fixated on results, and anything less than perfect pushed me to work harder, faster, and longer. Work became an obsession, and I continued sprinting in a race, unaware of where the said finish line was.

My hyperthyroidism, undetected at the time, aided a frantic energy and allowed me to outlast anyone. On most nights, my colleagues had likely donned their pajamas before I entered a dark, empty parking lot for the drive home. Decades after the culmination of my baseball career (such as it was), I still carried the "last one to leave the field" mantra.

It's no wonder, then, that I studied the Bible infrequently but enough to know God existed. I was unaware of him working behind the scenes. New opportunities persisted. If I knew these were his works, I would have asked why because I hadn't done much for him. Why would he keep looking after my best interests? I was a believer but only a novice on my spiritual journey. When astute scripture memorizers quoted verses, I fumbled through the pages to locate them. At least I could grasp biblical concepts, which seemed logical to an analytical person like me.

I was fortunate to have caring people teach me to believe hope existed beyond anything the world offered. I realized a higher power existed, a God who valued me. Why else would opportunity be inserted in my life after missteps from the past? Why would God stay with me when I hadn't done the same for him? This spiritual perspective had a nice ring to it, and believing in such a notion was intriguing. My journey of faith had just started—even if just one step at a time.

THE STORY OF GIDEON BEGINS WITH THE ISRAELITES HAVING done evil in the eyes of God. At that time, the Midianites ruled and oppressed them relentlessly, ravaging their lands for seven years, ruining their crops, and controlling their daily activities. The Israelites plodded along, weak and impoverished. It was so brutal that they cried out for the Lord to help them.

An angel appeared to Gideon one day, reminding him how God delivered them from the oppression of Egyptian slavery. They dwelled in a land that had been given to them, along with only one command: Do not worship the gods of the Amorites. The angel reprimanded Gideon for not listening to God. It was clear their current dismal situation was one of their choosing. The angel sat under an oak tree while a disgruntled Gideon pummeled wheat. The angel assured Gideon of God's presence and acknowledged he was a mighty warrior—courageous, battle-ready, and capable of managing the current situation and future challenges.

Gideon, a mighty warrior? The facts suggested otherwise. Wheat is typically threshed on a rock or elevated soil, allowing winds to blow away the chaff. Gideon, however, was threshing wheat in a wine press, a deeply dug pit. Not convenient for threshing, certainly, but suitable to avoid detection, perhaps? Was he hiding? Was he afraid the Midianites might steal his harvest? How could he be considered a mighty warrior?

Truth be told, Gideon wasn't a star-studded hero, and neither was he a mighty warrior, as many have mistakenly assumed, at times, down through the ages. He was ordinary—average, at best. It was only when God handled his conflicts that Gideon began to look like a mighty warrior.

WE ALL HAVE OUR BATTLES, BE IT A CRUMMY JOB WITH A cranky boss, a sarcastic family member, a strained relationship, an unruly child, a persistent addiction, or a list of overdue bills. Fighting these battles takes time, patience, and considerable effort. Sometimes we shoulder the warrior role, ready to fight.

Often, though, our victories, when they occur, are short-lived, and the same issues return, often with additional forces. Losing battles becomes our reality, and when losses stack up, they become mental blocks, leading to doubt. Powerfully negative thoughts strip away our armor of confidence, knowledge, and passion, raising new questions.

Do I have the right skills? Am I adequately prepared? Am I mentally and physically strong enough? Why does it appear as though I'm lacking? I'm not hero material, I'm not particularly brave or bright, and I'm not impressive or influential. I'm just a person with real struggles—how can I expect to accomplish anything?

All of this described me until I realized any significance or influence I had would come from other means. I gave little credit to God for the blessings and opportunities that surfaced in my life. I spent little time trying to embrace his love for me. Yet, behind the scenes, he kept looking out for me. When I perceived myself as failing, God viewed it as a teachable event. Every battlefield became a training ground to become a mighty warrior. Acknowledging I wasn't the strongest warrior, however, is when things began to change.

STILL LABORING IN THE WINEPRESS, GIDEON DIDN'T APPEAR receptive to the angel's words. He complained of their captivity and the whereabouts of all the wonders their ancestors experienced when they were freed from Egypt. He questioned why God had abandoned them and given them into the hands of Midian. Overall, a thoroughly predictable response. God's ability and willingness to perform miracles in the past didn't register with Gideon in the present. His ancestors' freedom from bondage didn't suffice as proof that God cared about the Israelites' plight in his time and could free them as well. He remained unsure and reluctant. Facing difficulty and fear, he retreated into a state of despair, convinced God had deserted them.

I could see how I might downplay the reality of Gideon's tendencies being evident in me since I had similar reactions to demanding situations. I questioned why God allowed terrible things to happen to good people, forgetting that the adversary, with all its power, is constantly stirring things up, and I neglected to consider God's presence and plans for me.

January 1999

Years of resume-building ultimately led to the opportunity of a lifetime. I received an offer for the pinnacle position in my profession, the Chief Financial Officer (CFO) of a two-billion-dollar public corporation. It came unexpectedly and required a speedy acceptance. What seemed an impromptu offer caught me off guard—I wasn't even planning to seek such a position till some years down the road. The suddenness of the overnight appointment seemed bizarre. Grasping its meaning and purpose puzzled me. I wondered: Why now?

Naturally, the inner voice of self-doubt entered my brain's executive functioning lobe. I had not been trained for the role nor did I possess any demonstrable experience. Of the six key functional responsibilities—Securities and Exchange Commission (SEC) reporting, tax, treasury, investor relations, international finance, and operational management—my resume touted qualifications for one. Career development plans included having two-year stints in the other five areas, meaning it would take another ten years in varying roles to adequately prepare me for this executive position. Again, I wondered: Why now?

I was far from being a seasoned executive. My tax experience was limited to Turbo Tax® and my treasury skills to personal bank accounts. I developed investor relations skills by watching movies like the crime drama *Wall Street*. My limited international finance skills were evidenced by a seldom-used passport with plenty of empty boxes and few customs stamps. I didn't care for the SEC regulations and accounting ramifications, especially after the near burnout from the CPA examination.

But breaking news stories of the Enron and WorldCom scandals prompted compliance concerns, and our board of directors required a candidate with an active CPA license to fill the CFO position. I kept my license active after passing the exam and completing twenty-plus years of continuing education. I never thought those patchy-fogged road trips across Florida would ever bear fruit. At least now, the opportunity existed.

My good friend, Neeraj Mital, would advise me later, "The beginning of wisdom is understanding the limitations of your abilities." This offshoot from a quote from Aristotle teaches that our lives reflect our views and beliefs, thoughts and attitudes, fears and concerns, and what we see in others and ourselves. Together, they coalesce to shape our mindset and determine who we become.

Was I entirely prepared for this new role? No way! Are we ever prepared for most challenges in life? Not likely. My past was littered with missed opportunities and setbacks, so this role was shaping up to be the ultimate test. A battle was brewing, and my resiliency would clash with my fears. I decided to let the battle begin.

Besides, the corporation was coming off record-breaking profits. I was due for a break and good fortune. What could go wrong?

WHEN I STARTED AS THE CFO THE FIRST WEEK IN JANUARY, a minor issue required my attention. I learned quickly that minor issues are a myth on Wall Street. Our company profits fell short of meeting analysts' expectations for the prior quarter. We went public with a prerelease on my second day in the office, a preemptive tactic used to control the narrative for any imminent lousy news.

Doing this before the regularly scheduled earnings announcement allowed us to avoid having to react to possible information leaks. Investors regularly—if nervously—waited weeks before an earnings release, hoping there would be no surprises. They always assumed that no news before an earnings announcement was good news, so, the prereleasing of bad news was simply the lesser of two evils.

We announced that a delay to some highly anticipated new products triggered the disappointing results and noted the issue was transitory. Engineering believed it had resolved the problems, and we were back on track. Most investors took our lousy results and somehow translated them into good news. They elevated their expectations, citing that a robust first-quarter market ramp would increase the stock price—a second lesson on my second day. Be careful and precise with your words. I didn't say too much that day.

After the news release, I began accumulating frequent-flyer miles with an afternoon flight to my first meetings with shareholders and analysts. It was my introduction to a whole new world involving Wall Street. In three days, I met investors comprising a third of our shareholder base. They were cordial and thankful I spent time with them under challenging circumstances, but I sensed their discontent with our financial results. It was the first week on the job, and I left thinking I had already used my one and only "get out of jail free" card. The business activities that led to the disappointing news we delivered didn't occur on my watch. But I felt as though everything going forward would be.

Our preannouncement of the financial shortfall was damaging but not irreparable. The hype of the temporary product delays appeared believable, especially with the credibility of having achieved record-breaking profits the prior year. The stock price took a quick dip from its $37 price, the same value I received for the large batch of incentive options in my executive contract.

But all was not well back in the engineering labs. I had scars from the past learning about new product launches in the technology industry. The real dilemma, especially with software technology, was finding the problems. The engineers were brilliant at creating solutions once the issues were known.

We closely watched problem discovery curves. If the number of new issues discovered didn't crest, that was a clear indicator that the designs were unstable. Unfortunately, our problems persisted and grew. The project teams agreed, however, that resource levels were adequate and insisted they were about to turn the corner, but intradepartmental confidence levels were mixed. The teams believed there was ample time to resolve the lingering problems and ship enough products to meet first-quarter expectations.

Those closest to the project had sufficient data to support their confidence. Two months into the quarter, a few of our executives and entourage flew to New York to ring the opening bell on Wall Street, an event planned well in advance. It was a great honor for the company and a marketing bonanza. The buzz it created lifted our stock price, topping $40 per share.

I didn't attend. For years I watched companies ring the bell on Wall Street and hoped I would do so one day. But my instincts told me it was unsuitable for the CFO to celebrate on stage when product problems still existed. I was head-down, looking at the first-quarter numbers firming up. Sales looked weak, reinforcing my concerns. A few usually reliable customers pushed orders to the next quarter, presumably waiting for product validation.

With a month left in the quarter, the new products had yet to be released for shipment. It would take a yeoman's effort in March to move the volume of product necessary to meet the first-quarter financial estimates. It was possible, but the likelihood dwindled with each passing day. My instincts sensed a shortfall was inevitable.

Unfortunately, my instincts were right. We missed Wall Street's expectations by a considerable amount. Wall Street expected we would earn a profit of forty-two cents per share. We barely broke even at six cents per share. Throughout the quarter, we tried fire-selling the inventory of older products in anticipation of the newly released technologies. Shipments of the newer products didn't begin until the last week of the quarter.

When we announced the financial results, our profits plummeted 86 percent. Investors punished us. Our stock price dropped from $39 to $18 per share. High-volume selling cut our market valuation in half by $2 billion. We implemented plans to axe five hundred jobs.

The profit shortfall was the second in as many quarters. The pressure from disgruntled shareholders intensified, and their phone calls were no longer cordial. I split my time between shareholders, the media, and employees worried about losing their jobs, all while implementing plans to fix a business model gone awry. The worst part? Missing a family who had seen little of me for three months.

Teresia, my administrative assistant, was a trooper. She informed me later of her attempts to manage one shareholder conversation. Responding to a demand to speak to me at once while I was using the men's room, the investor shouted at her, "I don't give a crap where he is. I want to talk to him right now."

What could she say? "Let me go in there and get him for you?" My honeymoon period as the CFO dissipated within three months.

For whatever reason, I took this personally. I didn't know if it was because of the investors' collective response, or if it came from within me. But I felt I was responsible, and I had to right the ship. I didn't know why or how, but the athlete in me stood tall and said, "Dang it, I'll show you! I'll prove to you I can make this work."

In May, mystified investors wondered why our company couldn't post better numbers. Seven months before the turn of the century, a Y2K buying binge for technology products like ours was in full swing. Companies continued throwing money at backup systems and redundant systems behind those, all because of the uncertainty about whether or not the world would come to a halt. Information technology experts prepared for the worst but remained cautiously hopeful because they didn't know if computers could react to a new century.

The shareholders, our harshest critics, took direct aim at us and what they viewed as ineptness on our part. Analysts poured fuel on the fire.

Gary Helmig was the first analyst I met on my initial road trip, and he proved to be an ally. In a *Wall Street Journal* article, he said, "They're running out of time."[9] Michael Geran of Pershing Securities added, "This time around, there's no room for shortfalls."[10] Shareholders and analysts turned up the heat. We began shipping the newer technologies. We had to deliver good news. We were in the batter's box, ready to hit. But I knew we had two strikes.

My inexperience continued to trip me up. By the time I could decipher the engineering lingo regarding problems, schedules, and commitments, I faced new tests on the legal front. A legal team member commented, "This case is a slam dunk winner for us." That came just before a federal appeals court ruled against our company in an earlier patent-infringement lawsuit we won. The appeals court sent the case back to the district court, and we subsequently lost that case. The check I wrote for damages was $70 million. We didn't have that level of cash and would need to secure a new line of borrowing. My next task was to convince the banks our credit remained solid.

There is one thing sports and business have in common: what has happened is over, and all that matters is what lies ahead. When a football team wins a game, their celebration lasts one night because they are quickly back working on next week's opponent. In business, financial results become historical information quickly, and future profits are all that matter. That was what we faced at the end of July.

Catching our breath after the lawsuit, we held our second-quarter conference call. We resolved the software bugs and began a rapid product shipment ramp for the new technologies. We ultimately met Wall Street's estimates, but the underlying reasons told a different story.

Two consecutive quarterly reports composed of terrible news put pressure on attaining those second-quarter numbers. Three in a row would be catastrophic. Decisions made provided short-term benefits but at the expense of long-term viability. These decisions, at a minimum, indicated organizational dysfunction. Temporary lucrative incentive plans were offered to the sales teams to accelerate business transactions into the current financial period.

Salespeople love lucrative incentive plans. They sold everything and anything in their pipelines, and in doing so, significantly reduced the sales levels for the next quarter. Business groups given full autonomy to grow their sales had increased hiring, leading to bloated expense levels, and keeping profitable returns distant. A multiyear sales arrangement that supplied nearly 20 percent of our sales approached its end, and replacement revenue streams lagged. The strategic plans made sense, but the execution of those plans did not.

The dam holding up our business soon sprung leaks. The sheer number of moving parts meant rough times lay ahead. My instincts signaled an incoming flood of bad news. We neutralized the short-lived good news by warning investors that the year's second half would be challenging and that profit expectations would be lower. Our already battered stock price tumbled further.

Word circulated about our financial woes. In August, loyal customers delayed multimillion-dollar sales transactions. I met with key customers to assure them of our financial stability and that resource levels were sufficient to weather our self-inflicted storm. I gave a straightforward message to everyone, but their reception was more complex.

Every week I packed a carry-on for multiple days, given a ticket the night before, knowing the full itinerary only after I boarded the plane. The long and late-night flights provided solitude to catch up with email. Occasionally, I pulled tattered pictures from my wallet of Lindy, Brooke, and Jamie. I hadn't seen them in weeks and wondered what they might be doing. I missed them and briefly pondered the direction of my life.

Following a customer visit with Florida Power & Light in Miami, I drove three hours to visit NASA at the Kennedy Space Center in Brevard County. Both were critical customers with sales opportunities. They appreciated the opportunity to speak with a company executive but still sought assurance of our financial viability.

I had a few hours to visit my parents before flying out of Orlando. The move to Colorado eight years prior had distanced me from my family. Lindy and I weren't wealthy, and our limited trips back home coincided with the Christmas holidays. My parents' finances made their travel opportunities nonexistent. I became the distant child of the family while my siblings filled the vacancy I had left behind.

I didn't expect this short visit would include troubling news, but it did—my mother was ill. She reluctantly told me her diagnosis as I nervously searched for an explanation. Cancer! She had reasons for not divulging too much information, and I surmised she did what mothers do, not wanting to burden me with worry. She equivocated, saying it was early in the process and she had several appointments scheduled. I discovered the diagnosis soon enough—pancreatic cancer.

By early September, investors' tones began to deteriorate further. The *Wall Street Journal* noted, "A leading investor was asking StorageTek to sell itself or seek a strategic partner to boost shareholder value."[11] The investor sent a letter to StorageTek's board of directors, claiming that since their initial acquisition of shares for their clients, the company's management had failed to create shareholder value while its competitors had prospered.

Letters like this are common. Shareholders often apply pressure on underperforming companies, whether operationally or financially. It became public information when they filed the letter with the SEC. Filing letters with the SEC at that time was uncommon. This investor was irritated. Other investors would soon join the hunt. When the idea of a potential sale of the company reached the media, new buying activity bumped up our stock price to $23 per share. Some thought this was the beginning of the end.

Days after this hit the news, Lindy received a phone call from her father. Her mother had been diagnosed with ovarian cancer—

just one month after news about my mother. I thought, *When will the bleeding stop?* Unfortunately, it wouldn't be anytime soon.

By the end of September, our business had spiraled out of control. We made too many mistakes, and our assessment of risk was flawed. Our strategic initiatives weren't well-balanced, and we had overly optimistic expectations that turned out way off the mark. The execution of our plans was far from successful. Our financial performance in the third quarter fell short as a direct result of operational miscues on multiple fronts.

The final tabulations provided an affirmation. We failed to meet Wall Street's expectations for the third time in four quarters, which was sure to shock our shareholders. Our longest-tenured investors had already lost millions of dollars. They held their stock positions because of their loyalty and belief in our company, but their concerns about our ability to turn the company around were justified. I assumed their only hope was if some other company made an offer to acquire us at a slight premium.

All I could think about was having to deliver this devastating news. I knew once these financial results became public, the share price would plummet when the stock markets opened.

The analysts viewed our explanations as excuses. They were correct. A.G. Edwards & Sons analyst Shelby Seyrafi responded, "Clearly, they don't have complete control of the many moving parts of their company…the problems at the company are a lot more systematic than the company had probably believed before."[12]

When the dust settled on our bleak news, the stock price sank 25 percent to $14 per share. Analysts slashed earnings expectations for the fourth quarter and the following year. We started planning for more organizational restructuring and layoffs. We hired two advisory firms, Goldman Sachs & Company and McKinsey & Company, to investigate options, including the sale of the company. Some analysts remained skeptical and didn't think any suitors existed.

PaineWebber's Kevin Buttigieg noted, "Shareholders no longer have an understanding as to what the depths of the company's problems are, and we're not sure that the company itself knows."[13] He continued, "The mere fact that they've put out this announcement is a sign to me that they don't have anyone knocking on their doorstep right now."[14]

Disenchanted shareholders and industry pundits believed we had given up.

I considered doing the same. I doubted I could ever be a "mighty warrior."

At two a.m. the day we released our third-quarter results, I sat on the edge of my bed, body slouched, feet dangling. My Bible sat underneath an alarm clock next to a lamp on the nightstand, where a few ibuprofen tablets lay every night for easy access, ready to nurse the inevitable headaches. A whole night of uninterrupted sleep never occurred during that time of my life.

I reached for my Bible. Like most people, I always felt comfortable reading it in times of difficulty, and the pull to do so was often accompanied by a hope God would be listening. My constant squirming usually disturbed Lindy's rest. But that night, she seemed at peace, sleeping comfortably. I continued praying silently.

Where are you? I need help. I don't know what to do. I need some indication that you are listening. I'm lost, void of answers. Please give me a sign that you are working with me.

In my hands, the pages fell to the book of Judges, chapter six—the story of when God planned to save Israel from the hands of Midian by sending Gideon. His struggles mirrored mine. Though Gideon was promised an escort guaranteeing him victory, he wasn't on the same page with God. He was too busy wallowing in his self-doubts. Unsure, weak, and afraid he wasn't good enough.

A highlighted verse showed Gideon's response. "If I have found favor in your eyes, give me a sign that it is you talking to me."

It sounded familiar. I had been here before. I went through similar periods of doubt and disappointment. I wondered, *When will it ever end? Is God working in my life?* I wanted a sign too.

Gideon then prepared a sacrifice before the angel of the Lord. The angel touched it with the tip of his staff, and fire flared from the rock and consumed the offering. The angel disappeared, convincing Gideon this was a sign and that he had seen the angel of the Lord. God then calmed the oft-afraid Gideon, assuring him he would live, but he didn't relieve him of the task to defeat the Midianites and save Israel.

That didn't satisfy Gideon. He wanted further proof as if a flaring fire wasn't impressive enough. Gideon then thought of something more unusual, more miraculous. He placed wool fleece on the threshing floor overnight. He sought another sign, suggesting there be dew on the fleece and the ground left dry.

This idea isn't ordinary now, and it certainly wasn't back then either. Then again, neither is God, nor has he ever been. God is extraordinary and again delivered a miracle, giving Gideon the sign he wanted, the proof that God was with him. He had every reason to be confident and primed to battle with the Midianites. You would think he was as ready to go as he would ever be, right?

Not exactly!

The brazen Gideon wanted more. He asked for the fleece episode again. But in reverse. He wanted dry fleece and dew-covered ground. He was bold enough to ask the Lord for one more sign. One more proof point. So that night, the Lord made it happen. He granted Gideon what he desired. Typically, we would scoff at Gideon. We would ridicule him for his cowardice and constant need for God's help. We would laugh at him for his ignorance and arrogance. Good grief! He just witnessed three miracles!

But are we right in doing so, especially when we do the very same thing? When our faith weakens, we are first in line, asking God for signs. We would be better off if we sought his guidance and trusted his plans. It's okay to ask for help, but God wants us to seek him, bringing him all our burdens and worries. He wants us to know he is with us as we fight our battles and will take care of us in his way and on his timeline.

God's word supplies limitless guidance for us to consider as we encounter life's experiences. We must plant his words in our hearts, letting them help us grow, prosper, and share our good fortunes while serving others. As the writer of Proverbs said, "Trust in the Lord with all your heart and do not lean on your own understanding. In all your ways, acknowledge Him, and He will make your paths straight."[15]

These simple verses carry compelling messages. Trust in the Lord wholeheartedly, not half-heartedly. Don't require signs like Gideon; don't depend on your knowledge. If our faith is weak, get closer to his word and learn of him. Acknowledge and trust he is in our presence. There are no guarantees we won't fail, we will have hills to climb, but the pathway will be directional and headed toward heaven.

THERE WAS A TIME WHEN KING DAVID WAS VACILLATING OVER his son Absalom, who had murdered his brother Amnon for raping their sister. His heart and his head were at war. He loved his son but knew what he did was wrong, and being expelled from the kingdom by his father was justified.

A wise woman from Tekoa was engaged to counsel the king. Having been coached on what to say, she tried to make something that wasn't the case appear to be true. She said, "Our lives are like water spilled out on the ground, which cannot be gathered up again."[16]

I believe her point is we cannot relive our past. We cannot take back any harmful words we've spoken or lackluster efforts we've produced. We cannot reverse the decisions or mistakes we've made.

The Tehoaken woman finished by saying, "But God does not just sweep life away; instead, he devises ways to bring us back when we have been separated from him."[17]

God doesn't just sweep things under the carpet regarding our future. Instead, he is ever considering ways to bring us back to him. He continues investing in everyone. Why? Because everyone is valuable to him. We are his creation, and he wants a relationship with those he created. When obstacles surface, with all their discouragement and dismay, have comfort knowing there is another pathway. What a great asset if we learn and use this simple principle. God gives this promise. Every setback starts a comeback. Every failure creates a new opportunity.

THE SETBACKS I EXPERIENCED FELT EXTREME WHEN THEY occurred, though they would likely be merely a walk in the park for many of you who have endured genuinely extreme difficulty and suffering. All the same, I still wondered why I had to go through trials. Was I being punished for something I had done or not done? How many times did something terrible have to happen to me?

But these hardships put me on a path to understanding. I could change my mind and heart, and I could change who I was and who I could become. But I was missing the formula to help me overcome the nagging feelings of inadequacy. I needed to find ways to move beyond those moments of insecurity, learn how to process failure, and understand how to conquer the difference between living life with *my* expectations rather than the expectations of others.

I wanted to make a difference, to serve others in ways beyond the thinking of mere humans, to be effective in building relationships in whatever role I played, to know what it takes to be at peace during life while preparing to be at peace approaching eternal life. I wanted to make an impact on the lives of others. But it would require a change in my life.

Jim Quinn founded Lifestream Incorporated in 1973, intending to inspire lives with his teachings and a mantra of transforming our planet one person at a time. He told a story about a four-year-old boy running down the stairs, joyfully shouting when his dad came home from work, hoping to play with him. His dad put him off until after dinner, when he headed for the living room to relax after an exhausting day at work, much to the toddler's dismay.

One weekend afternoon, the boy was optimistic about playing with his dad, who was positioning himself on the couch to watch a big football game on TV. The father loved his little boy, but with his mind set on enjoying the game, he created a little diversion to buy enough time to watch it. On the table was a magazine with a picture of planet Earth from space on the front cover. He asked his son if he saw this picture of the world as he ripped the cover off the magazine. He tore the picture into tiny puzzle-like pieces, mixed them all up, and gave his son a roll of clear scotch tape. Then he said, "When you put the picture back together, we'll play, okay?"

His son agreed and went to work while his dad slumped back on his couch to watch the game, figuring it would take most of the afternoon for the boy to finish.

Shortly after the game started, the boy came running into the living room shouting, "I'm all done, Dad. I taped the picture back together!"

His dad was astonished and asked how he did it so quickly. The little boy replied, "When you tore the cover off the magazine, I noticed a picture of a man on the back of it. I knew if I put the man back together, the world would come together too."

What a great message! If we can put the man together, the world will come together too. We are all broken people who need to be put together in some manner. I had to find ways to put the man—me—back together, and I believed I could accomplish this. More importantly though, I wondered whether my setbacks could inspire me to understand the bigger picture—finding the best ways to impact the lives of others.

I resolved to find out.

Turning Points

The turning point in the life of those who succeed usually comes at the moment of some crisis.

—NAPOLEON HILL

The incandescent lightbulb brought nightlife to the world, forever changing society's economic and social aspects. The automobile created ease of transport for personal and commercial purposes. The first computers solved complex problems and marked the beginning of the information age. The telephone made communications instantaneous and was at the front of the mass media revolution. Indoor plumbing brought the ease of transporting water for drinking and sanitation purposes and thankfully ended the need for the outhouse. All these inventions were turning points, significantly impacting societal behaviors.

Likewise, the birth of a first child or grandchild is memorable and begins the nurturing and guiding of a gift from God. Graduation from high school and college prepares one for a prosperous future. A first job begins a lengthy career, and the following promotion brings new challenges, opportunities, and rewards. A wedding is a joyous event, the first day of a new, hopefully lifelong, journey with a spouse.

The death of a loved one is a huge loss and a celebration of life. This person loved you, gave you more than you deserved, had been by your side through life's challenges, and instilled hope in you. They allowed you to pass along any benefits you received to others.

Any of these events, individually or collectively, can be turning points in one's life.

We often look back to moments when a singular moment or series of events brought decisive change. We altered our views, changed direction, or navigated through a relationship in a distinctly different manner from the past. A new mantra, stimulated by further clarity, replaced the old ways. We refreshed our hope because we saw that change was good. We convinced ourselves it was the right thing to do, the right way to go. Years later, we consider one of those moments a turning point.

Unfortunately, there are also turning points that send us in the wrong direction. Often, we have better choices at our disposal than the ones we ultimately make, and this flawed thought process steers us toward poor decisions. It becomes challenging to break free from something that has exerted control over us for an extended duration. These unhealthy habits or ill-reputed behaviors often entice us through a prism of pleasure. They are sweet to the senses, and their promising and urgent pleas are addictive because they know our weaknesses and how to break us down. Every time we try to escape, they pull us back, reminding us that what we once had is missing.

Take a moment to reflect on any turning point that may have affected you and your life's direction. Was it a person who said or did something that touched your heart, or ripped it apart? Did a specific event, good or bad, kickstart you to change direction? Did someone new enter your life, bringing inspiration and hope, or alternatively, did you encounter someone toxic and manipulative who led you down a dark and disillusioning path?

Did someone you cherish transition from this life to the next, leaving memories of virtuousness, or conversely, did you experience the painful loss of someone you deeply cared about, leaving a void that still lingers in your heart?

Was a new revelation injected into your thought process, bringing a better understanding of what is essential, meaningful, or worthwhile, or did you grapple with a devastating truth that shattered your illusions and left you feeling lost? Did specific experiences contribute to an accumulation of wisdom, bringing clarity to a better purpose for existing in our imperfect world, or did a series of mistakes and misfortunes leave you feeling bewildered and questioning the very meaning of your existence?

A single event can trigger change, though for some, it may take multiple incidents. Regardless, in some cases, many people don't know they're in the midst of a turning point.

January 2000

I accepted the CFO appointment with hesitation and excitement. The hesitancy came from an uncertainty of the unknown and a fearfulness concerning my ability to succeed. The excitement arose from the prominent position that would now give me an opportunity to effect change. My burgeoning career created an illusion of significance, and I leaped into the job. I was uncomfortable when employees, customers, investors, family, and friends viewed me as being a star of some kind. The exposure to high-profile people, CEOs, investment bank partners, politicians, charities, television anchors, university presidents, and deans was daunting.

Executives of public companies relinquish a lot of their privacy, thanks to the Securities Exchange Act of 1934. This legislation aimed to restore investor confidence in the financial markets following the stock market crash of 1929. It established reporting rules on the dissemination of information for all officers of public corporations to ensure a level playing field for investment firms and individual investors. Conference presentations discussing strategic and operating plans were broadcast simultaneously on public platforms. Information considered significant required immediate public release. Any purchase or sale of company stock I made required disclosure. Specifics about compensation and benefits were publicly filed. Every financial transaction, professionally or personally, became general information, as did a substantial part of my communications.

Speaking engagements were routine and often. Investors scrutinized my comments and critiqued my responses for tone. They interpreted my body language, moods, and facial expressions for informational truth or company direction. All of this made me uncomfortable, but none of it deterred me from seizing the opportunity to achieve success at a higher level, to prove I was good enough so that everyone could see it.

I had no idea I would endure a year of misery—again!

Frequently, sports figures and business executives are targets for journalistic beatdowns, as anyone in a leadership or performance-based position is often exposed to this criticism. I learned firsthand that I wasn't immune to these same tactics when the local newspaper published a scathing article about our company's dire situation. Public exposure is fine when all is well and positive statements are made, but it's a different story when the opposite is evident and harmful comments are made. It comes with the territory, but it gets complicated when you are attacked personally and unable to defend your record adequately. And it is especially tough when your teenage daughters at school hear about their father in the newspaper.

A two-part headline noted our stock was taking a beating, and the article included a quote from an interview with an investment analyst who covered our company. Referring to the entire management team, he said, "I think it's a total and complete mess. I don't see any reason to have faith in them at this point."[18]

Ouch! That hurt! I could only think of my daughters at school listening to the barbs about their father screwing up at his company. I was only one team member, having been in the role for a year, but I viewed it as my fault.

Exhausted, I reached a boiling point. My tank was empty, and I knew of no way to refill it. Rising stress levels contributed to sporadic sleep, and my family noticed my deteriorating health. If I wasn't depressed, I was close to it. I reflected on what I considered to be my past failures—not good enough to play pro ball, not smart enough to have my own business, and not experienced enough to help lead this company to success. I thought about what I might be missing and couldn't see it. I mulled over how much longer this could go on.

Portfolio managers who lose millions of dollars on their investments deserve answers from those responsible for results. They also need a plan they can believe in. So, we devised one that would return us to our strengths.

Only core businesses would remain. The experiments were over. We scuttled all unprofitable enterprises. A *Denver Post* article called it a "far-reaching restructuring plan."[19] It wouldn't come without pain. We would eliminate another 20 percent of our workforce. The cutbacks would include rank-and-file workers and middle- and upper-management positions.

We were no longer an acquisition target. We were unpredictable, and potential suitors couldn't understand why we struggled when our competitors enjoyed booming sales tied to the onslaught of redundant system requirements needed with the approaching Y2k turnover. Our newly devised methodical approach seemed sensible to investors, but questions remained: Was it too late, and was it enough?

Two tasks sat heavily on my heart. The first was communicating the full-year results for the disastrous year that had just ended. We lost $75 million, vastly different from the record-breaking

$200 million in profits we had garnered the previous year. We had missed Wall Street estimates in three out of four quarters. Thousands of employees received pink slips, with more to come. A stock price once above $40 per share was nearly in single digits, erasing almost 75 percent of the company's valuation in one year. Heck of a first year for a rookie CFO! It sure wasn't the best in my life.

It made my second task inevitable. At the same time, the *Denver Post* sports page included a headline printed in large bold letters, "At last, it's over." The Denver Broncos had just finished their lackluster football season, becoming the first defending Super Bowl champion to lose double-digit games the following season, going 6–10. It was as though they had thrown in the towel and given up.

I shared the same sentiment. At last, it's over. Except I didn't want a next season. I had no plans to come back and decided to resign. All year I had fought hard. I had battled the fear, the uncertainty, and the pressure, and it drained me so much that I needed to get out. It had been a heck of an experience, but at last, it was over. It was time to move on.

Sound familiar?

I privately approached the CEO, Dave Weiss. He was gracious, kind to all people, and worked tirelessly. Because of one dire year, the pundits instantly forgot the three successful years he celebrated leading the company.

My voice quivered. "Dave, I'm here to let you know I'm resigning."

He frowned as his chin jutted slightly forward, seemingly taken back by my announcement. He responded, "Why?"

"I cannot keep doing this. I'm sorry."

"You can't resign," he said, fidgeting as he took a few paces, hands on hips.

"I have to. I'm exhausted. I'm overwhelmed."

He would not let go. "You can't."

My head pulled back, and I thought, *Like hell, I can't.* "What do you mean I can't?"

Apprehensively, he released breaking news. "You can't…because I have already resigned. The company cannot afford to have the CEO and CFO resign simultaneously. We need you to stay in your role."

I greatly respected Dave and could only imagine how he felt walking away from his position. My head said his resignation and the implications on the company weren't my problems, so I had no idea why my heart said, "Hang in there; take one for the team." I couldn't let him down.

Thank God Lindy hadn't lost patience with me. Her support astonished me, and if any good came from this, it was because she stuck it out with me and never wavered. And I thought *I* was the executive with steely nerves and great composure!

Within days, the company began a search for a new CEO while the restructuring plan moved forward. Other departures included the Chief Operating Officer (COO), who had spent over twenty years with the company and negotiated several successful significant partnerships. At times, I felt alone on an island. But our transformation plans had to move forward. It was our last chance for survival and redemption.

The multiple executive departures sent shock waves and raised concerns that too many executives were bailing out. My attempted resignation remained a secret. With no imminent sale of the company, it didn't take long for the stock price to sink to new levels, plummeting to $8 per share. A $4 billion company valuation contracted to a paltry $800 million. The $37-per-share incentive options issued to me when accepting this executive position now appeared worthless.

Six months lapsed before we hired a CEO. Our cost-cutting efforts allowed minimal profits to return, and investors believed the worst was over. Our bludgeoned stock price jumped 23 percent on the news as new investors entered the picture, believing in our recovery plans and the potential for value creation. Wall Street loved turnaround stories, and ours seemed a reasonable opportunity.

Just as we could see clear sailing ahead, a supplier in the Pacific Rim miscalculated the timing of their new manufacturing plant and couldn't produce enough components for all their customers. Unfortunately, they were our sole supplier, and a $10 part prevented us from shipping several million dollars of equipment. We missed our profit forecasts but built enough credibility with the new investor base to avoid a market panic. The new CEO used his "get out of jail card." He wouldn't need another. The runway to success was cleared for takeoff.

The company responded favorably, but my job security remained uncertain. In sports, most newly hired coaches fire the prior staff to bring in assistants who share the same views. The tactics are similar in business. The process of replacing eleven previous management members had begun. Most of my peers had been in their roles for many years, while I had just completed my first.

But I was part of the prior year's disaster, and like my colleagues, my future waited in the wings. While waiting, a different storm entered my family's life. The last eighteen months of professional turmoil were over, but they were about to be replaced by eighteen months of personal misery.

LINDY RECEIVED ONE OF THOSE DREADED PHONE CALLS. Her mother's condition had taken a turn for the worse. She was on the first available flight to Florida, uncertain of what awaited her. She arrived at the hospital in time to be with her mother and let her know she loved her. Within minutes, her mother lost consciousness. A few days later, she lost her battle with cancer.

After Lindy boarded her flight, my daughters and I waited for an update on her mother's condition, though I knew what was coming. Brooke and Jamie, both teenagers, were extremely close to their grandparents, and I suspected losing their grandmother, Mee-Maw, would devastate them.

My intuition was correct. The impact on our daughters from her passing struck me when I delivered the news. It felt like Lindy's mother's transition to the next world was the beginning of my understanding of the significance of certain things in life.

When we arrived in Florida a few days later, it was the most difficult of nights. Brooke clung to her mother. Jamie could not enter her grandmother's house. She was no longer there to greet her with warm hugs, gentle smiles, and calm excitement. Instead, Jamie and I walked to the nearby Indian River, where we dropped onto the edge of a fishing dock. With legs hanging, we gazed over the moonlit waters of this mile-wide intercoastal waterway. We cried for hours. Head-throbbing, wailing, heart-wrenching sorrow. We wept until we had no strength or tears left to cry. That evening, the deep sorrow of my heartbroken daughters seared my mind forever.

I HAD LITTLE ENERGY AFTER THE FUNERAL AND SUFFERED beneath the weight of my family, who were beaten down by, and yet only beginning, the grieving process. In times like this, something or someone would send a subtle message that kept my candle burning. I would thank God for the comforting news and assume he had his hand in any minor win.

Paul warned the Corinthians about Israel's history with idolatry and the temptations they would encounter. He said, "But when you are tempted, he will also provide a way out so that you can endure it."[20] This "way out" is rooted in the Greek word *ekbasis* and is described as "a way of escape as afforded by God in case of temptation."[21]

Many read this as God only giving us what we can manage in real-life situations, meaning God will place limitations in our lives, as though regulating our pain and anxiety. Our financial issues will end, cancer will leave our bodies, or our marriage relationship will be reconciled. Yet, there is no promise that our hardships will be shortened or softened, much less that we will be freed from these difficulties before we die. We may never escape a life riddled with problems. But if we stay true to our faith in God until the end, nothing will be able to separate us from the love of God.

The grieving process helped me understand that I needed to be an inspiration and example to my family in a different way. I needed to set my mind on things above and let the earthly things run their course.

January 2001

For the moment, I didn't have to face the wrath of angry shareholders because the business finished the year on a high note. Long-overdue, profitable results gave me a reprieve, with time to support my family while they grieved. We entered the new year with great confidence, bolstered by the early success of our restructured business. Excitement returned, employees were upbeat, customers were encouraged, and bankers appeared confident. Investors were accumulating shares, and our stock price was rising. Our employees were laser-focused on the newly implemented business disciplines, delivering results and exceeding expectations. For the first time, I sensed we were on the right track.

Professionally, I had survived the storm and started believing in myself. If I could contribute to our turnaround success, I would be part of the success story. The cards seemed stacked in our favor, and momentum was building. Until I received a phone call similar to Lindy's a few months earlier. My mother's cancer had taken an aggressive turn, and so I took the first available flight to Florida to be with her.

The clouds below glowed from the moony sky as I recalled a motivational speaking engagement Lindy and I attended, delivered by the well-renowned Les Brown. He was a phenomenal orator and captivated audiences with his inspirational journey as an underdog who conquered challenging times during his rise to success.

During this engagement, Mr. Brown shared a story about one of his good friends, Jack Boland. Jack's vision was to serve his church and community, supplying resources to fulfill others' needs and helping people rid themselves of their addictions. Diagnosed with cancer, Jack informed his congregation he had endured the chemo treatments to the point of remission. But the cancer returned forcefully, and when Jack's vitals failed, his family rushed to the hospital to be with him. Most thought Jack would die before the end of February; some expected he would pass before the next morning. They questioned why he was still alive on the second day of March. At one moment in his hospital room, Jack regained consciousness, opened his eyes, and said to those surrounding him, "This is embarrassing. I'm not dead yet."

Jack finally passed on March 4th. In a tribute, Mr. Brown declared that Jack delivered his final inspirational message. By dying on March 4th, he told the people he loved to *"march forth."*

Regardless of your hardships, continue moving forward. When your mountains appear steep, know that you can reach the summit. Under the direst circumstances, know that hope awaits you. Continue striving toward excellence because you have much to learn and give. Jack Boland's message inspired everyone to march forth with their life.

It was the end of February, and I considered that my mother's last days on earth might coincide with March 4th. My family gathered around her. She was nonresponsive when she received her Catholic last rites. I knew from Lindy's recent loss of her mother that the last thing to go is one's hearing. As my family members lamented bedside, my mother regained consciousness. She opened her eyes, saw her weeping children, and blurted, "I'm not dead yet." The connection to Jack Boland's story was surreal. I exited the room to a moonlit evening. It wasn't March 4th yet.

Days passed, and my mother went in and out of consciousness. We briefly spoke on Sunday afternoon. With weary eyes, she winked when I said I loved her and would see her later. She seemed stable at the time and eventually dozed off. As she slept, my late-night flight home awaited. Some critical business milestones in our company's recovery required a few days of my attention. Thousands of employees were relying on management to secure their future. Climbing through the clouds, my thoughts wavered between staying or leaving.

During the flight, my mother rapidly sank into a coma. She would not return to this world. When I arrived home, I informed Lindy of the latest development. My intuition turned out to be correct. It was just before midnight, the night of March 4th. My mother remained comatose until she died a week later, on March 11th. Our family returned to Florida for a second funeral less than four months after the first.

OUT OF DESPAIR COMES HOPE. PERSONAL LOSSES ASIDE, OUR company profits continued in the first quarter of 2001 and persisted in the second quarter. Newspaper headlines noted, "StorageTek on a profitable roll."[22] Dataquest analyst Fara Yale said, "I think there's a new energy and vigor at StorageTek I haven't seen for quite a while."[23]

Third- and fourth-quarter financial results exceeded expectations. Our ability to perform did not go unnoticed as the media touted that our "Strategic changes had quieted the doubters."[24] By the end of 2001, StorageTek had capped a remarkable two-year turnaround when most technology companies were struggling since the Y2K hype had left customers with excess equipment.

It was more of the same when we entered 2002. We continued surpassing expectations, and the future seemed limitless. With each successful quarterly result, enthusiasm grew. I was riding the wave of jubilation, knowing we had more great news to share as we continued to baffle Wall Street with our consistently strong financial performance. We were the darling of Wall Street, with loads of momentum.

Equally noteworthy was the fact that I was finally comfortable in my role. I had overcome many of my fears and was pleased that

I played a small part in our turnaround. The future looked brighter than ever before. Professionally, I had weathered another storm, and on a personal level, my family and I had moved through the grieving process of losing two mothers.

Or so I thought.

During the previous three years, which included the business downturn and the loss of two mothers, my sister had been battling ovarian cancer. Twice, it had gone into remission. The third time, she wasn't so fortunate. A year after my mother's death, she celebrated her 51st birthday. The next month, she followed my mother's footsteps to heaven. This was the third member of our family we had lost in eighteen months. The adage that "everything comes in threes" proved true in this instance.

During this time, Lindy tended to Brooke, who was dealing with some health issues. Still suffering from losing both grandparents, Jamie insisted on being with me at my sister's funeral. It wasn't easy living far from our family. Our flights back home to Florida were becoming routine. We were visiting ill family members—or burying them. I prayed again, for hope to follow despair. For the next four years, my family evaded further tragedy. We had time to grieve and time to recover. We grew closer together and closer to God.

From a business perspective, we achieved phenomenal success. We produced eighteen straight quarters of profitable growth, eliminated nearly $500 million in debt, and accumulated $2 billion in cash. For several years, the trade magazines ranked us as one of America's most admired companies to work for. The technology industry recognized our success, and we restored credibility with Wall Street. A higher stock valuation rewarded loyal investors. We received significant attention, enough for the technology giant Sun Microsystems to move strategically, acquiring us in a $4.1 billion transaction. The business tale had a fairy-tale ending and provided time for recuperation.

October 2007

Two years after the acquisition, Lindy and I shared a late dinner with my brother Tommy and his wife Debbie. We both sensed something awry, eerily like something we had seen before. Tommy didn't look well, slightly jaundiced. By Thanksgiving, he was undergoing tests. By Christmas, he was severely ill. On my birthday, January 15th, I received yet another phone call. Tommy's diagnosis was precise. He had cancer. Pancreatic cancer. Just like my mother.

It is difficult to tell of his escape from this world.

I wanted to run away and dreaded going through this again. Whenever I crossed a bridge over troubled waters, another wood plank fell off, and I swayed over the depths of raging waters, trying to reach the other side. He was closest in age to me, and I loved him dearly. We were teammates on the same Little League and Babe Ruth baseball teams and played ball for the same junior college. We worked at the same company for a time. Undoubtedly, he put in a good word to help me land a job after baseball was no longer possible for me. I loved him because we grew up together and were close to each other.

In early February, the doctors considered surgical alternatives, but the risks were too onerous. Over the next few weeks, his condition worsened, which placed him in hospice care. Nobody thought he would live beyond the first of March.

I could not remove March 4th from my thoughts.

But I knew he could.

Tommy had other plans. He was determined to deliver his last message of respect and love. Tommy was closest to my mother. Living across the street from our parents' home, he never shunned her calls for help. I never heard him complain about his time and effort helping our mother, and now he hung on for his life to continue. He was withering away slowly.

He outlived the prediction of an early March demise and passed by the March 4th date cemented in my head. Though he couldn't speak a word, I knew his plan. He would not leave this world until the time was right. Tommy crossed over to his new life precisely six years to the day after our mother passed away. It was March 11th. It was his way of honoring our mother, and he marched forth until that day.

Losing our parents or a loved one is something we all will likely endure in our lives. As I mentioned, my story is common to most people but unique to me.

I learned through these difficult years that no one event, loss, disappointment, or squashed dream would decide my destiny in life. No single event could influence me one way or the other. The turning point for me wasn't singular. The multitude of adversities that I lived through shaped who I would become and how I could survive and thrive in the remaining years of life.

Overcoming fear didn't come overnight. Conquering the premonition that I wasn't good enough didn't come from mastering something once. The turning points became apparent over time when I worked through the various difficulties life brought me: suffering through the losses that fell on me, resolving the issues that confronted me—thinking, believing, and knowing I could overcome—and understanding that fear can be mastered if you don't let fear master you.

IN THE DAYS OF NOAH, PEOPLE WERE CELEBRATING—EATING, drinking, marrying, and living rebelliously—until the flood wiped them out. In the days of Lot, the lifestyles of the people were similar, and in the end, fire and sulfur rained down, annihilating the city of Sodom.

Jesus addressed the coming of the kingdom of God in similar terms. He said, "It will be just like this on the day the Son of man is revealed. On that day, no one who is on the housetop, with possessions inside, should go down to get them. Likewise, no one in the field should go back for anything. Remember Lot's wife!"[25]

Jesus's message was simple: Lot's wife loved earthly pleasures too much, and this proved to be her undoing. They had received a warning when told to flee for their lives: "Do not look back; run entirely through the plains and continue until you reach the mountains." The consequences would be severe if they did not follow these instructions.

The story's end is familiar. Running for her life to escape the destruction of Sodom, she could not help but think of the lifestyle she was leaving behind, so she turned back for a peek. Her scriptural demise is described succinctly. "She became a pillar of salt."[26] Pulling away from sin was difficult. But the pleasures of sin had deadly consequences.

What factors come into play in our attempts to rid ourselves of inappropriate behaviors and sinful living? What allows this powerful pull to return us to our past practices? What convinces us that the unpleasant habits we give up outweigh the benefits of what lies ahead in our new course of direction? Is it hesitation? Are we reluctant to change from the outset because our desire for certain pleasures is too deeply rooted? Do we regret no longer having what we once enjoyed or doing with so much fondness? Do we feel bitter, resentful, or deprived? Are we prone to reassess our decision, wondering if we made the right choice? Are we stubborn, unwilling to sacrifice our time to try and change? Author L. Thomas Holdcroft once said, "The past is a guidepost, not a hitching post." Learning from the mistakes and hardships of our past is valuable. Holding on to them is dangerous.

The apostle Peter boasted of his loyalty toward Jesus, declaring he would die for him if necessary. Jesus knew Peter was more talk than action and would collapse under pressure. He told Peter in short order that he would deny him three times. Jesus was present for the third denial. As Peter finished his final repudiation, the rooster crowed just as Jesus predicted. At that moment, "The Lord turned and looked at Peter."[27] Peter remembered. The look from Jesus devastated Peter. He had failed his Lord, exposing his weakness. His bravado silenced, Peter left, weeping bitterly. For Peter, it was a turning point in his life, turning away from concentrating on himself to focusing on serving his Lord.

Mary Magdalene also had a significant turning point in her life—one with substantial ramifications for believers in Jesus Christ. Mary's background was quite interesting. After Jesus cured her of evil spirits, she toured with him and his disciples, contributing her resources to support them as they went from village to village. She followed and ministered to him in Galilee and Jerusalem, watched the events preceding his crucifixion unfold, and was one of the few who remained at the cross.

She didn't fear any potential wrath as she watched Jesus's death and burial. She prepared the proper spices to anoint his body and went silently in the morning to perform this ritualistic duty. Likely the last one to leave Calvary's hill and the first one to visit the grave, she was unafraid to accept the reality of her Savior's dead body. She did this freely, expecting nothing in return. No fees. No thank-you from anyone. She wasn't tired of being the one who cared. To her, this was important. She would have it no other way.

Through the early morning mist, she approached the tomb. Still dark, she was surprised to see the enormous stone removed from the entrance to the grave. Physically and mentally exhausted, she peered inside and discovered the body of Jesus was missing. In search of help, she darted away to get Peter and John, who hustled to the tomb without hesitation. The younger John arrived first, squatted at the entrance, and glanced inside to see the linen cloths. Peter barged in, wondering what had happened. John joined him but was silent. Did they even think that Jesus might be alive? Hold that thought for now.

After the rush of excitement from the morning's events, a discussion of what steps to take seemed logical. Rally the troops and create a game plan to find the underlying reason for the missing body. Instead, the two disciples decided differently and simply returned to their homes.

Mary didn't budge. She stayed at the tomb, crying. She watched in dismay as her two friends left the scene. She was alone, but something more substantial trumped her emotions—her determination. She wanted answers, and until she got them, she wasn't budging.

Peering back into the tomb, two angels surrounded the spot where Jesus once lay. They asked Mary why she was crying. She neither feared them nor viewed them as ghosts; instead, she responded that someone had taken her Lord away, and she was unaware of his whereabouts.

A light shuffling prompted Mary to peer over her shoulder. She assumed the local gardener, with a rake and shovel in hand, was there to complete his early morning duties. The gardener asked why she was crying and whom she was looking for. Mary responded respectfully, hoping he was the one who took the body. She pleaded for the location and vowed to take Jesus's body away. Miraculously, whether blinded by tears or the circumstances themselves, Mary didn't recognize it was Jesus.

Then came a pause, and Mary looked back into the tomb.

How often do we get distraught over a tricky, lingering situation or relationship? We search for answers, analyzing every aspect of our dilemma. We look for evidential clues to solve our predicament or search for novel approaches to avoid what is unpleasant or unrelenting. We get upset when resolutions aren't prompt. Hours, days, or weeks are spent searching for the correct answer to put our issue to bed. With self-reflection, we sometimes realize the answer was right in front of us—if we had only searched the right way and for the right reason from the start. It is incumbent upon us to start every search focused on Jesus. Our hope of heaven rests on him.

Mary's deep thoughts at that moment will be forever known only by her.

Finally, the gardener-looking Jesus spoke. "Mary."

Perhaps she tilted her head and squinted, curious and concentrating. The voice behind her seemed familiar. It sounded like…

Mary turned toward Jesus, a turning point so significant it will remain forever in memory. She cried out, "Teacher!" It was Jesus! He was alive! Jesus was alive!

Thankfully, Jesus is *still* alive!

It's hard to imagine the elation Mary must've felt seeing Jesus. The sheer joy of knowing her Savior was alive, the adrenaline rush. Once pierced by nails to the cross, his convincing return restored her hopes. Jesus conquered death because it had no dominion over him. It's no surprise that Mary jumped for joy and wrapped her arms around him. Who wouldn't?

Jesus told her not to cling to him, however, but to tell his brothers. Imagine the jubilant celebration when everyone who followed Jesus heard of his resurrection, a joy we share today, centuries after it occurred. Jesus was, is, and will always be present for anyone searching for him.

History has a way of making us think about the past. I looked back at what I thought were turning points in my life only to find out they ended up being something different than I expected. When I failed, I thought the world viewed me as unsuccessful. I tried to make every failure a turning point in my life. Each misstep added to my insecurity and convinced me I wasn't good enough in the eyes of the world. It increased my fear of subsequent failure. There were times I was paralyzed by those escalating failures. I doubted my decisions.

At one point, I researched the top ten signs of a person who was dangerously depressed. I had nine of the ten. The tenth reason never crossed my mind—the consideration of suicide. Thank God! The pressure to please and succeed was self-inflicted. I fought off every two-strike pitch life threw at me but would not give in to the naysayers nor give up on those who depended on me. My faith needed more growth.

I thank God for planting a seed in my heart and mind. It kept me away from the dark hole. He had a better plan for me, and he gave me the time to figure it out. He wanted me to learn the joys of living life under the influence of Jesus. He wanted me to live with the restored hope of Mary Magdalene, emboldened and unafraid.

There is a common thread with those involved in the gravesite scene after Jesus's resurrection: fear! All three gospel writers made a note of it. Luke said the women bowed to the ground in fear. Matthew mentioned Jesus saying they shouldn't be afraid but to tell his brothers to meet him in Galilee. And Mark explained they left quickly because they were full of fear. Why might this have been important to them at that time? And to us, today?

When Mary Magdalene first saw Jesus alive, it made sense that he would tell her not to cling to him. Putting her joy and excitement aside, Jesus had not ascended to his Father yet, and Mary needed to help take advantage of his remaining time on earth by sharing the good news with his disciples.

William Barclay, a world-renowned New Testament interpreter and scholar, suggested the manuscripts might have been copied incorrectly. He noted, "Some scholars think that what John originally wrote was not *me aptou*, do not touch (or cling to) me, but *me ptoou*, do not be afraid."[28] A slight variation of a few symbols written with archaic writing tools. But a different conclusion since the verb *ptoein* means to "flutter with fear." Both translations make sense coming from Jesus. Both have true meanings. But if the latter is correct, Jesus told Mary, "Don't be afraid."

That profound message should resonate with us today. By conquering death through his resurrection, Jesus is saying, "Do not fear!" He is alive. He will be with us always through our hardships, struggles, and failures. He will be next to us when we suffer and grieve, and he will be with us in our joyful times, celebrating our good fortunes. Jesus wants us to put our fears aside.

God had a better plan for me, a different plan, which didn't require me to be famous or have a prominent position. The world had pulled me in, and I had allowed myself to be enticed, to enjoy it. I had lived through the thrill of victory and the agony of defeat. It took decades of disappointments and myriad setbacks to understand the importance of enduring every one of them, to *get it!*

What happened over forty years—coming to understand and know God was always there, working behind the scenes and looking for the best in me—created in me a new spirit. Unfortunately, I didn't see it at the time because of the enormous pull to either remain in or turn back to the ways of the past, believing I could fix or change things in my way, on my time frame, but all while seeking to gain approval from those setting expectations based on worldly parameters.

God's parameters, however, are not of this world. He remained with me the whole time, patiently waiting for me to realize where my ambitions truly dwelt. He created me in his image and didn't make a mistake despite my stumblings and shortcomings, whether perceived or actual. I was the one who made mistakes, and God revealed his power through my weakness. His love never fails, and he saw value in me even while I looked for the world to see the same in me.

There was no singular turning point where I can say, "That was when everything in my life changed forever." Instead, my turning point resulted from an accumulation of lessons that occurred over decades. I didn't work through a single incident of difficulty or a specific circumstance and then decide to move on. My turning point came when I realized God saw me as one of his precious treasures. I'm thankful and fortunate that I didn't lose hope when I felt discouraged and disconnected. He was willing to watch me work through the process and help me get to the finish line.

My desire through all these disappointments—whether it was baseball, a business of my own, or even the hardships of an executive position—was to find a way to impact the lives of those whose path I crossed. I learned valuable lessons to be effective in doing so. Throughout each of the storms I weathered, I learned and built upon seven principles.

Each one is distinct but linked with the others. They all connected through my hardships and disappointments, and I needed to grasp their importance. They became my tricks of the trade to understand why all my efforts and resiliency kept clashing with the fears embedded in my appetite for success. These guideposts helped me work through and move on from the battles. They helped me become more effective and provided a framework to influence and impact the lives of others.

Ironically, I remember these principles by the acronym IMPACTS. Each letter represents an important attribute to remember if you desire to weather the storms in your life so you can impact the lives of others. In the following chapters, I hope the practical application of these IMPACTS will make your finish line more transparent and reachable, as it is for me.

THE I.M.P.A.C.T.S.

5

Identification—Determine Who You Are

*If you don't know who you truly are,
you'll never know what you really want.*
—Roy T. Bennett

Jill returned from the pool and lifted the towel from her chair to see her purse missing. Terry finished a four-week project and discovered his boss had taken full credit for it. Amy had her grade lowered because her views and principles differed from those of her teachers.

Jill was robbed, Terry was exploited, and Amy was violated. If you've ever felt that way, you are not alone. These are common occurrences.

Identity theft continues to be a growing challenge in the electronic age. Millions of people are affected annually, with billions of dollars stolen. The Federal Trade Commission reported that in 2021, $2.3 billion of losses occurred from impostor scams, 2.8 million customers reported fraudulent activities, and 1.4 million people submitted identity-theft claims.[29] Identity theft claims a new victim every two seconds; 30 percent of the time, they endure a repeat occurrence.[30] Seniors are the most common victims, but sadly, so are children.

Past television commercials depicted an individual looming on dark streets seeking personal information. Data destined for the landfill is left innocently in a curbside garbage can, ripe for the picking. But that's old school. Forget having your personal information exposed during an eerie stroll at night; it's easier to secure that information from the comforts of one's home. In the dark. Undetected. Unseen.

Thieves seize credit card information through unsecured networks and old or shared passwords. Once in hand, the perpetrator spends freely and quickly. Reviewing a credit card statement a month later reveals the damage. By then, the thieves have finished their spending spree.

There is little difficulty calculating the financial losses, but the effect of compromised personal information is unmeasurable. Email addresses and passwords get hacked frequently, and cyberpunks send embarrassing and confusing messages to a user's complete contact list. It can take months or years to recover financially from such crimes and much longer to reestablish one's reputation or credibility. Again, older adults become easy prey.

Most individuals have received a phone call from their bank asking about specific purchases. An attempt to buy $23,000 of electronics got charged to my credit card, and the next day, another $16,000. Thieves stole my credit card data while I conducted business abroad, and I struggled for weeks to find out which country and in what way. My bank representative informed me the hack attacks occurred in Saudi Arabia, but I never stepped foot there. Fortunately, fraud prevention processes squelched the attempts, and I averted financial damage. Unsurprisingly, identity-theft protection and fraud services have exploded into a multibillion-dollar industry.

Have you ever had your wallet or purse stolen? Yes? Me too. Restaurant in Boston. Business discussions over lunch. Briefcase by my side. Unzipped pockets. The thief charged thousands of dollars before I recognized my wallet was missing and notified the credit card companies. All in fifteen minutes. If it hasn't happened to you, it likely will. If not, it will occur to someone you know.

A crisis? It seems that way. Your identity is stolen. Your electronic footprint is seized. The assets you own are taken, and an impostor's gain comes at your expense. Even if the odds are in your favor and financial damage is averted, that feeling of being robbed or violated by someone you don't know is bothersome. Sometimes panic sets in. *How could this happen? Why me?*

Jolts like this prompt immediate preventive steps to ensure it doesn't happen again. You secure the issuance of a new credit card, change and strengthen your passwords, and insist on being more diligent. Chalk one up for a lesson learned to be more careful. And then, a return to normality, the same routines. As far as you know, the identity crisis is over. At least for the moment.

But is it over?

Author Stephen Covey wrote, "We often hear about identity theft when someone takes your wallet, pretends to be you, and uses your credit cards. But the more serious identity theft is to get swallowed up in other peoples' definition of you."[31]

Take a moment to list the nontangible assets that define you. The moral persona that allows you to bring value to our world. Attributes that define your life. Traits that distinguish the quality of your character. Thoughts that direct your mental activity. Motives that cause you to act. The innate dynamics that characterize who you are as a person every day, no matter what circumstances or crises you face on your journey in life. With your friends, throughout your career, or at your place of worship.

These characteristics help craft your identification badge. You wear it every day, like an access badge for your place of employment. You check in with it, knowing that these principles will guide your influence on others. When your day is complete, you check out with it, having the peace of mind of knowing you were true to yourself—whatever "true to yourself" means to you. Focus on that ID badge and what it represents to you. Ask yourself, "Who am

I?" Don't respond with who you say you are, but instead, who you really are. Answer honestly. Refrain from responding to what other people think of you. It's not up to them, because it isn't their badge.

Everyone has their own set of fingerprints, their DNA, and their identification. Your parents cannot decide your identity outside of your name. Nor can your teachers, friends, bosses, or ministers. It's your call and only your call. Others can only confirm that your actions match up to the badge you're wearing.

St. Augustine, a Christian writer and philosopher from the third century, once said, "In order to discover the character of people, we have only to observe what they love."[32] What is it that you love? How are the things you love used in your life? Do they inspire, influence, and affect change? Do they make an impact?

If making money is a top priority, those with the same vision will be attracted to you. If you are willing to do anything and everything to get to the top of an organization, then the way you choose to work with others will be scrutinized or given credence. If your promises remain unfulfilled, then your credibility will be questioned. You will not gain trust if you say one thing but contradict it by doing something else.

Likewise, if you're consistent, others will note you are serious and not just going through the motions. If you dress neatly or poorly, then your followers will mimic you. If you speak kindly or harshly, so will your followers. If you are the same person outside the walls of the church building as inside its hallowed walls, then your ability to influence will be considerable. Every aspiration you have will be seen through the lens of those on the journey with you.

Want to have a lasting impact on others? Reconsider the question, "Who am I?" Your answer will have a significant bearing on your ability to influence them. Go through a vetting process of yourself. Challenge the commitment you are making to yourself. This is foundational and a necessary first step.

The story of Moses depicts a man trying to find himself as a person. Early in the Old Testament, God saw his people's suffering under Egyptian bondage. The Israelites were at the mercy of their slave drivers. Oppressed. Overworked. Undernourished. Nasty working conditions. Moses however, spared from the pharaoh's decree to drown all infant boys, lived with an alternate identity that was given to him. He was the son of the pharaoh's daughter, and he reaped all the benefits of being her son: good fortune, tasty food, fine wine. Sounds like a great life.

Until his outward identification was exposed.

When he saw an Egyptian soldier ruthlessly abusing one of the Hebrew captives, he took matters into his own hands. Seeing no witnesses, he murdered the tyrant and buried the body. The next day, evidence from his crime scene was exposed when he tried breaking up a fight between his fellow brothers. Instantly, his identification changed. He was no longer recognized as an Egyptian but rather a Hebrew, just like those who served the pharaoh. And now he was a fugitive in the eyes of the pharaoh, whose daughter claimed him as her son.

What now? Who was he, and who would he become? What would he do? Faced with this dire situation, the pull to run away was powerful. Should he run from his problems, his past, and his privileged lifestyle? Isolate himself? Hide? Live under the radar, deep within the mountains? Running seemed like Moses's only option for escaping his predicament, so, he did just that.

But God saw more in Moses than Moses saw in himself. God saw the opportunity for him to lead by example, to be bold, and to serve. The opportunity to develop his character, to look deep within himself. This plan needed faith, included struggles, and required time—all of these aspects would help define who Moses would become.

That was true for Moses then, and it remains true for us today. God sees value in each of us. He created us without making any gaffes. There is no island for misfit people because God created everyone in his image. He has plans for us, just as he did for Moses. Better plans. Fruitful plans.

Like Moses, our character isn't determined by a single event, be it an achievement or failure. It's developed over time by the decisions we make and the actions we take. How we react and plan for life's roller-coaster ride in an imperfect and unfair world becomes our testimony to others. The patterns we form substantiate our character, giving clarity and preciseness to those watching. Their perception of you and me becomes their reality, not ours.

In exile, tending his flock, Moses had to face his destiny. No more running or hiding. God stepped in and gave him a directive: step it up and do what is right; do something good. From a burning bush, the Lord told him to secure the release of his people. (Imagine how you or I might feel about the prospect of explaining this scenario to people in today's world. People would think we were crazy!) Moses, reluctant, had one question: "Who am I that I should go to Pharaoh and bring the Israelites out of Egypt?"[33]

Years had passed since Moses escaped from the grasp of the pharaoh's soldiers. He had minded his own business, simply poking and prodding sheep, living the secluded life, lying low. He hoped his past had been forgotten and that his future would be kept secret. Like Pumbaa in *The Lion King*, his aim seemed to be *hakuna matata!* No cares, no worries.

What was the underlying reason for his reluctance to follow God's directive? Initially, it was fear, and Moses struggled with this new role. Leading people was not his forte, and he had no experience or training to do such a task. Why did he get this onerous assignment?

I experienced a similar fear, and I'm sure you have as well. We ask similar questions. What is going to happen to me? What could go wrong? What if this doesn't work out? What is the worst that could happen to me (and this was not asked flippantly, but from a place of deep-seated worry)? And if the worst happens to me, what do I do? The same fears that agitated Moses troubled me.

Moses recalled his earlier crime and escape, and the thought of the pharaoh's wrath overwhelmed him. Fear of the unknown was enough to send him to the hills. God's plan for Moses, however, went beyond facing the pharaoh and releasing the Israelites; God's plan laid the foundation for Moses to become a leader. He committed to be with Moses each step of the way. He wanted Moses to answer the call, to step up to the plate, ready to swing for the good of his people.

Moses knew he had to do something. He saw his friends being treated horribly, yet he remained hesitant, uncertain whether he could handle an interrogation. But why? Was he questioning his abilities (I cannot do this.)? Did he need more confidence (I need to be trained to do this.)? Low self-esteem (I am not good enough.)? Insufficient desire (I wonder if I even want to do this.)?

Whatever the reason, Moses's internal struggles continued, and his self-evaluation was inconclusive, just as it often is with you and me. Whether you are a student, athlete, parent, employee, churchgoer, or someone or something else entirely, facing inevitable challenges with a sense of fear and uncertainty is as certain as our need to breathe. Moses's uncertainty, however, wasn't solely from a lack of understanding about who he was and what he could accomplish. At least not at that time. There was a missing link—a connection with God.

God knew Moses could lead his people out of captivity, despite Moses having a diminished opinion of himself, so He waited for Moses to let him into his life so he could then use his talents purposefully. Moses inquired as to how he should reply if he was asked who had sent him. God responded to Moses, clearly establishing His identification. "I AM WHO I AM. This is what you are to say to the Israelites: I AM has sent me to you."[34]

Many will read God's identification and wonder what it means. But those connected to God will see a God of power and a source of strength. This God created the universe, pitched stars across the sky, and arranged the sun for warmth and rain for moisture. God might just as well have said, "Just tell them I AM has sent you!" Nothing more needed to be said.

God planned to test the Egyptian leaders and pledged to give his people favor. Moses, of course, had no clue of the plagues that were soon to be released on the pharaoh and the Egyptians, but he would not be engaging in the confrontation empty-handed and needed to trust God's plan. Moses had God's assurance, after all, and that was all he needed—if only he would realize it, let God be God, and let him rescue, protect, encourage, and save them.

Despite God's assurances and demonstration of power, however, even though God showed confidence that everything would work out as he wished, and although God was in control, Moses continued to doubt, questioning his speaking abilities, uncertain if he could convince the Israelites. Rather than feeling confident and empowered because God was with him, he still felt powerless.

FEAR, UNCERTAINTY, AND DOUBT ARE THE SAME TACTICS THAT have stymied personal growth for millennia. Bookshelves across the world are stuffed with self-help books written to help conquer these issues, but they remain obstacles for struggling individuals.

Every one of us grew up with a unique set of circumstances. We didn't get to decide the events (good or bad) that occurred in our lives, choose those who would attend school alongside us, or cherry-pick our next-door neighbors. But there are things we have and can choose to do, including having sufficient abilities to lead and serve others. Like diamonds in the rough, however, we need to polish our skills and learn to collaborate with people effectively to positively influence them.

Start the process by asking, "Who am I?" Write it down so you can read it to yourself. I am someone who will work hard and refuse to quit. I am committed to maintaining high ethical standards without compromising my principles. I am willing to sacrifice for the good of my team, even at my own expense. I am going to help those in need, to make a positive impact on their lives. I am going to be honest with others, trustworthy, dependable, compassionate, and caring.

Now look over your list. Add to it wherever necessary and take away from it if you won't commit to a particular trait or idea. But in all cases, personalize it. Eventually, you will be tested by your peers—those who look up to you and those who don't.

Consider the apostle Paul's assessment of himself. He reminded the Corinthians of all the appearances Jesus made after his resurrection: first to Peter and then to the twelve disciples, and then more than five hundred brethren saw him at one time. Then came His brother James and all the apostles. Then, "…last of all, he appeared to me also, as to one abnormally born. For I am the least of the apostles, and do not even deserve to be called an apostle because I persecuted the Church of God. But by the grace of God, I am what I am, and His grace to me was not without effect."[35]

Any of Jesus's followers would have wanted to be the first to see him after his resurrection. Peter denied Jesus three times but was the first in line to receive comfort from Jesus. Paul was the last and the least. The reference to himself as abnormally born is derived from the Greek word *ektroma*, meaning Paul likened himself to an aborted child,[36] one who was born at the wrong time, prematurely, yet given a chance to live. He felt insufficient and unworthy to be associated with the other apostles. And because of his past aggressions toward believers, Paul considered himself undeserving of attention.

But Jesus still came to Paul. Why? Because Paul made life-altering adjustments. He no longer identified himself with his past ways and past life. He no longer placed himself on a pedestal to rule over those he deemed beneath him. Paul sought a new identity, one with Jesus stamped on his heart.

His resultant turnaround was so extreme that others questioned if it was real. Those seeing him were mesmerized because this was the guy who had done all those horrible things to Christians. Yet through all of Paul's efforts, he gave credit where credit was due, admitting that God's grace made him who he was. With God, he was strong, powerful, and confident in his new identity in Christ. He became an influencer of people and a leader by example.

There may be times we feel unwanted, unappreciated, or undeserving, whether as a parent, employee, teammate, or even a believer. Paul's discomfort came from how he felt about himself. If similar thoughts creep into our minds, we should remember that by God's grace, we can cultivate and produce enormous impacts within ourselves and in the lives of others.

CHILDREN ARE JUST AS SUSCEPTIBLE TO IDENTITY THEFT AS adults are. Their character develops as they grow in age and understanding. Leaving home for college or trade school is usually the first time most young adults will begin to face the task of discovering the individual they will become. No more parents, neighborhood watchdogs, or even church monitors looking over their shoulders to ensure they stay on the straight and narrow. It's their time to develop a skill or trade to earn a living and meet new people who hold views that may or may not be similar to their own. They will be inundated with new experiences, challenges, ideas, opportunities to make friends, and yes, temptations.

I met a new high school graduate determined to attend a college that was right for her. She had decided to go out of state, away from home. She researched cities and campuses, investigated upcoming events and concerts, and explored sororities she could join. Her father told her all those criteria were available at the local university and asked why she felt compelled to attend an out-of-state school. She answered, "I need to find myself, and being away from home will allow me to do so." The father reasoned she could find herself at the local university near home without the elevated out-of-state tuition costs. Truth resided in what the young woman said to her father.

The way we approach life, business, school, friends, marriage, and even our moral being, depends on the character we develop, given the circumstances we face. This power lies within each of us. The people we hope to influence, spiritually or secularly, will look at our words and the character revealed in how we consistently live.

I had a boss introduce himself to his staff on the first day of the job, saying, "You may think I am the nicest guy in the world or the biggest SOB. Whichever opinion you hold, I commit to being the same every day." That was his identity badge. To be the same person every day. I knew who he was when he came to work. I knew what he would stand for and not tolerate. He wouldn't waffle on his principles, whether good or bad, or treat people differently. He would be who he said he would be. He was persuasive. And successful.

I tried to live this consistency principle throughout my career (though not the SOB part). Hundreds of people across the globe directly involved with the financial integrity of our company reported to the CFO's organization. I had to ensure there was a consistent approach to the financial disciplines in dozens of countries having different languages, cultures, and educational levels.

The then-current corporate scandals of fraud and insider trading with Enron and WorldCom were putting extra scrutiny on public corporations' financial organizations and personnel, so I knew I was being watched more closely than ever. I may have been the nicest guy in the world for some employees, and to others, I may have been the biggest jerk (hopefully not). Regardless of the differing opinions, I always tried to be the same every day, because by doing so, people knew what to expect, and the consistency in my behavioral patterns made working on common goals easier for everyone.

Jesus Christ set the record straight as to who he was. His ID badge stood firm and clear. In John's book, he stated, "**I am** the bread of life.[37] **I am** the light of the world.[38] **I am** the resurrection and the life.[39] **I am** the way, the truth, and the life.[40] **I am** the vine; you are the branches. If you remain in me and I in you, you will bear much fruit."[41]

Jesus never drifted away from any of these identifying statements. He focused on doing his Father's will and was devoted to teaching—doctrines considered to be radical both during those times and by many today. Because of his keen sense of purpose, he became a well-known (not necessarily favorably) and acclaimed person. Peter acknowledged him as the Son of the living God, as did the demons who feared and knew him.

Even the governor, Pontius Pilate, recognized Jesus as "The King of the Jews" in the trial he presided over. He confirmed his view by ordering the inscription to be placed on the cross of the crucified Jesus. The chief priests who battled with Jesus didn't want him to be identified as such and demanded that Pilate change the inscription to say Jesus "claimed" to be the King of the Jews. Pilate reiterated, "What I have written, I have written."[42] Pilate understood—Jesus was who he said he was.

Jesus never relinquished his identity. He was fully aware of his mission, his consistency was irrefutable, and his friends and followers who had contact with him knew what to expect. The same could be said for those who tried to intimidate him, adversaries who opposed him, and those who feared him. Whether you agreed with his teachings or not, you at least knew where he was coming from, every time. What a model of consistency! And an excellent way to be influential and impact humanity.

The same holds for any spiritually minded person in today's world who is trying to help others. Speak and act as if your identification is at stake because it is! Inconsistency will reduce or eliminate your ability to influence those who closely watch you. The persona you bring to church on Sunday must be the same one you bring to work on Monday.

Three influential and successful people—poet Ezra Pound, chewing-gum founder William Wrigley Jr., and the automotive icon Henry Ford—have been credited for a quote I read early in my career: "If you and your boss always agree, one of you is not necessary."

The best way to improve as an individual or an organization is to challenge one another respectfully. When peer agreement is constant, it is typically coupled with a lack of diligence and creativity, resulting in complacency. People begin to settle rather than stretch for results. These "yes" people do whatever is asked of them. Whether it's their boss, parent, teacher, counselor, or coach, they look to please or help someone look or feel good. It may be done to avoid conflict or to elevate themselves and their career.

Unfortunately, in doing so, they often disregard their principles and beliefs. When they compromise their beliefs because of pressure, their character becomes suspect.

Those watching will notice this concession. They will see the inconsistency. They will recognize someone who says one thing but does something different. The words they hear will lose meaning because someone's identification is contradictory. This inconsistent and changing identification diminishes one's ability to influence others.

Be aware of how you react in demanding situations or adverse conditions. When times are good and problems are nonthreatening, don't be complacent during these moments because it seems they're irrelevant. Remain on guard, because when the stuff hits the fan and emotions are elevated, people will watch and remember how you manage any chaotic situation. The influence you have developed over a prolonged period can be wiped out in just a few moments of panic.

WHEN A TEAM STRUGGLES, THE COACH IS ALMOST ALWAYS THE first to get the blame, usually in the form of the team's owners firing him or her. Then the newly hired coach often replaces all the existing assistant coaches. Why? The assumption is they're all connected to and responsible for the previous lack of success, so dismissing the whole staff of losers creates the opportunity to erase the past and provide a fresh start.

I faced that when StorageTek hired Pat Martin as its new CEO following my dreadful first year as the CFO. Pat's objective was clear: turn this company around and recreate the value it once had. He had decades of business experience and a demeanor the board of directors coveted. Straight out of the Bronx, he was staunch as steel, all business, knew how to get every ounce of effort out of everyone, and taking prisoners wasn't an option. In his world, you didn't get benched for not making the necessary changes or delivering results; you got cut from the team.

The existing management team began updating their resumes, as it was highly likely the new boss would bring in some of his former colleagues. The case for my potential ouster was more likely since the board of directors would have informed Pat of my intent to resign six months earlier. I figured it was only a matter of time.

Pat laid the groundwork when he visited our corporate headquarters before the official press release announcing his appointment. I assumed he wanted a deep dive into the business before coming on board. On a Saturday morning, he arranged individual reviews with a few current executives spaced a few hours apart. I was first in line, meeting him off-site, starting at 4:30 a.m., Mountain Standard Time. It was a late start for him, having just arrived from the East Coast.

He pressed me the moment we shook hands. His deposition-like questioning amazed me. His inquiries were exhaustive and came from every angle. He had every report, project status, and collection of meeting minutes for every organization, region, country, and person in management. You name it, he had it—and he comprehended it. He had an incredible memory, thanks to the vast amount of reading he had done, and he understood the information I shared with him as well as, if not better, than me. Having set out to learn the business and my understanding of it, he wanted to know if I had enough game to play in his new world.

Three hours later, I drove him from Boulder to Louisville for his eight o'clock meeting with his next victim (how I felt), except the individual didn't show up for personal reasons. I stood there with Pat, in an empty building, with three more available hours. My second deposition lasted until noon. We poured through business topics, functional processes, country-by-country operations, and strategic initiatives. If I hadn't prepared and learned from all the prior years' miscues and misfortunes, our time together would have been useless. I didn't know this would start a new way of thinking and believing. I didn't know if I was up to the task and wasn't even sure if I would be around.

Shortly after Pat came on board, it didn't take long before I saw frequent visits to the corner office by some of my peers. Challenging him was taboo, so people avoided saying anything to upset him, at least directly. Some management team members who used to speak their minds soon became "yes" men. Staff members would now say things they thought he wanted to hear, and the fear of losing their jobs caused changes in behavior and principles previously held. It appeared as if their identity underwent a sudden transformation.

Three months later, my day with the boss eventually arrived. His first quarterly report to Wall Street would come with disappointing news. A supply issue from vendors unable to ship flex circuits and chip components caused a temporary shortfall in our sales. We would miss earnings estimates.

Before we preannounced the results, he summoned me to his office so I could explain the financial shortfall. He reminded me that missing quarterly expectations would cause market turmoil and trigger a stock sell-off—as though I hadn't just survived the brutal process of surprising Wall Street's investors in a bad way and then being bombarded by questions after millions of dollars of value had been erased.

This bad start for the newly hired boss wouldn't sit well with the shareholders, much less him. He asked what I could do to improve the numbers, hoping for a way to meet expectations.

That kind of comment often lends itself to doing something akin to fixing, or changing, the numbers to improve them. That wasn't the case here as the story unfolded.

Our discussions heated up when my response didn't include reporting additional sales and profits. A phone call to one of his former employees in a position similar to mine gave false hope there were alternatives to consider that could improve the results.

His phone call ended, but our debate raged on. There was nothing else I could do. With no sign of the pressure ceasing, I lost it. I had had enough. With a clenched jawbone and bulging eyes matching his, I pointed my finger and sternly rebuked him. "I am going to tell you what you need to hear, not what you want to hear. The results are final."

Silence.

The meeting ended abruptly.

I knew it was time to leave and presumed my tirade wouldn't be tolerated. Several staff members would eventually depart, and I figured to be next on the list. Distraught, I left the building immediately. Rather than resigning, I anticipated I would be fired.

I called Lindy and mumbled, "I think I just got myself fired." I knew right from wrong, and what I said to my boss was right. Though pointing my finger at him may have crossed the line, I was unwilling to compromise the principles I was taught and grew up believing. I stood my ground, true to my identity, even if it meant losing my job and the financial security that went with it.

As the company continued its recovery, I recalled that day of reckoning with my boss during those challenging times and finally grasped his motive—he was evaluating and teaching me. He sought those who would stand up for what they believed. He wanted to know who would challenge the status quo and anyone who sought it out, even if that included him. He wanted to know whom he could count on to stand up for what was right, who the strong people were who would risk themselves for the company's good. He wanted a different culture—one that delivered positive change—and in doing so, he set out to influence people, extracting value from them to create value for the company.

There were twelve executive team members when Pat came on board. When the dust settled, only one remained—the guy who previously tried to resign. The lesson I learned and my new boss's impact on me, was instrumental in my career. More importantly, it helped me in life. I always looked for mentors who would help me grow—leaders who instilled hope and confidence, demonstrated composure when handling adversity, and pushed me to new limits.

JESUS WAS THE ULTIMATE LEADER. NOBODY FACED MORE PRESsure-packed situations during or near the end of their life than he did. The Hebrew writer said, "Jesus Christ is the same yesterday and today and forever."[43] The inspiration Jesus provided will forever be a source of empowerment to all who serve him. Jesus led firmly but fairly. Whether tempted by the devil or challenged by governmental authorities, Jesus wasn't a yes-man and thus didn't give in to their enticing promises or fall in line with their improper ideals. He lived his life with one purpose—doing his Father's will.

I began to change as a person after I discovered my true identity and the expectations of others stopped dominating my existence. A good friend once told me, "You have to respect yourself if you want to be respected by others." If I didn't, nothing else would matter.

God created and chose you. He sees value in you and in your destiny to do remarkable things. He selected you to bear long-lasting fruit. When you go through your identity process, do so carefully. It is a valuable asset, your prized possession. Protect it. Wear your ID badge proudly, without fear, uncertainty, or doubt. Wear it in your life's peaks (successes) and valleys (failures). Wear it in the calm and in the chaos.

Let your deepest desires—those that define you—illuminate your life and the lives of others and be sure to guard against those who don't share your values. Let the love of God be more than a part of your identity; let it be the core of your identity. It is the critical first step to unleashing your ability to influence and impact the lives of others.

6

Motivation—What Moves You?

Motives reveal why we do what we do, which is actually more important to God than what we're doing.

—Joyce Meyer

"Talk is cheap!" some will say.

Not exactly.

Fees for motivational speakers are in the five-to-six-figure range. Athletes and authors, coaches and celebrities, executives and politicians actively put their names and stories to work during and after their careers. The Leading Motivational Speakers Agency's website explains the speaking circuit in terms of A, B, and C lists when revealing the costs for a celebrity speaker. Estimates for high-profile figures like Bill Gates and Oprah Winfrey may garner between $500,000 and $1,000,000; entertainers like Reese Witherspoon and Ron Howard reap in the range of $250,000 to $500,000; athletes like Peyton Manning and Magic Johnson collect between $100,000 and $250,000.[44] According to Forbes, treasury-secretary Janet Yellen earned more than $7 million in speaking fees over a two-year period.[45]

It's no surprise the motivational business is a billion-dollar industry. Bookstores are full of shelves with how-to manuals and DVDs. Audiobooks offered on Amazon cover every subject imaginable. Patrons pack auditoriums eager to hear motivational speakers deliberate on topics specific to their needs while breaking news stories activate drama in our daily lives.

Speakers aren't necessarily hired for their ability to articulate eloquently. Their prominence, personal encounters, or expertise in a chosen field drive demand. Success stories, comeback tales, and legendary achievements of an underdog feed the enormous appetites of those wanting to hear awe-inspiring, true-life stories. Targets include anyone seeking help or hope, and there are few better ways to seek answers for nagging and prolonged problems than from someone who has conquered the same issue you currently face.

Ask a handful of people to define motivation and you will receive a wide range of answers. The law of physics describes it as the motion of a moving object, measured by its mass and velocity. Aside from the scientists, most will respond in terms of personal experiences, like a sports team changing the momentum when making a comeback. It's been said, "The loudest noise in golf is the swift change of momentum."

Motivation is a strange force that takes over a situation with great strength or electric emotion and continues building and growing. It goes beyond sports comebacks. Novelists create ever-building tension with each page, leading to a thrilling conclusion. Patients recovering from an injury gain momentum with each therapy session that shows improvement. Addicts grow confident every time they walk away from demons that are desperately trying to keep them hooked. Troubled marriages begin to heal as couples seek therapy and learn to work through disagreements. Christians strengthen their faith with each trial, knowing God is present and ready to help. In each case, there is optimism, growth, and strength. Perceived impossibilities turn into high probabilities.

Motivation stimulates us through a combination of internal and external influences. These emotions or energies encourage us to work harder, take extra steps, and test our limits, so that goals once considered insurmountable are now perceived to be achievable. Its presence is undeniable, and its absence all too familiar, reminding us that the driving force within us can propel us to great heights and transform the impossible into the possible.

WHY IS THERE A CONTINUOUS SEARCH FOR MOTIVATION WHEN the incredible offerings of God, such as the hope of heaven and the promise of eternal life, are available to every human being? Aren't the promises of God sufficient inspiration for all? Hasn't God proven his care for those who are following him? Isn't God's grace shown in our lives when we receive gifts of kindness, even though we haven't done anything to deserve them?

If the answer to these questions is yes, then why does there exist the need to be motivated by anyone or anything other than God and the promises he made to us?

Explore the Bible, find the word "motivation," and see what the scriptures say about it. Keep looking. You may need help finding it. I sure couldn't. Why not? Because motivation, the word itself, is a noun, merely an idea. The biblical terms supporting the concept of motivation are verbs requiring action. This was intentional. Our lives are to be active. We are supposed to do things.

Encouragement is a way to inspire bravery and confidence, stimulating others in their endeavors. It is why we comfort those experiencing trouble, console those amidst sorrow, build one another up, and treat each other respectfully. We pray, forgive, inspire, love, and exercise patience. All of these are active choices, and as such, they are the force and strength that encourage individual and spiritual growth. They are the "how" we can motivate.

What drives you to motivate others or even yourself? The answer lies in your motives—the reason you do something. Motives persuade, incentivize, or prompt you to act a particular way. A promotion might convince you to relocate for a better job opportunity.

If you are a sales agent, bonuses are structured to incentivize you to sell more. A desire or need to lose weight might prompt you to start a regular exercise program or engage in a healthier diet. Motives are beneficial, especially when self-sacrifice is coupled with opportunity.

But motives can also be immoral. Thieves steal because they need or want money. Students cheat because they failed to prepare. A spouse lies, fearful of being caught in nefarious behavior. Sinners hide when guilty of sin.

Good or bad, motives come from within a person.

How can we guard our motives? How do we ensure they effectively build relationships with those needing help? What standard do we measure ourselves by when evaluating how we live, what we do, and how we speak and treat others? Do we see ourselves as better because we do more for others and give more from our accumulated resources? Are the parameters we use for measurement established by our own unchallenged bias? Do we conclude that we are in decent shape and see ourselves as okay?

The book of Proverbs offers guidance, even a warning, to consider: "All the ways of a man are clean in his own sight, but the Lord weighs the motives."[46] In scripture, "motives" and "spirits" are interchangeable. The motives being "weighed" are translated in Hebrew as *ruach*,[47] which takes on many attributes, including a spirit of courage, desire, and moral character. Our views may seem right, but God is the ultimate judge. God weighs the spirits or motives of our thoughts and actions. He knows our thoughts before we act. He searches our hearts, as only he can, to see if we operate with a spirit of integrity and love.

We see *ruach*[48] reappear in David's lament after committing adultery with Bathsheba: "Create in me a clean heart, O God, and renew a right spirit within me."[49] David admitted his mistake, learned from it, and sought forgiveness. There was a reason, a motive, for him to change.

God wants the same from us, knowing our inner spirit and motives genuinely reflect our hearts. Barclay wrote, "To examine one's own motives is a daunting and shaming thing, for there are few things in this world that even the best of us do with completely unmixed motives."[50] It is challenging to evaluate ourselves, especially without outside feedback and critique. God's word and Jesus's life are our best measuring sticks.

Our motives are lifelong and linked with our hearts and minds. It's best not to pass judgment prematurely because the Lord "will bring to light the hidden things of darkness and disclose the motives of men's hearts."[51] *Vine's Complete Expository Dictionary* states the heart used in this verse, *kardia*, "came to stand for man's entire mental and moral activity, both the rational and the emotional elements."[52] In simple terms, our heart is intelligent. Everyone has a heart capable of understanding, reasoning, thinking, and believing. The human heart is connected with the human mind.

God knows the motives of our hearts. If we are truthful and have come to grips with our identity, our motives will coincide with a love for God. Every day, we choose between spiritual or worldly values, and how we choose to live confirms our preference between material treasures today or eternal blessings forever.

In both Greek and Latin, the root word in "motivation" means "to move." Our motives come from something that moves or drives us to act. So, what moves you? Recall your ID badge and what you decided was critical and of value to you. What do you want your legacy to be? What causes do you stand for, and what makes a difference in your life? What allows you to endure your roller-coaster life and keeps you strong? What bridges have you built that let you cross over troubled waters?

A GRADUATE STUDENT RESEARCHING FOR HER DISSERTATION interviewed me shortly after I assumed the CFO role. She was interested in the process that preceded my appointment to this position, and I told her my story.

I was at an off-site business meeting when given a note to return to meet with the CEO immediately. It seemed strange for this request to come late in the day, but I made the twenty-minute drive back to headquarters. Within minutes, I was informed the current CFO, my boss, had resigned unexpectedly, effective immediately. He left for a similar position to launch a European start-up company with an impending announcement scheduled the next day. For security reasons, he exited the building at once.

At the end of the briefing, with encouraging words and flattery, the CEO proposed a replacement for the CFO role. I was taken aback when an offer for this high-profile executive position, ready for signature, was dropped in my lap. Using baseball jargon, this came clear out of left field and reminded me I had been in this position before—contract to sign, colossal career potential, and significant money on the line. There was only one difference from before, however: there was no time to kick this can down the road. A decision had to be made quickly, within hours.

Any critical information or development in a public corporation requires disclosure as soon as possible. Our communications team prepared two press releases covering the resignation and replacement. One announced I was the new CFO, and the other divulged I would be the interim CFO while the company searched for a replacement. It was eight o'clock, and I had the night to decide which release would cross the wires before the markets opened the following day.

Whenever a corporation's top financial executive resigns, especially in a surprising fashion, it brings apprehension to the shareholders. The board of directors and CEO wanted to alleviate those fears by communicating that a plan was in place involving a well-trained replacement. Though I had no formal training, I was that backup plan. Earlier succession planning discussions indicated I was several years away from being considered for a role like this because I needed more experience and seasoning in several facets of the job. I never knew that "fast-tracking a career" meant immediately.

Separately, the executive vice president of human resources told me accepting the position would be rewarding for many reasons. But there was one caveat—I would be married to the company. At the time, I didn't understand her point; eventually, I would. It was almost midnight—two o'clock on the East Coast, where Wall Street would soon rise— and six hours remained before I had to make a life-altering decision.

Lindy and I pored over the pros and cons deep into the morning hours. I didn't fully consider or understand the downsides of taking the position, though I presumed it would take only a short time for me to do so once I was engaged. The upsides were attractive, and I rationalized this could be a terrific career move with lucrative financial incentives.

Two things stood out when finally deciding. First, though the company was dealing with some operational challenges. I understood them to be manageable and thought I could help. The second and more critical factor was remembering that I walked away from the chance to play for the Chicago White Sox three times twenty years prior and had vowed never to turn away from any significant opportunity in the future. No matter what. No matter when. No matter how difficult it appeared or what fears I had.

I signed the executive contract by sunrise.

Unfortunately, I came to understand that the issues I had thought were easily solvable had worsened, causing severe financial problems. The rating agencies planned to lower our credit rating, banks were reluctant to loan us money, and suppliers began raising prices. The media outlets were writing awful reports about us and longtime investors were selling their stock. Customers were questioning our viability, competitors were like sharks swimming in bloody waters, and lawsuits threatened to drive our company into bankruptcy.

"So why did you take the job?" the graduate student asked at that point. "It couldn't have been for the money or prestige."

No, it wasn't. That might seem odd to a grad student. You will soon be looking for a job, doing something you enjoy, and making as much money as possible. But I had been with this company for twenty years and had seen dozens of layoffs affecting thousands of people, including many good friends. With over twelve thousand employees, assuming an average family size of four, I was now in a position that could impact the lives of nearly fifty thousand people.

She sunk into her chair, unsure of the answer she was looking for.

What helped get me through the challenging times was the idea of making an impact on so many people's lives.

This last statement was important to me. It was my motive. It was what moved me.

SCRIPTURE TELLS US THERE IS A YEARNING INSIDE OF US, AND that in Jesus Christ, "we live and move and have our being."[53] This inner urge, or hunger, moves us to act. Jesus said, "Blessed are those who hunger and thirst for righteousness, for they will be satisfied."[54] Considering our blessings, it's hard for us to fathom being hungry and thirsty. But that is the intensity we should have when looking at what moves us to be our best—the deeper your hunger, the grander your feast.

When seeking motivation from external sources, remember that your motives stem from what moves you, so take the time to establish the right motives. Albert Einstein was motivated by curiosity as a physicist to develop the general theory of relativity, and Eleanor Roosevelt by her achievements with human rights. Adolf Hitler, sadly, was motivated by power. While different studies with opposing views debate whether money is a true motivator, obviously it can lead to problems down the road.

It's also vital to understand there is a difference between building a reputation and developing character. Reputation is the belief or opinion that someone has of you. Others will look at your reputation and let it determine who they think you are based on their scrutiny of you over time. Their viewpoint may be right or wrong because of limited observations or improper information, and their assessments may be fair or unfair, but there is often little that can be done about this.

God doesn't get caught up on your reputation; instead, he is concerned about your character. He knows your true nature, regardless of what others think or say about you. God is good, wise, and understanding. He knows what is best and will always care for you. He works plans for you, even though you don't understand how your future will unfold. He sees your next problem, letdown, or setback, but he rewards those who seek him, especially in those trying situations. Your accomplishments will contribute to your reputation. What you do with them will mold your character. Constantly challenge your motives. Guard them. Be careful what soaks into your mind and seeps into your heart.

Who in their right mind would build an ark in the middle of nowhere? It couldn't have been for pleasure, not one over five hundred feet long and fifty feet high. It's doubtful there would have been any competition to see who would be the first to produce the biggest chunk of floating wood. And there certainly wouldn't have been any financial gain to consider, without any market for cruise ship revenues at the time.

So why did Noah do such a thing? Fear!

"By faith, Noah being divinely warned of things not yet seen, moved with godly fear, prepared an ark for the saving of his household.[55] Deep faith and godly fear moved Noah. This fear, translated from the Greek *eulabeomai*, is a verb. Noah "acted with the reverence produced by a holy fear"[56] of God, who planned to destroy the world. Noah, moved by love, fixated on saving his family. Faith, godly fear, and family. What better motives can one have?

Our world has a way of producing disheartening fears in our lives. Unemployment, financial strains, medical issues, family quarrels, divisiveness in our country, drugs, and crime are just a handful of the fear-inducing activities and realities that plague our world. These fears are real and relentless. But we must fight them. We cannot let them become the reason for what moves us. Nor should we allow other momentum-killers to influence our motives, like toxic or self-centered people, critics, or pessimists. Let godly fear, blended with reverence and love of God, guide our reasoning. In this manner, we can be builders of momentum rather than blockers, and a force that fosters movement rather than a barrier that stops it.

It's easy to become comfortable when everything is going well. You may have worked hard, achieved your goals, and done much good. Your life may be fine, or at least acceptable. It is in these moments when you must be careful to maintain sight of the brevity of life.

Too often, we focus too much on what we are trying to do in this world, the possessions we wish to accumulate, and the trips we plan to enjoy. As we do, time doesn't just pass on—it accelerates. Years pass, and we wonder where the time went. Reflection becomes a daily habit because we can't do what we could in the past.

Barclay mentions a conversation between an ambitious young man and a wise older man.

"The young man said, 'I will learn my trade.'

"'And then?' said the older man.

"'I will set up in business.'

"'And then.'

"'I will make my fortune.'

"'And then.'

"'I suppose I shall grow old, retire, and live on my money.'

"'And then.'

"'Well, I suppose that someday I will die.'

"'And then,' came the last stabbing question."[57]

If you are not motivated by life after this world, you will be unfulfilled and devastated in this one. There is a litany of Bible characters in the book of Hebrews that served God admirably. These incredible people were motivated to do amazing things spurred by their faith. It led them to serve, help others, and do God's will.

Does your faith do the same? Is it at the forefront of your behavior? Routinely relying on faith only at times of difficulty, persecution, or suffering is reactionary. Something happens, you need help, your faith kicks in, and you pray "God, I need help!"

There's nothing inherently wrong with this sequence of events, But what I'm suggesting is you look ahead to your reward. Let your hope of heaven be active. Let it move and motivate you, releasing the distractions that come with the pleasures of this life so you can exchange them for everlasting rewards.

Let love be a motivating factor in your life. Speaking of the Corinthians—and himself—Paul said the "love of Christ controlled us."[58] The Greek word *sunecho* used in this setting means they were constrained by the effects of their love of Christ.[59] It was holding them together, securing them. They no longer lived for themselves because their love of Christ was sufficient motivation for them. It's why we abide in faith, hope, and love, knowing love is the greatest of all.

When I was in high school, I wanted to be the captain of our football team. I had many buddies on the team and a decent support base. I played cornerback, could deliver punishing blows to running backs, and was respected by teammates for my tackling skills. I wanted the captain's role, thought myself deserving, and was motivated to be one of the leaders. I was excited by the idea, prestige, and glamour that went with the title. Not to mention the attention I might get from the cheerleaders, especially one named Lindy.

I wasn't aware of any requirements to be worthy of this title, but I quickly discovered that the election process wasn't a popularity contest. Instead, the decision on captains came from battles between players in "the pit." It was a chalked-out circle where all the prospective captain candidates would enter, surrounded by the raucous noncaptain participants, and engage in a two-way brawl with another candidate. Inside the ring were the most intimidating, gigantic athletes, and I suspected they should be in their third year of college. After facing them, I would be comfortable with any of these guys being captain and willing to refer to them as "sir" if I could get out of this alive.

When the coaches announced the pairings, they matched me up against a dude named Curtis Harris. He was a mere five feet, six inches—four inches shorter than me—but had a body fat content of less than 1 percent. This kid was made of granite, meaner than a junkyard dog, and appropriately nicknamed "Rock." There was a reason he was our starting nose tackle. He could throw any 280-pound lineman around like a sack of potatoes. I asked myself, "Why should I go through this?" and finally decided it wasn't worth it. Thank goodness our match didn't last long. I was down and out in a matter of seconds. I learned that motivation doesn't always get you over the goal line. Something else may be necessary.

Having survived my day in the pit, I laugh at that story, but it introduces a more serious thought for those who are struggling as they approach their long-awaited finish line. There's something needed in the toughest of times, when the issues you are dealing with become unbearable, when the odds are not in your favor, or when those you trust—your friends, even the world—seem to be against you. Everything is arduous, and you are at your lowest point, at the edge of giving in or giving up. It is then that you ask yourself, "What possible motivation do I have to keep moving on?"

Shortly after the last supper with his disciples, Jesus entered the garden of Gethsemane with Peter, James, and John. He was overcome with sorrow and asked them to pray and watch. Jesus walked a stone's throw away, where he dropped to his knees, faced the ground, and began praying. The intensity of the moment was complete and unprecedented. His agony was overwhelming, knowing the brutality that would occur shortly. He prayed for the possibility of being spared from the impending torture. It's what he wanted. In that situation, who wouldn't? Instead, however, He chose to do his Father's will, putting his desires aside.

Returning to the trio, he found them asleep, exhausted from the overload of several daunting days. Would it have mattered if they were awake? What could they have said to motivate Jesus? What else could they have done? Even if they fully understood the ridicule and suffering Jesus would soon endure, what encouraging words could they have spoken that would have been effective for Jesus? The bottom line? There were no words that would suffice. So why did Jesus drag them along with him?

Think of a time when you or someone you knew was extremely sick. The pain is terrible and relentless; the suffering is long-lasting. You wait for medications to kick in and supply relief. You don't know when the anguish will subside, much less end. You don't know what else you need or can do. Entertaining visitors is out of the question, as you only want those who are closest to you to be around you. You don't want to speak to anyone or necessarily want anyone to talk to you. You only want them there. The comfort of knowing someone you love is with you. They support and pray for you, think of you, and do their best to share your pain and anguish.

This is the comfort Jesus wanted.

Why, then, did Jesus go through this torture? Why go through the trial, the betrayals and beatings, the crown of thorns, the ridicule, the long trek to the hill carrying a cross, and the crucifixion to follow? How can anyone be motivated to go through all of this? What were his motives?

Jesus had a willing spirit, which he demonstrated throughout his life, serving his Father. Training from an early age, Jesus prepared himself extensively so that when crunch time came he could draw upon the reserves he had accumulated in a life of service. Jesus didn't need to be motivated by anyone or anything, at least not in the way we think of that word, but he did have a motive. What was it? Why did Jesus go through with this devastating plan of death?

Because to Jesus, it was worth it! He did it for us! Though we are selfish and sinful, Jesus did it to save us. His love for both his Father and us was the powerful motive that pushed him to complete his mission. His purpose included dying for us so we could be reconciled to God and live eternally. And to him, it was worth it!

DO YOU HAVE THE RIGHT MOTIVES IN YOUR LIFE? THERE WILL be times when people will attack and oppose you. Times when people will ridicule and harass you. They will say evil things about you and lie to you. People will pretend they are on your side when they are not. There will be times when it seems the entire world is against you, ridiculing and wanting to destroy you. These things will happen during your lifetime. More times than you want or expect. So always remember: the motives that drive you must be worth it!

Life is exceedingly difficult at times with a blend of highs and lows. Decide what is important and of value to you. Know the reasons for what you do and who you want to be. By doing so, you will understand your real motives. Your motives, if properly aligned with a godly value system, will help you move through the inevitable hardships and disappointments. Whatever in life moves you enough to make a difference, keeps you strong in times of trouble, or enables you to walk by faith and not by sight—whatever it is, find it! Treasure and hold on to it. Build on it. Share it with others. When you do, your motivation will come from within—from the person you have chosen to be.

Preparation—Master the Fundamentals

There are no secrets to success. It is the result of preparation, hard work, and learning from failure.
—Colin Powell

Good fortune lands on the doorstep of someone we know, even though they have done nothing to deserve it. We shake our heads in disbelief, questioning why some people seem to have all the luck. We hope for similar good fortune. Instead, something dreadful happens to us, a major disappointment or significant setback, maybe a problematic trial we must face. We think the world is against us, and the odds are not in our favor. We meander around as if afflicted by something strange or unfair. We ask, "Why me? Why did this happen to me?"

Well, why not you? Who would you prefer or wish this upon in your place? Perhaps somebody you don't like because they offended you? Or someone you know who is lazy, selfish, or narcissistic? Why not them? They deserve it more. Do we hope they get what's coming and wonder why terrible things happen to good people? Are we naïve, hoping for a life without hardships? Is hope really a plan, or does a plan give you hope?

An oft-used quote defines luck as "preparation meeting opportunity." Preparation requires planning, deciding which direction to take, and the necessary steps to get there. It involves building and creating value. It takes time and endurance because it contends with failures, doubts, and discouragement. Preparation embraces the daily grind, not as ordinary but as a necessary part of growth. It patiently waits to breach a roadblock, topple a limitation, or achieve a breakthrough. That is when preparation meets opportunity, and luck is unleashed.

Preparation contrasts with the classic definition of luck—circumstances activated by chance. Luck doesn't do much of anything. It doesn't plan, create, endure, grind, or grow. It merely waits for something to happen. At some point. Good or bad. By chance.

Careers don't happen by chance. Nobody wakes up on a given morning and becomes a teacher, doctor, or attorney. There are required educational degrees, certification tests to pass, continuing education, and training renewals to remain licensed. Essential skills and subject matter expertise are merely the starting point in preparing for these roles.

What about the desire to be a good parent? No requirements exist, although there are distinct types of parents—foster parents, volunteer parents, child-life-specialist parents, and even nanny parents. But no diploma or license is necessary to be a good mother or father, much less a bad one. How-to books are plentiful, offering considerable advice and value from experienced parents who have dealt with temper tantrums, teenagers, dating, and a never-ending list of forbidden behaviors. You can recall what your parents, or others, did that was effective during your childhood. But in this role, as critical as it is, there are no clear-cut prerequisites. The world doesn't view parenting as a profession. Unfortunately, it doesn't value it appropriately, either. Parental preparation comes mostly through trial and error.

Want to be Christ-like? The same principles apply. No degrees or licenses are required. That's not to say there isn't plenty to learn from biblical scriptures. The inspired word of God is extensive, and the only prerequisite is an open and surrendering heart. Even then, Christians must exercise careful consideration. Humans are imperfect, and differing interpretations of scripture can be misleading or taken out of context.

Preparation is a common theme, personally and professionally. Teachers prepare lectures so students understand facts and principles relevant to their career interests. Students prepare for examinations through diligent study to prove they know the essential skills. Athletic teams that consistently win are better prepared, both physically and mentally. Corporate ladder-climbers learn their trade and make preparation paramount.

Well-prepared speakers impart knowledge and enthusiasm to their audiences, while unprepared presenters confuse their listeners and make them irritable for time wasted. Political candidates debate, and those who prepare purposefully are likely to garner favorable poll results. The effectiveness of one's influence will often depend on their preparation. Those who prepare have the upper hand over those who don't.

Preparation started for me in Little League when baseball was a summer game for kids to play together—when putting on a uniform with a proud local sponsor lettered across your chest and sliding into a base to show a dirty uniform was a badge of courage. Playing in front of parents, friends, and neighbors, who cheered whether you hit a home run or struck out, was the ultimate thrill. Winning or losing didn't even matter; it only supplied bragging rights to half the parents.

What mattered most were the fun and the twenty-five-cent treats we bought at the concession stand after each game—enough for a snow cone, baseball cards, and a stick of bubble gum we reused, lasting for days. Our innocence kept us from knowing that any other benefits beyond playing even existed. We studied the rules—how to pitch and catch, the mechanics of hitting and fielding, and running the bases. We became teammates and found ways to encourage one another when someone dropped a fly ball, or we lost a game. We didn't know we were starting to master the fundamentals of the game while absorbing valuable lessons we would use later in life.

At Mississippi State University, consistently an NCAA Top-25 program, baseball mattered more than anything else to their fans. This small college town of Starkville had friendly, supportive Southern people who loved baseball. Located in the dry county of Oktibbeha, anyone interested in a cold beer had to cross county lines to get one—or a few extras for the thirstiest consumers. Lin Lou's was the first dive in the next county and profited from its pinball machines, pool tables, and the patrons' beer consumption. But the brews were second to baseball, which was more than a game to the diehard fans.

It was a highly competitive and, at times, intimidating environment where there was an added pressure to win. The game represented more than simply a nice day at the ballpark. My hometown support system was a day-and-a-half drive away. I was no longer the best player on the team, and neither was I the hometown hero. Everyone playing at MSU held similar credentials. My workout routines and mental approaches required reaching a higher level. The evaluations tested my limits and exposed flaws. I began to understand the importance of preparation and recognizing the attributes necessary for success on and off the field.

The key to winning in any sport hinges on having a team that plays with discipline. Talent and ability are undoubtedly critical, but these are only some of the requirements for success.

I've known many successful baseball coaches at the collegiate and professional levels who all advocate for sound fundamentals. Legendary coach Ron Polk was instrumental at MSU, and major league managers I knew—Clint Hurdle, Buck Showalter, and Bruce

Bochy—all stressed fundamentals in baseball. They believed preparation for all game-type situations wasn't an option and mastering the fundamentals was essential.

It's true across sports and careers. Former Boston Celtics great Larry Bird said, "First, master the fundamentals."[60] Football coach Lou Holtz advised, "Build your empire on the firm foundation of the fundamentals."[61] Probably the ultimate competitor ever to play the game of basketball, Michael Jordan, noted, "Get the fundamentals down, and the level of everything you do will rise. The minute you get away from the fundamentals, whether proper technique, work ethic, or mental preparation, the bottom can fall out of your game, schoolwork, job, whatever you are doing."[62]

Successful people apply the fundamentals in their trade consistently. It's so etched in their minds that they don't need to consider them. Mastering them is of the utmost importance. Without them, the foundation anyone starts with will eventually bear cracks, weaknesses will stand out, uncertainty will rise, and opportunity, once promising, may vanish.

College students have often asked me the number one reason behind successfully reaching the executive level, and I always respond that it is preparation. Nothing is mysterious about success, and no magical Disney ride will drop you off at your desired position. But preparation will help you along the way.

My oldest brother served in the Merchant Marines. His officers drilled discipline and preparation into everything they did. Early in my career, he told me that successful career-oriented professionals build their resumes over time, and I followed his counsel.

I wasn't an expert in any specific field or business. Those with extensive knowledge and ability in limited discipline areas are specialists—think brain surgeons, tax specialists, and patent attorneys. Their careers can be very lucrative but limited to an extent. It is their calling, what they love doing, and very few will leave their profession.

I took a different pathway. Every two to three years, I changed jobs or added new responsibilities. I learned a little bit about a lot of things as fast as possible. It was a constant push to take ownership of my career. I immersed myself in the fundamental principles across the spectrum of organizational operations in business. It took time and included failures and even embarrassing situations, but it helped me transition from thinking something special might happen in my career to believing my destiny would emerge. Those who work the hardest at preparation have the highest potential for long-term success.

ANYONE FORTUNATE ENOUGH TO PROGRESS THROUGH MULTIPLE phases in their profession will face headwinds. Every level of achievement faces increased levels of competition, and the further you progress the more the numbers begin stacking up against you.

Little League benefits 2.6 million children playing baseball and softball every year.[63] Of the 800 or so active roster spots on the thirty Major League Baseball teams, less than 10 percent of those participants are rookies. One extrapolation of this data suggests that for every 30,000 Little Leaguers, only one will make it to the major leagues. It doesn't take a genius to recognize these razor-thin odds. Similarities exist for all professional sports, including basketball, soccer, and football. And it doesn't matter what profession, goal, or dream position because the odds are more or less as small.

Why don't we get it? Why don't parents understand that the odds of living their childhood dreams of playing a professional sport through their children aren't very good? Approximately one hundred thousand contestants try out for *American Idol*. Only one gets the crown, and only a few become major recording artists.[64] IBM has nearly three hundred and fifty thousand employees worldwide but only one CEO.[65] Many will seek the pinnacle, but few will reach it. When the pursuit comes up empty, it can be difficult and disappointing. But it's reality. All pyramids come to a point.

What can we do if this is our reality? The pyramid's point shouldn't stop anyone from dreaming and pursuing their destiny or calling. My point isn't to suggest that dreams don't come true because they do. Instead, it's intended to express that the road to success will be difficult and demand relentless preparation. Professional athletes, top executives, and those best in their field don't reach the pyramid's top solely because of their abilities—they do so because of their relentless preparation.

There are three ways anyone can approach their trade every day. The LIFO view represents the individuals who are last into work and the first out. These employees are there to get a paycheck and do as little as possible to get as much as possible. They look for shortcuts instead of working through processes that produce long-lasting results. They struggle to get to their job for many reasons, doing the minimum to keep their job.

The FIFO person is the first in and the first out. They are punctual and put in their time but only do what is necessary. Nothing more, nothing less. They are satisfied with their position and will stay there as long as they can survive. Their interests are outside of their daily job requirements.

Those who prepare relentlessly take the FILO approach. They are the first one in and the last one out. They take extra time to review past work, learn new skills, discover better ways to change processes, or hone a craft. Feedback is welcome, because they want to know where they stand in order to prevent being surprised to learn later on that they weren't on the right track. They don't resent input nor the person giving it. They know it is best for them. They relish it, knowing it can produce personal growth. They accept the departure from their long-held comfort zone and confidently cherish the entryway to new challenges. They don't think about success—they believe in it.

I dreamt of playing Major League Baseball. I'm glad I did, but that dream didn't come true. The disappointment of not being one of the roughly eight hundred people who play professional baseball each year was real. Although I didn't fully recognize it at the time, what mattered was learning from falling short. Pursuing the dream while going up against the disproportionate odds helped me become a better person. It helped me understand the value of working hard. At each level, I improved. My commitment to preparation was merely a first step to other benefits I would receive later. I was able to let go of the past and move forward, setting the stage for new opportunities to unfold. Progression brought challenges and introduced another by-product of preparation—perseverance, the ability to work through difficulties and achieve success.

THE SAME IS TRUE FROM A BIBLICAL PERSPECTIVE, WHERE WE see the domino effect of embracing tribulation. Working through difficulties produces perseverance, which shapes character, gives hope, and doesn't disappoint if it is appropriately focused. Our misfortunes, sorrows, and calamities aren't meaningless if correctly connected with God.

We learn to be honest with ourselves when communicating with others. We understand the need to be persistent and consistent. We treat people with respect and sacrifice for the good of others. Along this journey, we grow, and we produce fruits from our efforts as we serve others. The benefits of preparation encompass progression, perseverance, and production.

Remember Noah being moved by fear as he prepared an ark to save his family? He was supplied instructions, including the type of wood to use, the specific measurements for the rooms, windows, doors, and even the cargo to bring on board. It took over half a century of progress and perseverance to produce the finished product, not to mention the apparent ridicule of doing such a peculiar task.

Preparation, not luck, made his mission worthwhile when relentless rains flooded the earth, sparing his family. The unprepared suffered deadly consequences.

There were others, inadequately prepared, who similarly suffered. In the book of Amos, the Israelites ignored God's pleas. They weren't bothered when God brought hunger to every city and famine to every town, nor were they fazed when God withheld the rain before the harvest. He brought disease upon their gardens and vineyards, yet they showed no concern. He sent plagues like those used to afflict Egypt. Still, they didn't bat an eye. He destroyed their cities, yet they remained clueless about their desperate position.

With each hardship, they remained shortsighted and didn't return to God. They were unaware, unafraid, and unprepared. Then came God's ultimate warning: "Therefore, this is what I will do to you, Israel, and because I will do this to you, be prepared to meet your God."[66]

How daunting for Israel, to face God—who knows all your thoughts, your motives, the words you speak, the secrets you hold—and yet to be unprepared! Noah was prepared and avoided harsh consequences. It was a much different outcome for Israel.

One day, we will have to meet God. It won't matter if we are rich or poor, cultured or not, famous and influential, prepared or not. We will stand before God.

THERE WERE MOMENTS DURING MY CAREER WHEN I WAS JUGgling my time between preparations for career opportunities and learning more about my relationship with God. This story gave me a healthy perspective.

The Grand Trunk Railway company held a contest to see who could create the best slogan for a railroad-crossing sign. The only requirement was that the tagline be short. A $2,500 prize awaited the victor. The winning slogan was "Stop. Look. Listen." Since the 1800s, when the first trains started running, thousands of people have undoubtedly been killed because they didn't stop, look, and listen when approaching a railroad crossing.

As we prepare for life beyond this world, we must stop, look, and listen to God's word. Accept this as a fundamental part of our lives, knowing its eternal promises or consequences, and realizing we will come face to face with God, eventually.

THE GOSPEL OF MATTHEW ADDRESSES THE NEED FOR PREParation. John the Baptist came preaching in the desert of Judea, saying to those there to repent for the kingdom of heaven was near. He referenced the prophet Isaiah who said, "Prepare the way for the Lord; make straight paths for him."[67] An understanding of what paths are being referenced is essential.

These people knew that when a king or a high-profile person traveled to another country, preparations included improvements to the roads for the ease and comfort of the guests and decisions on routes to ensure safety from potential ambush by bandits. But John's message was different. He let them know of their need to prepare for the coming Messiah. A check on their moral behavior to start, but more importantly, a spiritual preparation that included repentance, forgiveness, and a recognition of the need to be saved. With an opportunity approaching, John declared they should prepare for the incredible gift of salvation.

In his second letter, Timothy discussed preparation with respect to three distinct types of people.

First, he implored the soldier to suffer hardship as part of his service and to focus on sacrifice and loyalty. Second, he compelled the athlete to compete with discipline, according to the rules, and to be professional in preparation and competition. And finally, he instructed the farmer to prepare for work at any hour, to be patient waiting for the crops to progress, and to be determined to persevere through water shortages and insect infestation.

These three examples give guidance concerning sufficient preparation, encourage perseverance, and reward production. What helps these three kinds of people endure this drudgery? For the soldier, it is the expectation of victory. For the athlete, it is the vision of the champion's crown. For the farmer, it is the hope of a bountiful harvest.

Without question, these examples are relevant today. Parents often don't see the fruits of their parenting labors demonstrated in their children's lives until they have matured as adults. It takes a long time for kids to recognize (or admit) that their parents did know a few things about raising them as children, teenagers, and young adults. Parents are willing to work endless hours, watching, waiting, hoping, and praying their demanding work will eventually bear fruit. Parents are farmers.

The same can be said for the career-seeker who keeps plugging along and produces results yearly until the reward comes through a promotion with more responsibilities, or the student who learns the subject matter over time and earns a degree in their chosen field. Mastering the fundamentals and discovering the idiosyncrasies unique to your profession can produce the edge you need on your journey.

ONE OF MY MOST THRILLING AND NERVE-WRACKING EXPERIENCES as a CFO came during each quarterly conference call when we reported our financial results. The call targeted Wall Street investors but was open to the public, and the discussions covered the quarter's business results and provided guidance concerning future expectations. After our prepared remarks, investors called in with questions to help figure out the potential for future stock-price appreciation.

If they were direct investors, they would make decisions at once and, depending on their outlook, buy or sell stock the next day of trading. If they were equity analysts, they would draft reports that evening, recommending to their clients whether to buy, hold, or sell their positions in our stock. For days, investors executed hefty trading volumes.

In a closed conference room, a single phone was centered on a massive table with individual speaker lines stretched to the CEO and me. The technology was so pristine it could pick up the turning of a page, and this prompted the other half-dozen supporting team members to sit beyond an arm's length away in case they needed to sniffle. A deluge of reference information was scattered before us in anticipation of both expected and unexpected questions. And I thought hitting a ninety-five-mile-per-hour fastball was hard!

Intense investors would listen closely to the tone of our voices. The importance of what we said was matched by how we said it. Both gave credence to the investors and analysts buy or sell recommendations. Millions of dollars of investors' value were at stake. A simple word spoken or misspoken could lead to a misunderstanding or, even worse, uncertainty. And with any stock market, uncertainty is a catalyst for volatility. Stock market movements can be quick and dramatic. People's net worth and livelihood are linked to their investments, and our words and tone could severely impact their financial well-being.

We aimed to drive clarity with our explanations of past results and future plans by portraying a professional and confident demeanor. We had to be on top of the details of our business and competitors and articulate the latest movements in our industry and the markets we served. We needed to understand the conditions of the global environment and potential geopolitical impacts that could help or harm our business. We did our homework on the analysts covering our company, knowing their expectations, key indices, and investment goals. We had to be crisp in explaining our strategic direction to them, knowing our competitors lurking in the shadows of the call were listening for hints of information they could use against us in sales activities.

How could we handle something like this, where the stakes were high and the ramifications potentially severe? We needed an edge and that came from our preparation!

EVERY DAY BRINGS NEW POSSIBILITIES, SO WE SHOULD CONstantly be looking for ways to better prepare for the unfolding future. We can't control what opportunities will appear, or when. But we can take matters into our own hands by preparing, learning, and growing, plus gaining knowledge from our preparation and wisdom from our experiences.

How many of us as parents would love to raise our children again now that we've had the experience of already doing so? Our experiences, both good and bad, have given us the wisdom to manage temper tantrums, ridiculous clothing, loud music, unsafe friends, pouting and whining, selfishness, pie-in-the-sky dreams, and mundane college degrees for jobs that don't exist.

Unfortunately, we cannot replay that record, but we can impart the wisdom we have accumulated to those going through the same process now. We can help our children understand the realities of the world and the importance of preparation for the failures to come and dreams that don't materialize. We can steer those needing direction, encourage those whose plans are derailed, and guide those with mistaken ideas. We can inspire people to dream and teach them to do good work in diverse ways. We can impress upon them the importance of preparation. We can be "instruments for special purposes, made holy, useful to the Master and prepared to do any good work."[68]

It's okay to celebrate successes without dwelling on them and to enjoy the benefits of arduous work and preparation. We run into danger, however, when we consider our accomplishments grand

and worthy of recognition, when we seek a trophy to place on a bookshelf or a plaque to hang on a wall. Instead of seeking such things, continue preparing, constantly make progress, and produce good things for others. That is the ultimate objective—serving others and giving glory to God.

I didn't stop dreaming when playing Major League Baseball stopped being an option, and neither should you. Seek new dreams, goals, and ways to achieve and serve. Continue looking for opportunities, and pursue pathways to living life to its fullest, to prosper and enjoy.

There is power in the process of preparation. We are a work in progress with plenty of ways we can improve. Even if we don't see results, we are still growing. We weren't put in a dismal position accidentally by God. He is always working behind the scenes with a plan and purpose to better us. Don't allow any shortcuts you discover to undermine your journey. Let the process of preparation lead you to growth. Don't give up on it. It will carry you to the endgame. When life throws you a curve ball, hang in there. Fight it, learn from it, but stick with it.

The National Sleep Foundation once conducted sleep polls which generated interesting ideas. Some of its findings suggested people slept longer and felt better when their bed was made and the sheets had a fresh scent.[69] To test this theory and concurrently teach the importance of chores, I instructed my then five-year-old daughter Jamie on how making her bed was an excellent example of learning this important concept.

One night, with the sheet and blanket corners barely turned down, I kissed her good night and sent her off to sleep, reminding her about her task the next day. I was amazed the next morning seeing her bed perfectly made, blanket corners squared nicely back in place, not a wrinkle at all. The next few days, the same result.

I couldn't believe the bed-making skills of this young child.

I decided to watch her technique and walked to her room before she woke up, only to find her on the floor, wrapped snuggly in her sleeping bag. When I asked her why she slept in her sleeping bag, not her bed, she told me it was easier to make. While I appreciated her creativity, I hadn't expected to learn about the art of taking shortcuts that morning.

Tolerating the preparation process or unconsciously going through the motions of it is a nonstarter because it's nothing more than taking a shortcut. Relentlessly pursuing and embracing preparation, however, will produce unexpected benefits beyond our imagination.

The sister of a dear friend of ours was diagnosed with terminal cancer, and the two were having discussions about preparing for the future. Deep in their conversation, the sister remarked, "We all have to endure some disease, illness, or old age to graduate and transition to our eternal destination." Such a phenomenal perspective to hold while suffering in grueling times, that our earthly garments, the bodies we have, will become increasingly worn until the day God clothes us in eternal garments. This courage highlights our need to "Consider it all joy when we encounter various trials, knowing that the testing of our faith produces endurance."[70] Let this endurance run its course.

Jesus knew of his impending doom when he entered the garden of Gethsemane. He asked his Father to let the cup, the suffering that would be his fate, pass from him. He asked if he could avoid his death sentence. Nobody in their right mind would want to experience this ordeal, with its mental, emotional, and physical anguish. Jesus was no different.

But he prepared for this occasion through a life of service. While in the desert for forty days and nights, he was tempted to satisfy his hunger by turning stones into bread, to test God's protection and seek public acclaim by jumping from the pinnacle of the temple, and to gain worldly power and wealth by compromising his devotion to God.

Yet he remained committed to his Father. His adversaries sought to confuse, convict, and cast him out. They tried to test, trick, and threaten him. Jesus was betrayed, denied, questioned, and rejected. And now, his rivals and most of the people in that land wanted to kill him. But Jesus chose to finish the task he had been called to do: to serve his Father and save humanity. He had always known it would come to this, that it would all boil down to him enduring all that suffering and being crucified on a cross. Knowing this, Jesus relinquished everything, forfeiting his own desire in order to honor his Father's desire.

What message can we glean from his sacrifice? Where does the courage come from to acquiesce to such brutality? What goes beyond the sheer motivation to serve and suffer?

Jesus was teaching everyone that there will be times of progression during the preparation process, but progression will also bring new trials and difficulties that require perseverance if we wish to overcome those obstacles. Doing so will produce growth personally, professionally, and spiritually. There are no shortcuts in this process. You must endure the preparation process to reach your goals, ambitions, and purpose in life. You cannot cut corners to be complete, perfected, and prepared. Master the fundamentals. Complete the entire process with every step of growth. Shape your view with confidence, believing something good will happen. Recognize that hope by itself will not be your plan, but your newly prepared plan will surely give you hope.

Accountability—Measure and Own It

*On good teams, coaches hold players accountable;
on great teams, players hold players accountable.*
—Joe Dumars

The dreaded performance evaluation! The once-a-year review to find out what the boss thinks about your job performance. Trudging toward the office brings similar trepidation to when you visit a dentist you haven't seen in years, but instead of dreading dental drilling and extraction, you think about deflating self-confidence and destroyed self-worth. Precise tools or gauges for measuring won't be necessary. No stopwatch timing an athlete's speed, calipers firming up dimensions, scales for weights, or even the wooden ruler used as the behavioral measuring stick in my parochial school days. In these settings, it's just you and your boss.

Positive feedback is offset by constructive criticism, areas of proficiency contrasted with those needing improvement. An evaluation will cover the accomplishments of goals, job knowledge, decision-making, and time-management skills. Then come the soft, usually unmeasurable, criteria when opinions get formed on interpersonal skills, leadership, initiative, and flexibility. A performance-level rating may indicate you are outstanding, satisfactory, or substandard. By the end of the review, you'll know how you measure up and where you stand. So will every other employee who has to endure the same ritual.

Companies frequently use statistical models to evaluate their workforce. One such tool, the bell curve, got its name from its shape. Picture the Liberty Bell, with a circumference around the crown of about seven feet and twelve feet around its lip at the bottom. The bell curve modeling suggests up to 80 percent of a company's employees are ordinary achievers, perform their jobs equally well, and collectively comprise the bulk of the bell (results).

The left and right tails on the bell represent 10 percent each for those exceeding expectations and those not performing up to par. This is akin to the "80/20 Rule," which suggests that 80 percent of results attained come from 20 percent of efforts expended. These tools highlight the most critical elements for achieving the best results.

Most of our world's daily activities operate under this theory. Eighty percent of Major League Baseball players have similar talent, 10 percent are superstars, and 10 percent will be reassigned to the minor leagues.

In other sports, Tom Brady, Michael Jordan, Tiger Woods, and Serena Williams are clearly in the elite as the greatest of all time in their profession. In business, 80 percent of sales are closed by 20 percent of the salespeople. In politics, roughly 80 percent of people, whether Republican, Independent, or Democrat, are between right- and left-center in their beliefs. The other 20 percent have views considered to be extremely to the right or the left.

The bell curve suggests the majority of employees should be near the middle of rankings, performing their job satisfactorily. The outliers are smaller in number and extreme in performance, whether outstanding or substandard. It isn't a perfect model, but it does have merit.

Technology companies face a constant battle when releasing new products in fast-moving industries. I joined StorageTek (STK) through its 1980 acquisition of Documation, a small printer company in Florida.

Technology wasn't the primary reason for the deal. Instead, it was the thousands of sales and service personnel having access to most of the Fortune 500 companies and their decision-making executives. STK had an appetite for growth, and the acquisition was a means to expedite its vision. The company's sales that began in the mid-1970s were approaching $1 billion annually. This hypergrowth and success gave credence to a desire to develop new products in different market segments. It opened the door to an opportunity to compete at the next level, in a new and much larger market, against the behemoth IBM.

While the strategic vision made sense on paper, the execution could have been better. The three-year experiment to challenge IBM took its toll as development issues arose. Resources were overextended, time to market was slow, and much energy was wasted. Mainstay product offerings needed more focus, and sales couldn't keep up with ongoing costs. Financial losses swelled, and bill payments stretched beyond due dates. When creditors demanded payment, the company filed for bankruptcy protection, giving them time to develop a survival plan.

The board of directors replaced the company's founder with a new CEO, Ryal Poppa (pronounced Poppy), a turnaround specialist recognized for helping distressed companies survive. Poppa quickly sought to understand STK's past achievements, because a company is only as good as its workforce. Performance rankings for fifteen thousand employees painted a lopsided picture. Eighty percent of the employees were rated outstanding or superior, 15 percent satisfactory, and 5 percent substandard. In an address to employees across the globe, he shared this information and bluntly said, "If 80 percent of our employees are outstanding or superior, then why am I here, and why the hell are we in bankruptcy?" A drop-the-mic moment

I will never forget.

How could this happen? Many could share in the blame. Why did this happen? Because too many employees believed, or were led to believe, they were among the few on the right tail of the bell curve, considered excellent and superior. It was only a short time before our employee rankings formed a properly shaped bell curve, and most people were right or left of center.

Working through bankruptcy is a long and arduous task. Companies that survive the process become leaner, stronger, and highly focused. Three years later, we emerged from bankruptcy in what was touted as one of the most remarkable turnarounds in the technology industry.

In an interview with *Forbes,* Poppa mentioned the company only had a three-month life expectancy when he came on board, and if the existing customers didn't come back, STK would have been forced into liquidation. He told management the first question customers always asked was, "Are you going to make it?" Reshaped and resized, the company did survive. Over six thousand furloughed employees did not. Many left, having held or once held superior and outstanding performance rankings.

Several thoughts stuck with me from that ordeal. The first was the importance of measurements and a time-tested truth—if it doesn't get measured (correctly), it doesn't get done. The process of evaluating people needed more rigor. Managers needed training in establishing meaningful and measurable goals and in the art of critiquing personnel. Crisp objectives were vital to provide a clearer view of accountability for employees.

We remedied these issues quickly, and from then on, the expectation of measurements prompted every individual to engage in a deep, thorough self-examination. If a weakness was acknowledged, an improvement plan was determined. If strength was evident, a maintenance plan was devised to prevent decline over time. Retraining, continuing education, researching new methods, and constant improvement were all integrated within the workforce to sustain sharpness in fulfilling roles. Everyone expected to be tested on their goals, knowing there were rewards for achievements and consequences for missing expectations.

We reconfigured measurement standards. No longer would anyone be measured against their ideals. Instead, established goals came from the business, its customers, and competitive threats in the industry. Everyone understood the requirements for success and was accountable for doing their job adequately.

God made accountability an essential part of a healthy, whole life from the very beginning of mankind's existence. He created a masterpiece when he unveiled the Garden of Eden, and he gave Adam total freedom with one exception—he could not eat from the tree of the knowledge of good and evil.

God knew Adam couldn't go it alone, so he created Eve as his partner and helper. The couple were free to roam and enjoy their blessings. They pranced around the garden naked, feeling no shame. Everything was going well. Life was good. Until the crafty serpent entered the picture and coaxed Eve to nibble on the forbidden tree's fruit, convincing her she could be like God, knowing good and evil. There was no obvious or immediate transfer of godlike knowledge after Eve's first bite, and she handed the scrumptious fruit to Adam.

When both finished tasting, their eyes opened to their nakedness, and the cover-up began. When asked if he had eaten from the forbidden tree, Adam pleaded innocence, criticized God for putting Eve in his life, and blamed her for giving him the fruit. Eve testified her shortcoming was the fault of the serpent's deception.

When we see others deny accountability for their deeds, it's simple to identify the source. We can point to somebody or something and ascribe guilt. But when we are the ones making excuses and assigning blame, it's more difficult to grasp. There is no masterful design or definition of accountability. It means we must account for, or answer to, our actions or inactions. We often reason, and correctly so, that to account for something is a form of reckoning. Metaphorically, taking something into account is "a reckoning of characteristics or reasons."[71]

The parable of the unjust steward in the book of Luke speaks to the depletion of a rich man's possessions. The rich man accused the supervisor of lacking management and wasting resources. He called him in for a performance appraisal and told him to give an account of his leadership. The steward had little ground to stand on, was held accountable for his deeds, and terminated for lack of performance. Accountability includes the use of intelligence. But the lack of intelligence provides no escape from personal responsibility.

When God told Moses to challenge the pharaoh, Moses pleaded for someone else to be sent. When God told Jonah to preach to the great city of Nineveh, Jonah ran away. Pilate had a choice to free Jesus and stop the call for his crucifixion, but instead, he left it up to the multitudes to decide. All three were able to act independently and intellectually. All three tried to shirk their responsibilities.

Accountability is hard, and sometimes undesirable, but this doesn't give anyone license to neglect an ability to respond to and answer for one's actions. Nobody desires to be the victim. Everybody wants to be innocent. It's why we either use excuses to show it's not our fault, blame to avoid guilt, or utilize distraction to change the subject. Thousands of years later, these patterns continue.

SINCE BOSSES HOLD THE KEYS TO PERFORMANCE EVALUATIONS, should there be a reliance on them for our career opportunities and growth? Don't bet on it.

The 40 percent workforce reduction from STK's early bankruptcy days opened up new opportunities. With reduced staffing levels, we had to streamline processes to complete all essential tasks. The resume-building mantra I followed earlier proved to be worthwhile. I volunteered for new roles nobody was interested in, adding new responsibilities and breadth to my curriculum vitae (CV). The long hours stemming from the FILO mentality were exhausting, the challenge of trying to pass the CPA exam over a three-year period burdensome, and the birth of both our daughters exhilarating and draining. There aren't enough words to describe the importance of Lindy's support during these times.

As in baseball, my progression turned some heads at corporate, and for several years, the executive management team floated subtle hints to determine my interest in transferring to Colorado. That would require moving across the country and taking away Lindy's parents' only two grandchildren. Leaving home took much thought to justify. We were hesitant but did it anyway. Lindy's parents supported our new journey, although I'm sure, reluctantly. For years, I assumed I was in their doghouse.

Moving from an off-site location, with its casual approach and freedom, to a corporate office, with stricter rules and regulations, was complex, but the transition appeared seamless. The executives included me on the HI-POT (high-potential) list, a designation that suggested additional responsibilities, likely promotions, and monetary rewards could be in my future.

One year passed, and soon it was time for my initial performance review. It had been ten years since the bankruptcy. New executives were in place, and with their arrival a relaxing of the performance review disciplines previously implemented under Ryal Poppa had come into the picture. During my annual performance review, I probed my boss on career planning. I told him how I had continued building my resume and done something new and different every two years. I stayed active, constantly pushing myself to reach the next level. I was okay with the increased competition, figuring I would outwork everyone. I focused on being ready to take on a new challenge the next year and continue climbing the corporate ladder, and at times, my ambitions were detrimental to my family. I was naïve, expecting my boss to make these career plans for me.

My boss hadn't considered any of this. After I pushed the conversation along, he promised to reevaluate me in six months. Convinced he would care for me, I put my career in his hands and left it up to him.

Six months later—eighteen months in my current position—I was back in his office. "What have you come up with? Which opportunities should I consider next?"

"To be honest with you, I haven't had time to think about it," he replied. "Let's reconvene in another three months."

So much for being a HI-POT! So much for taking care of me! I sensed he was uncomfortable with my assertiveness, hoping I might back away and let it go. Three months later—twenty-one months in the new job—and only three months shy of my second anniversary, I marched into his office again.

"Hello, sir. I'm ready to discuss the new responsibilities I might be undertaking in the next few months. I've been in my current role for almost two years. I took on corporate responsibilities and blended well with the breadth of organizations. My department has either met or surpassed all the requirements we've been assigned. I moved my family across the country and helped them get settled. I would like to know what's next in line for me."

He looked at me like I was crazy, and his response was unsettling. "I'll tell you what. Since your next annual review is only three months away, let's discuss it then."

I asked on three separate occasions yet received no response. I reverted to my baseball mentality. Three strikes, and you're out. Before my second anniversary, I resigned, having accepted a new job on the East Coast. I was fortunate to learn early enough that I was accountable for my career. I couldn't depend (different from seeking help) on someone else to plan for my aspirations. I needed to pursue what I wanted. I needed to take things into my own hands and seek other alternatives. I alone was accountable for myself.

This is true for all of us. We are responsible for our words, ways, and deeds. For maximizing our talents and skills. Each of us must account for our conduct, our decisions, and the mission in life we have chosen. We will answer for what we do in our circumstances, how we handle success or failure, how we deal with joy or hardship, and how we cope with stressful situations and address crises. Accountability starts with me, just as yours does with you.

The story continued after our move to Boca Raton, Florida. I accepted a position with German-owned Siemens, a massive conglomerate with whom I had previous business relationships. Siemens was the majority owner in a joint venture with none other than StorageTek. Within a few months, STK called and offered a multilevel promotion to have me return as vice president of finance for the worldwide sales and service organizations, an offer I accepted. My appreciation and love for my family was off the charts. Within three months, we lived in three different homes.

I THOUGHT I WAS A GOOD GOLFER UNTIL I PLAYED A ROUND with golf professional Paul Azinger during a customer event. Ouch! "Embarrassing" might be the understatement of the year. I played terribly! Zinger, as he is called, was the ultimate encourager, an absolute riot to play golf with, especially since we had ties, having attended the same junior college in the late 1970s. I simply collapsed under pressure, aided by an inactive (and poor) golf game.

The same thing happened again when I was asked on short notice to fill in and participate in the Pro-Am event at The International at Castle Pines. I was the CFO, working six to seven days a week, and hadn't golfed in a year. I had no business playing, but we had two Swiss customers playing in the foursome, and they were hoping we could discuss a little business during the outing. They didn't look athletic, and I figured I could compete with them. Let me repeat. Ouch!

Paul Stankowski was the pro in our foursome, and, out of sheer luck, the lone ball on the par-three seventh hole green belonged to me. It was the only green I hit in regulation all day.

Because of many undulations from the mountainous terrain, even the pros need help reading a few greens. For amateurs like me, their difficulty is my impossibility.

Paul queried me about the break of my thirty-foot putt, and I responded that it would be about five feet. He strolled to the apex of the green and had me aim for a repaired divot, indicating the putt would have a fifteen-foot break. I thought he was joking, but what was I going to say? "Nah, Paul, you've got it all wrong."

I missed his spot, low by one inch, the same length my putt stopped just below the cup. Aside from Zinger and Paul being great guys to play golf with, I have a greater appreciation for just how good they are in their profession.

Everyone has standards they live by. Unfortunately, our imperfections often preclude us from measuring up to them. We branch out and begin measuring ourselves against others. Somebody will always be better, and somebody else will not be as good. We often think, "I'm as good as the other person," and sometimes that may be correct. But does that make it right? We must be careful when comparing ourselves to others and consider why we do such a thing.

ACCOUNTABILITY BEGINS WHEN WE RECOGNIZE OUR SINFUL nature and acknowledge that we "fall short of the glory of God."[72] The Greek word for "falling short" is in present tense, meaning everyone will continue falling short as long as we live. Knowing our weaknesses will persist, and that the brevity of life is unchangeable, we have good reason to focus on living to the ultimate standard. A heavenly and perfect standard. A Christ-like standard.

Accepting full accountability for our actions does more than have a positive influence on our own lives; it is also one of the best things we can do for those we wish to influence. It is a great gift, but even more valuable than most because it seldom occurs. If those we are trying to influence can count on us to do our best, they will trust us. They will respect our convictions when we fail but still do what is right. When we fix what we've broken or comfort those we have hurt, they will find solace in their relationship with us. We can nurture hope in the lives of the downtrodden by serving them.

Serving and enabling others are two distinct concepts, especially when determining accountability. We often hear how we are to "bear one another's burdens," as noted in the sixth chapter of Galatians. We say it and do it because it sounds right—it's the Christian thing to do. But in the same context, it states that we shall "bear our loads." In both cases, bearing means to support or carry. The key is understanding the difference between a burden and a load.

The "burdens" of others we are called to bear is translated from the Greek word *baros* and described as "anything pressing on one physically or making a demand on one's resources."[73] These hardcore difficulties are so demanding they make it difficult for a person to function. The person feels they are carrying the world's weight on their shoulders.

Consider the widow who has lost her husband on a tour of duty, the single mother struggling to make ends meet, the abused wife, the depressed child, or the late-stage cancer patient. Their lives are filled with physical and emotional suffering. Their lives are complicated, circumstances dire, and, like the dawgpile, they are smothered to the point that they can scarcely breathe.

It's easy to become distraught and feel lost, with neither hope nor end to their misery in sight. Their cry for help is real and vital for existence. In their book *Boundaries* (Zondervan, 2017), Henry Cloud and John Townsend refer to these burdens as "boulders."[74] They are heavy, extreme, punishing. And without a support structure, these boulders will continue pressuring and overwhelming the downtrodden.

On the other hand, the loads we carry are the tasks we face throughout life. They are like the ante in a poker game, allowing one to play the next hand. Life offers us cards from a shuffled deck, and we don't know what will be tossed our way. Sometimes we'll be dealt aces and high cards and have a leg up on the world, our competition, and our goals. Other times, we will be dealt the duds, with little chance of success, and think the best thing to do is fold and give up. Either way, we must work with the cards we have, which means doing so regardless of the issue or circumstance we encounter.

The weight associated with these so-called loads is light, translated from the Greek word *phortion*.[75] They are things we do daily and should carry ourselves. They may be mundane, annoying, or dreary. They affect our feelings, alter our moods, shape our mental attitudes, and influence our behavior. These daily loads are the "knapsacks we carry by ourselves."[76]

Cloud and Townsend suggest two scenarios when problems arise with people. The first is when they act like their "boulders" are daily loads and refuse help. The second is when they think their "daily loads" are boulders that they shouldn't have to carry. The results of these two instances are either perpetual pain or irresponsibility.[77]

I've known individuals who have gone through extremely rough times, with divorces involving minors, and who made feeble attempts to work through the consequences of separation without getting the help they needed. I've been associated with older adults who have lost a lifetime spouse and are involuntarily forced into isolation. Yet, they refuse support from close friends and family, or professional counseling, and avoid medical attention. I've known addicts who didn't believe nor wanted to admit they had a problem. They allowed their addiction to fester while their family was torn apart, and they neglected to seek help too. One addict told me, "I don't need any help. That's for weak people." Such senseless machismo.

Our destiny will include suffering, struggling daily, and making tough decisions that impact our personal, professional, and spiritual well-being. These inconveniences and unfortunate events will occur often. It's okay to seek help when you have a sack of heavy rocks bearing down on your life. The most extensive problems can be broken into smaller pieces with the proper support, thus becoming a more manageable daily load.

Accountability is assigned differently. The scriptures tell us we must gently restore those who have been overtaken by sin. The Greek word for restore is *katartizo*[78] and means "to mend or repair," meaning we should help the person who messed up get back on their feet. They are still accountable for their actions, but we must mend, not judge. Repair, not replace. Help, not enable. Provide resources and encouragement but let the individual take steps to recover. It can be a fine line to draw, and unfortunately, some outsiders may think it's not a Christian way to handle these situations.

Ultimately, we are all accountable to God. Though we cannot fathom what God has done from beginning to end, everything he has made is beautiful, including setting eternity in the human heart. Every human heart. God wants everyone to live life to its fullest. Every day is a gift, never to be squandered. If we keep our eyes fixed on eternity, every day will count.

Gospel preacher Jack Hobby was as close to an angel on earth as I have ever known. He spoke of an individual nearing the end of his life, stressing the importance of taking one day at a time. Don't procrastinate. Don't put off reconciling an issue from an argument. Don't forget to say you love or care for someone. He would always say, "Make Today Count! MTC!" What a great way to approach every day.

Spiritually minded people must be leaders and examples outside their church building in order to seize opportunities with those who have drifted away from God or who don't have God in their lives. Sometimes accountability will rest with us, and sometimes we must work to hold others accountable. In the end, "We must all appear before the judgment seat of Christ, that each one may receive the things done in the body, according to what he has done, whether good or bad."[79]

Nobody can sidestep their responsibility, even though it's a common mindset for many today. Since we are God's creation, he has authority over us, and there will be no escape from meeting him. What others have done won't matter. What matters now, and what will matter on that day, is the choices we make and what we have done. God will hold each of us accountable.

THE DISCUSSION ON ACCOUNTABILITY ENDS WHERE WE STARTED— the annual performance evaluation. Goals are set, deliverables understood, measurements made, and ratings assigned. Accountability might be financially rewarded when it's all said and done. Regarding your expectations, career, goals, and even your life of service to others, which is better: setting the bar low so you consistently achieve your goals, or setting the bar high and missing your objective? It could be somewhere in between. Where do you set the bar?

My first performance review with Pat Martin came six months after he joined our company. We appeared to be over the worst of our business struggles, and I walked into his office feeling good, seeking feedback on my goal achievement over the last year.

I worked profusely. Seven days a week. Long hours every day. I had a list of accomplishments to gloat over and relished the tasks completed. My organization helped secure a $500-million-dollar loan, completed a $1-billion-dollar stock repurchase plan, received board approval on a comprehensive strategic and financial operating plan, reestablished the company's credibility with the shareholders, and completed all the regulatory requirements of the newly enacted and extremely onerous Sarbanes-Oxley legislation, which was infiltrating and causing havoc within corporate America. I did…I accomplished…I fixed…I finished…I, I, I!

I concluded I belonged on the right side of the bell curve, worthy of a big pat on the back, and merited a stellar review and even a sizable financial reward. I deserved it. How could anyone argue my case? Certainly, it was evident to everyone that I deserved to be rewarded. At least it was to me. With my bloviating complete and my chest puffed up, I asked my boss, "What do you think about all of this?"

His response seemed heartless. "About what?"

"All of my accomplishments, the things I did."

He paused. Our eyes met. He responded. "What the hell do you think I'm paying you to do?"

Red-faced, I thought, *Are you kidding me?* He had riled me up. After all my accomplishments, this is what I got in return? I had no response, however, because I couldn't argue his point. I had done what I was supposed to. Clearly another drop-the-mic moment.

It took quite a bit of time to recover from that spanking. Eventually, I understood his message. I had no reason to boast about doing something that was my duty. No reason to come across as though I had done great things. I had only done what he expected of me. I recalled Luke's reminder, "When you have done all those things which you are commanded, say, 'We have done what was our duty to do.'"[80]

I eventually understood my boss was pushing for excellence. For years, our company remained mired in problems: engineering issues, supply-chain failures, manufacturing delays, and financial shortfalls. He wanted the organization to exceed expectations, not just meet them by doing what we were paid to do. He wasn't just setting the bar; he was raising the bar. We needed to go beyond the ordinary and move on to the extraordinary. We could no longer think in terms of limits but instead think beyond our limits—unlimited products, unlimited production, unlimited results, unlimited efforts, and unlimited potential. Achieving the ordinary was a given. It was the ante. He demanded extraordinary steps with higher expectations because both would lead to excellence and business growth.

The concept of accountability goes beyond the simple act of setting and raising the bar in our lives. To truly grasp its significance, I had to delve deeper into how I felt about this idea, contrasting my initial perspectives with my evolving understanding. Initially, I approached accountability with the notion of personal growth in mind. It felt like a solitary pursuit, where I set my own bar and worked diligently to surpass it. However, a significant realization occurred along the way. I began to understand the profound impact of sharing this journey with others. Rather than guarding my achievements and aspirations, I recognized that extending a helping hand to lift others up was equally, if not more, fulfilling.

The turning point in this realization was a series of moments where I witnessed the inspirational power of collective growth. It became apparent that success wasn't just an individual endeavor but a shared voyage. When we extend our successes to others, it has a ripple effect, enhancing not only their careers but also the overall quality of their lives. The joy derived from enabling others to reach their potential far exceeded the satisfaction of personal achievements.

H.E. Bates's inspiring short story titled "The Good Corn" provides insight into this point, clarifying our role of being accountable for the success of others.

"Once upon a time, there lived a farmer who grew high-quality, award-winning corn. He would enter the state farmer's fair every year and win a gold award for his exceptional corn.

"The farmer's high-quality corn was praised all around the state. Finally, the success story of his exceptional corn reached the ears of a journalist, and he wanted to interview the farmer. While learning about the farmer's agriculture process, he discovered that the farmer shared his best-quality seeds with his neighbors.

"'How can you afford to share your best corn seeds with your neighbors when some of them compete with you in the agriculture fair?' asked the curious reporter.

"'Why wouldn't I, sir?' asked the farmer. 'Didn't you know the wind picks up pollen from the ripening corn and swirls it from field to field? If my neighbors grow inferior corn, cross-pollination will eventually degrade the quality of my corn too. So, to grow high-quality corn, I must help my neighbors grow good corn too.'

"The farmer's answer made the reporter realize how aware the old farmer was about connections in life.

"It is the same with our life. Those who choose to live in peace must help others around them to live in peace too. The one who wishes to be loved must learn to love others too. The one who chooses to live well must help make others live well, too, as the value of a life is measured by the lives it touches. Those who choose to be happy must let others find their happiness, as the welfare of each is intertwined with the welfare of all."[81]

If you are fortunate and in a position to impact the lives of others, share your success with them. Help them get better. Help them be successful. Support them as they raise their bar to achieve higher excellence. I can attribute successes in my life to those who helped and supported me. My teammates and coaches in sports, teachers at school, colleagues at work, my wife and family at home, spiritual leaders, and friends—all of them have helped make me a better person. I only hope I have done the same for them.

GROWING UP, I WAS A HUGE TREKKIE AND WATCHED EVERY episode of *Star Trek*, starring William Shatner and Leonard Nimoy. In their 1982 movie, *Star Trek II: The Wrath of Khan*, the Starship Enterprise is dangerously approaching destruction when Spock enters a radioactive chamber to fix a mechanical issue to save the ship and its crew. Separated only by a clear cylindrical tube, Spock nears his demise and strenuously utters, "Don't grieve, Admiral. It is logical. The needs of the many outweigh…"

Admiral Kirk interrupts, completing the thought, "...the needs of the few."

Spock replies, "Or the one."[82]

I'm not suggesting you go out and die for anyone, although many say they would give their life for someone they love. The men and women of our military make a similar pledge to our country when they join the armed forces, and sadly, it's a pledge that is fulfilled by far too many. They are heroes to all of us, but the needs of many, even a few, outweigh the needs of one.

THE GREATEST ACT OF ACCOUNTABILITY CAME WHEN JESUS volunteered to die on the cross. Jesus didn't deserve to suffer through His crucifixion. He lived a perfect life and was innocent of the crimes levied against him. From the time Jesus taught in the temple, he laid the groundwork for all humanity to live righteously, think purely, act humbly, and serve eagerly. Even with all his teachings, patience, and forgiveness, the only way he could make a lasting impression on us was to die for us. He took our shortcomings—all the things we repetitively do wrong, all the unkind acts and words resulting from our imperfections—and placed them on himself. He took ownership of our sins on the cross so this gift of salvation would be available to everyone. For Jesus, the needs of the many outweighed the needs of the one.

There is power and goodness in accountability. When life is exhausted, we will be held accountable for our deeds. What we should have done or planned to do will have no significance. What will matter is what we did. Any suffering resulting from personal accountability provides tremendous value. Strive to initiate change in this world. Be willing to take responsibility for your actions, to be accountable, and then help others do the same.

9

Compassion—Be There When Needed

Compassion. It's not just a word. It's a way of being. It's not just a concept. It's love in action.

—Jeff Brown

The red-eye flight from Denver through Dulles to London Heathrow landed without a hitch. The boss and I took the same trip every three months for a half-day business review with all our European sales teams. It was a brutal turnaround to and from Europe done so quickly that my body couldn't process any jet lag. Our United flight departed Monday evening around dinnertime, briefly stopped in DC before the jaunt over the big pond, landing around 11:00 a.m. London time. Being an annual United Premier 1K frequent-flier for years seemed glamorous, but only to those who weren't members of this elite group.

The road-warrior experience taught me how to travel lightly. I never ate or drank on these trips because the sugar intake would further inhibit the few hours of interrupted sleep I collapsed into. Earphones playing zero music and a mask over my eyes would only dim the light and soften all the surrounding noise. I would ask the flight attendant to wake me in time for juice and coffee and to freshen up before arriving. The freshening up consisted of splashing water on my face, a little deodorant and body spray, brushing my teeth after a long night breathing stale airplane oxygen, and knotting on a tie. I still had a full head of hair then too, so I did the best I could with the bedhead look and called it good to go.

After clearing customs and immigration, we would meet with a dozen country managers to review their prior quarter results and analyze their sales forecasts. Such meetings were the best way to understand where we stood, straight from the horses' mouths. One at a time, we watched their posture and tone as they presented their forecast. We could tell who was confident and who wasn't. And we used their information to guide the expectations of Wall Street analysts. We saved enough time for an extra-late dinner before returning to a hotel for a short nap. We would board a midmorning flight a few hours later, landing us back in Denver roughly forty-eight hours after the trip had begun.

Everything seemed normal on this particular trip when our taxi dropped us off at our European headquarters just after the scheduled 2:00 p.m. start, with one exception. It was just after 9:00 a.m. on the East Coast, the morning of September 11, 2001. During our drive from Heathrow Airport, American Airlines Flight #11 plunged into the north tower at 8:46 a.m., and United Flight #175 crashed into the south building at 9:03 a.m. A half hour later, American Flight #77, which left half a day after our brief stop at Dulles the night before, crashed into the western side of the Pentagon.

Our colleagues' stunned faces greeted us as they escorted us to a room where we watched in shock as the horrific assault unfolded on television. Our business associates were simply friends that day, grieving in disbelief over the attack on our country. With all flights grounded until it appeared safe enough to fly, it was a week before we returned from our scheduled two-day trip.

A week before this European trip, Director of Investor Relations Karla Kimrey and I ascended the south tower elevators for introductory reviews with potential investors. When I returned to the US after the attack, she reminded me we had been a few floors below where the planes struck the south tower. We also visited our sales office on the 34th floor in the One World Financial Center, just across from the south tower at 200 Liberty Street.

Days after the attack, Vice President of Sales Michael McLay required an escort to retrieve backup data tapes because the building was considered unsafe. He saw rubble four stories high at the entrance of the building, and the windows I previously peered through to view the New York City skyline were completely blown out. For months, I could neither shed those images nor dismiss the thought: *What if I had been there that week?* My heart still aches for the families of those who lost loved ones that day.

THINK OF THE BEST SCENES IN ONE OF YOUR FAVORITE MOVIES or a chapter you read in a thrilling novel. Have you ever replayed that scene and envisioned being one of the characters facing challenging conditions but who find ways to rise above their circumstances and overcome their hardships? Your mind processes the sequence of events, and as the movie or chapter closes, your imagination drifts off, and you marvel at what it would have been like to have been there, sharing the experience. In some cases, the scene's ending is predictable. In others, you get caught off guard. Either way, you are engaged in the moment and its surroundings.

I absorbed the drama of historical characters in my elementary years. I wondered how thrilling it must have been to sail the seas with Christopher Columbus, with a dream of discovering a new land. I thought how cool it would have been to hunt with Daniel Boone, see the citizens' rage at the Boston Tea Party, and witness the horror and devastation of the Civil War. I was fascinated by the legends who helped build and shape our country, fantasized about meeting them, and wondered what I would say if I ever met the likes of Benjamin Franklin, Abraham Lincoln, and Thomas Edison.

I would often fly to visit my aged father before he passed away. He was eighty-eight years old when he died but still had an episodic memory of key places and events from the 1920s. His family lived in poverty during his childhood. He would tell tales of the Great Depression, standing in food lines holding his father's hand, waiting for a loaf of bread to bring home. I would wince at the stories of starvation, the hardships the stock market crash brought, and the financial ruin it caused so many.

Today, we laud events like our child's birth, graduation, and wedding. We grieve over catastrophic events like hurricanes and tornadoes ripping apart homes, the exploitation of drugs, drunk drivers taking innocent lives, or stories of spousal abuse. Whatever the occasion, we often reenact a scene in our minds, ponder the moment and wonder, *If I had been there, what would I have done? What would I have said? Could I have...*fill in the blank.

I experienced one of these moments in my late twenties. My sister's teenage stepson had become despondent and isolated, battling depressive thoughts. He may have felt pressured or unsure of what to do with his life. Perhaps he didn't fit in with his peers or had little self-esteem. Nobody will ever know what was bothering him, but something did. My previous interactions with him seemed normal. Though quiet and subdued, he enjoyed riding motorcycles and did so speedily. Yet he appeared to be a responsible young man.

Something may have troubled him one day, at least enough to spur a visit home. A knock at the door went unanswered, but his key gave him entrance. Perhaps he wanted a conversation with someone. He left remnants of a sandwich he had prepared on a plate beside the kitchen sink. Time elapsed, and he was still alone. Eventually, he drove his motorcycle around the pond, backing up to the lot where his parents' home stood. He completed his ride in a heavily wooded isolated area. Away from everyone. It was there that he took a gun and his life. So young. So senseless to all who knew him. So much opportunity dissipated as quickly as an early morning fog.

A few days later, I stepped onto the back porch and could see where the tragic scene took place in the distance. I reenacted the final ride, rehearsed the mogul-style bumps the young man soared over, the breeze-swept cattails he raced through, and the spot he chose to stop. I imagined him on the other side of the lake, looking back, across the lake, to an empty porch. I dropped my head, closed my eyes, and processed the imagery of him pulling the trigger and the terrible climax.

"Heartbreaking" is a colossal understatement. His father loved him, and I'm sure he did everything possible to help his son. The scene from the lake was etched into my brain, as was the playback of the father's words. As he painfully tried to put together the sequence of the last steps taken by his son, he repeated to me, "If only I had been there, if only I had been there."

Could he have persuaded his son not to do this? Could he have figured out what caused his son to think he had no other choice? Could he have been there to listen and comfort? And help?

Those words stuck with me—*if only I had been there*—a phrase this father used to grieve, and a reminder that when someone is hurting or suffering, we need to be there with them. Helping others is a conscious decision combining our awareness, capability, and desire, and it requires deliberate mindfulness to recognize the need. I didn't think about compassion often in my earlier days, much less consider myself compassionate. But the suicide, the south tower meetings, and the 9/11 European trip soon branded me with this "need to be there" mentality.

SCRIPTURAL COMPASSION HAS A MORE PROFOUND APPLICATION. Its Latin origin means to suffer together or the sharing of affliction. It isn't feeling sorry for someone (sympathy), sharing the feelings of another (empathy), or forgiving someone within your power to harm (mercy). Compassion is *suffering together with someone*.

This sentiment spurs one's desire to alleviate another person's suffering. The Bible doesn't give a textbook definition of compassion. It merely shows its application in the lives of those experiencing it. Most Old Testament verses refer to God's compassion toward his people, the Israelite nation. Most New Testament verses refer to Jesus's compassion toward those in need.

A scene in the New Testament illustrates this notion of compassion. Jesus and his disciples were leaving the city of Jericho with a large crowd following them. Two blind men were sitting by the roadside. No telling how long these guys had been in this spot nor why they were waiting. It's likely they knew of Jesus and heard of his impressive miracles. They probably heard Jesus would pass by, and this could prove to be their only chance to regain their sight.

They must have felt it was their lucky day because they wasted no time when the opportunity presented itself. As the old saying goes, "If you feel froggy, jump!" They did. At the right time, they shouted, "Lord, Son of David, have mercy on us!"[83] The mercy they sought is translated in Greek as *eleeo*, which means "kindness."[84] Jesus used the same application in the Sermon on the Mount when he said the merciful (kind) will be shown mercy. The blind men believed Jesus's kindness was the ticket to restoring their sight.

The throng of people rebuked them, thought they were annoying, and told them to shut up. But it was now or never for the blind pair. Unintimidated, they shouted louder for Jesus to be kind. When Jesus asked them what they wanted, they begged to be freed from their blindness.

Mercy involves a recipient and a donor. The blind men wanted their sight restored, and Jesus could fulfill their request. If they had any faith at all, it was far from perfect. But they viewed Jesus as a physical king with extraordinary powers and were hopeful they could be the recipients of some of his capabilities. But Jesus went beyond dispensing the kind of mercy they were seeking: "Jesus had compassion on them and touched their eyes. Immediately they received their sight and followed Him."[85]

The Greek word translated as compassion on this occasion is *splanchna,* which describes an internal yearning toward the suffering of another.[86] This wasn't just an act of kindness or a show of mercy. It was a heartfelt reaction, deep inside Jesus, to their suffering. Author Glennon Doyle Melton describes it this way: "Compassion does not just happen. Pity does, but compassion is not pity. It's not a feeling. Compassion is a viewpoint, a way of life, a perspective, and a habit that becomes a discipline. And more than anything else, compassion is a choice we make that love is more important than comfort or convenience."[87]

Compassion requires our inner self to go to the places where others are their weakest, most vulnerable, or loneliest. Too often, we see someone in need and try to minimize their suffering by avoiding it or finding a quick fix. When we enter their turf in their world, however, seeing their hardships through the same lens, they are more apt to be encouraged and willing to be influenced. Why? Because they believe we seek their best interests.

Compassion was a way of life for Jesus. When teaching in the synagogues, he had compassion for the crowds of harassed and helpless people. Before feeding the five thousand (and this was just the adult males—there were likely thousands more in attendance!), Jesus saw the large group, had compassion on them, and healed their sick. He felt compassion for the widowed mother whose only son had died. He was moved with compassion for the man with leprosy in Galilee. This compassion came from his heart, a deep yearning and willingness to suffer with hurting people.

For decades, I focused on being successful. I found ways to stay busy, feeding on resume-building opportunities and constantly pushing the needle to get ahead. Nobody would outwork me, and the long hours became routine. Employees heading home after a family dinner would drive by darkened buildings only to see my office light still illuminated.

When a text from my boss came across at three in the morning, I responded. I wanted him to know I was adamant about proving myself and outworking him. I was addicted to work, and I wore the reputation like a badge of honor. Many who had access to me—employees, shareholders, Wall Street analysts, bank executives, customers, and reporters—saw me as destined for success. I used it as fuel to overcome having failed too many times. Success became imperative.

I often justified my workaholic ethic as being essential so I could best benefit my family. Though partially true, the reality was my ambitions were for me. I didn't pursue or push for prestige, but I enjoyed it. People respected my position and opinion. Thousands of employees worldwide knew me by name, but I had difficulty remembering theirs. My career roles were launching pads to tell a story wherein I communicated a vision and plan, persuaded investors, and raised money. Wall Street always loved a good stock pick and the company executives capable of making them a ton of money.

In an interview days before he died, Albert Einstein advised a young student, "Never lose a holy curiosity. Try not to become a man of success, but rather try to become a man of value. He is considered successful in our day if he gets more out of life than he puts in. But a man of value will give more than he receives."[88]

I knew my focus slanted toward being a man of success rather than one of value. If I measured my time and efforts, the evidence would be overwhelming. My professional ambitions dwarfed my personal life and stunted my spiritual growth. The purpose I had chosen for my life wasn't the best indicator of value. As the desire for advancement grew in importance, so did the necessary emotional, intellectual, and financial development that went with it. Being aware of the limitations of my abilities kept me grounded, but accountability and confidence became traits I believed in. They seemed valuable to me. Yet I was still missing something.

Diamonds, Deals, and Divine Guidance

The apostle Paul summed it up perfectly when he wrote: "Do nothing out of selfish ambition or vain conceit. Rather, in humility, value others above yourselves, not looking to your own interests but each of you to the interests of others."[89]

The Greek meaning for valuing others means placing them above yourself, metaphorically, so they rise above you.[90] Selfishness isn't part of the equation.

I had difficulty reconciling this concept, however, because I was the one working long hours, giving up my interests, family time, and vacations. This approach to having compassion seemed unfair. It was a giant pill to swallow because it was more about others and less about me. Help an individual at a lower level on the organizational chart to the extent they surpass and become superior to me? Preposterous! This compassion was at a whole new level.

Biblical stories sparked new thoughts and a deeper search for the significance of compassion. In the parable of the good Samaritan, a man was making the trip from Jericho to Jerusalem. Jericho was an exciting city; its Hebrew meaning, "a fragrance," was augmented by the fact that it was referred to as "the City of Palms."[91] The two cities were just over fifteen miles apart, with a 3,500-foot elevation disparity. Anyone traveling on this road would go from the chilly temperatures of Jerusalem to the sunny and warm resort-like climate of Jericho, situated below sea level. The road to Jericho was treacherous in some parts, with sections of vacant paths surrounded by rocks and hills—the perfect place for bandits and thieves to ambush wealthy tourists heading to the resort. But this carefree man chose to go at it alone, without the comforts and safety of traveling in numbers. Unsurprisingly, he fell victim to robbers who beat him, leaving him half-dead and motionless while he waited for someone to rescue him.

A priest eventually came by on the same road, saw the victim, but crossed to the other side of the path. This is similar to when you see someone coming whom you want to avoid, so you look down or turn your head away. We have all done this before and likely more than once. Similarly, a second traveler soon came along, but as he got a little closer he also avoided the situation and chose a different pathway.

Next in line was the Samaritan, a member of a community group the Jews of the day despised. The level of animosity felt toward Samaritans was so bad, in fact, you would think this guy was part of the band of thieves who had ambushed the now-injured traveler. Though aware of the risk that the robbers could return, this Samaritan was overcome with compassion. He saw the need and seized the opportunity to help. He was willing to share in the suffering of this mutilated man, bandaging and comforting the victim. He took the time to take him to an inn for further observation and care. He supplied resources to cover the costs while the man healed, and he promised to return and check on his recovery.

Demonstrating compassion to others is a choice, demands time and resources, and sometimes involves risk. This story of the good, compassionate Samaritan offered me a new perspective on how to use my time, strength, and resources.

The story of the prodigal son sheds a similar light. A gathering of tax collectors and sinners waited to hear Jesus while the Pharisees and teachers of the law murmured about how Jesus welcomed and ate with sinners. Jesus had already told parables of a lost sheep and lost coin by this point, and now this third parable was about a missing son—all three bore messages about recovering something that had been lost.

I am in the camp that argues this parable should be named after the compassionate father, however, rather than his wasteful son. As the story plays out, it makes sense.

In this parable, a father had two sons. The younger son approached his father and demanded he fork over his share of the inheritance. Given that his father was still alive, and yet he wanted his portion immediately, such a request was indeed crass. I, like most parents, would have a huge problem with my child telling me to hand over their inheritance while I am still alive.

Yet, without hesitation, the father divided the estate and relinquished the portion due to his son. Jewish laws dictated the firstborn son would receive a double share of his parents' estate, while the other brothers received a single share.[92] In this case, the older brother would get two-thirds, with this reveler-to-be receiving one-third—still, a sizable valuation.

The younger son eagerly set off with his plunder to a foreign country, away from his hometown and anyone who might know him or be able to watch his rebellious behavior. He squandered his newly supplied wealth with reckless abandon. Saving for a rainy day was a foreign concept to him—but a storm came anyway. Famine spread across the land he was calling home. The tide had changed.

Penniless and in desperate need of help, he sought employment. His first job was feeding pigs, and before long, he gladly would have eaten the slop destined for the pigs too, except nobody offered him any. He was at a low point in his life. Starving, he recalled how his father's servants had food to spare, and he decided enough was enough. He would return to the land where he came from, return to his father, and he would admit his mistakes and beg forgiveness. It was time to go home, even if that meant giving up his namesake, asking to be a lowly servant, and suffering the consequences of his poor choices—anything to get out of this predicament.

Undoubtedly, the father prayed for his son's safety after his departure and hoped for his return the same way parents do when their kids leave for college. One day, he saw his son approaching in the distance.

Is this happening? Is that my son I see on the horizon?

After confirming it was true, he was filled with compassion. Immediately, he ran to his son, hugged and kissed him as if he had returned from a tour of duty fighting a war. Indeed, tears of joy were flowing as he touched his son.

The reaction probably shocked the wayward second-born son. Instead of hearing, "I told you so," his father greeted him joyfully. Instead of being informed, "You are on your own, and this is not your home," his father welcomed him with open arms. With this glorious reception, he could have pretended everything about his past behavior was no big deal. He could have reasoned that his escapades went undetected since he was in another country. He could have altered his approach, expecting everything to be like it was before he left home.

But this shamed young man had changed. He took responsibility for sinning against heaven and his father, saying he no longer deserved to be his son. Before he could ask for servant-like treatment, however, the father was already planning a welcome-home party. He clothed him with a fine robe, put a ring on his finger, and fitted sandals for his feet. He prepared a fattened calf for a celebratory feast. The compassion for his lost son, now found, was as real as the son's changed life.

When the older son returned from the field, he saw the jubilee dedicated to his brother. He refused to attend the party. His anger prevented him from seeing the joy in his father's eyes and from acquiescing when his father pleaded with him to join the celebration. The older son could only rehearse all he had done for his father over the years. He hadn't taken off any extended time or indulged in his inheritance. He always obeyed his father. The son who squandered his share of the family's estate was being honored with a party, while the loyal rule-follower wasn't getting squat. To the older son, this was ridiculous!

The father's love for his eldest remained strong. He acknowledged his efforts and longstanding dedication, assured him the remaining estate would secure his future, and explained why he advocated this celebration. Until then, he had assumed his son was lost and dead. But on that day he had been found and was alive.

I view these parables with consternation. How often have I neglected to be like the good Samaritan, staying in my lane and avoiding opportunities to help? Why did I see myself siding with or behaving like the older brother, unwilling to encourage and elevate someone seeking another chance to make things right while drowning in self-pity and jealousy? When did I show compassion like that of the Samaritan or the father of the lost son?

I still struggle to be compassionate with those whom I consider undeserving. It's not that I don't have pity or share my sympathy for them, and it's not that I haven't shown mercy by giving financially to fulfill their needs. But to have compassion, deep inside, from my heart, for someone who has repeatedly shown no regard for what is right, who claims they have turned the corner? Or the person who has wronged my family, stolen from my company, or slandered me for their gratification in the past? But when they have righted their ship and fallen into hardship, I'm supposed to elevate them to a point where they surpass me? Easier said than done.

Martin Luther King Jr. once said, "Life's persistent and most urgent question is 'What are you doing for others?'"[93] We sometimes say, "I understand your problems," or "I can imagine what you are going through." Do we understand? Have we experienced the same issues under the same circumstances? Do we even know the events causing their hardship? Have we suffered as they have suffered?

In the last of three stories told in Matthew's twenty-fifth chapter, Jesus lays out, for those blessed by God, the standard to receive an inheritance in the kingdom. When someone is hungry, give them a meal. If thirsty, a drink. If a stranger comes, welcome them into your company. Get some clothes for those who need them. Take care of the sick. Visit and encourage those living in a prison of discouragement or hardship. Aim to do these simple tasks consistently. There is no mention of our achievements, degrees we have earned, records we set, careers fulfilled, or wealth accumulated.

Jesus knew the righteous-thinking people would be flabbergasted, and that they would claim they were unaware of having seen him hungry, thirsty, in need of clothes, or any of the other examples he mentioned. He responded truthfully—what they did for others, they did for him. If they didn't provide a meal for someone hungry or a drink to one thirsty, welcome a stranger, clothe the naked, care for the sick, or visit the imprisoned, then they didn't do it for him either. What was his point? It's not a question whether you were there for others in their time of need, but rather what you did when you were there. Did you share yourself sufficiently to suffer with others?

I HAVE BEEN FORTUNATE TO HAVE THREE PEOPLE WHO SHOW genuine compassion in the way they live. The first one is Lindy. Unlike me, she isn't a competitive person. She refuses to play games with me because I play to win at all costs. If (make that when) I win, she says I am mean. Lindy doesn't have a mean bone in her body. She is an avid reader with a soft voice, and she has a wonderful way with words. She is the kindest person I have ever known, spreading her goodwill toward people everywhere, even displaying a frontal license plate that states, "Be kind." People come in droves to talk to her, sharing their problems, revealing their secrets, and exposing their troublesome circumstances and extreme situations.

I'm talking about people she doesn't even know. She can be at an airport or grocery store and start a conversation with a stranger. Before you know it, the person is so intrigued with her knowledge and tenderness that they drop their stories of divorce, abuse, addiction, or familial problems on her. She is a magnet for those needing a tender heart and open ears, something these people don't have in their homes.

The other two are my daughters, both of whom entered the medical field.

My oldest daughter Brooke, though a kickboxing instructor on the side, is a speech-language pathologist (SLP). The stories of her patients, both in-house and home-care individuals, amaze me, but the most touching one came during her internship while attending to a stroke victim diagnosed with a swallowing disorder. Nerve damage can result in aspiration pneumonia, which means anything swallowed can fill the lungs and can go undetected without proper tests.

This elderly patient wanted to eat but couldn't and nourished himself through a feeding tube. He and his large Italian family loved their food and hoped they could share what might be their last Thanksgiving meal together. A patient's diet is upgraded only with a successful swallowing test, and with each unsuccessful trial, the family's hopes for a potential last supper dwindled.

Brooke worked extra time with the patient, strengthening his swallowing muscles to a point where she believed he could pass the test. However, political issues with Medicare payments prohibited incremental tests.

When a patient leaves the hospital, the nursing facility housing the patient must absorb the costs of any new studies. With money often tight, these facilities must adhere to strict cost controls, and so most SLPs' requests get turned down, especially those coming from usually risk-averse interns.

Brooke convinced three seasoned SLPs that the patient could pass the test and finally received approval from a reluctant executive at the facility.

On the day before Thanksgiving, with the whole Italian family in attendance, they encouragingly counted aloud each repetition of the father's required swallowing test. The family's jubilation at his success, knowing he could eat Thanksgiving dinner with them the next day, wouldn't have been possible without the compassion of a young intern willing to help a patient and his family.

Our youngest daughter Jamie is the boy I never had. From the outside, she looks like a competitive powerlifter, but inside resides the softest of hearts. Coaches oppressed and saddled her with an inferiority complex as a freshman in high school. We transferred her to a new high school, hoping for a new beginning. As a sophomore and junior, she became a starter on the varsity basketball team. Small-college recruiters inquired about her interest in competing at the next level.

By her senior year, her interests had changed. She asked if I would mind if she chose not to play basketball in her final year. Grimacing, I wondered why. Her reason was very telling. She wanted to enroll in the nursing classes designed for seniors interested in the medical field. I had no choice but to agree.

After graduating, Jamie coached in high school, taught in elementary school, owned her own business, and worked extensive hours. It wasn't until COVID forced the business closure that I discovered she was simultaneously volunteering in a hospice facility. She knew well before me that everything was coming full circle.

Jamie completed her nursing program and worked in a downtrodden Level II trauma emergency department as part of her internship. How can someone have the head for toughness in an emergency department and the heart for hospice care? Because both disciplines have people who need the compassion she can offer. Today, she provides comfort to those in hospice and their families. She leaves every one of her transitioning patients with a plastic fork tied with a bow, reminding them that dessert is coming. In their new life, the "best is yet to come."

Three strong, compassionate women. All willing to suffer alongside those in need. All making a significant impact on my life. I am blessed beyond measure with them, and, thankfully, I keep learning from the best.

Reach out to those in need. Look for the afflicted and anxious people. Be aware of those feeling depressed, defeated, and discouraged. Watch for those appearing confused, fearful, forgotten, or frustrated. Seek those who have been mistreated or misunderstood. Console the sad, sick, and suffering. Actively seek them out rather than waiting for something to drop in your lap. The bottom line? Commit to being there when needed.

SELF-SACRIFICING COMPASSION INCLUDES SELF-SACRIFICING love. There are two prominent types of love mentioned in scripture. The first is rooted in the Greek word *phileo* and is described as having a tender affection for someone.[94] It is a sincere and caring love that shows the feelings one has for another. Reasonable people have this love and display it regularly.

God wants a love from us that goes beyond this, deep within us, as with compassion. He seeks an all-encompassing love, one that is self-sacrificing, not self-filling. This love seeks the benefit of all and no harm to any. It pursues the opportunity to do beautiful things for the good of all. It places others over you, and it allows others to surpass you. In Greek, this is called *agape* love.[95]

They are both differentiated in John 21. The resurrected Jesus had appeared to his disciples, granted proof to a doubting Thomas, and performed a miraculous catch of fish for the disciples to reap. It was like the good old times before the crucifixion. Their Savior was alive, and seeing Jesus again renewed their hope. It was the third time Jesus appeared to them after being raised from the dead.

Jesus knew he needed to have a discussion with Peter. The disciple had boasted about how courageously he would support Jesus, even to the point of giving his life for him. But ultimately, he caved to the pressure of the crowds and denied any affiliation with Jesus. Peter was at a low point, undoubtedly struggling with not only his last words about Jesus but also how diametrically opposed they were to his prior boasts about his loyalty. At the end of dinner, Jesus began to restore Peter.

"'Simon, son of John, do you love me more than these?'

"'Yes, Lord,' he said, 'you know that I love you.'

"Jesus said, 'Feed my lambs.'

"Again, Jesus said, 'Simon son of John, do you love me?'

"He answered, 'Yes, Lord, you know that I love you.'

"Jesus said, 'Take care of my sheep.'

"The third time he said to him, 'Simon son of John, do you love me?'

"Peter seemed upset that Jesus asked him the third time. 'Do you love me?' He said, 'Lord, you know all things; you know that I love you.'

"Jesus said, 'Feed my sheep.' And then, he went on to indicate the kind of death Peter would encounter and how Peter would glorify God. When finished, he said to Peter, 'Follow me!'"[96]

After Peter's disappointing comments and actions, his love for Jesus remained under scrutiny. It is easy to understand why Peter might be feeling the blues. But what is this back-and-forth "love for love" exchange between the two all about? The Greek usage of these "love" terms connects the dots.

On the first two occasions, Jesus asked Peter, "Do you *agape* me?" Do you love me more than anyone? Are you willing to put me at the forefront, ahead of everything? Are you ready to sacrifice your life for me, do my will rather than yours?

To both questions, Peter responded, "Yes, Lord, I *phileo* you." I have a sincere and tender affection for you and care about you. I have feelings for you, and I show them often. Without hesitation, I *phileo* you.

On the third attempt, Jesus changed his final question to Peter. "Do you *phileo* me?

Peter knew Jesus lowered the bar on the type of love he was pursuing. Grieved, he responded, "Yes, as you know, Lord, at this moment, all I can say is I *phileo* you." Peter knew he lacked a greater love for the Lord—he just wasn't there yet, and he wasn't going to claim that he was. His mission in life, daily steps, and whole inner self would need to strengthen and grow. Peter's work was unfinished.

I don't know if Peter understood Jesus's point when he indicated the death Peter would suffer to glorify God. But their exchange made an impression because Peter would eventually have an *agape* love for his Lord, strong enough to fulfill his earlier commitment to give up his life for him. This he did when he was hung on a cross, upside down—unworthy to die like Jesus, but boldly proclaiming him as Lord all the same. John wrote, "Greater love has no one than this than to lay down one's life for his friends."[97]

When we read the crucifixion story or hear tell of it, it's natural to put ourselves there at the various scenes. We think, wonder, and consider: *If I had been there…*

If I had been there at Jesus's Last Supper with his disciples, would I have understood what he was teaching when he washed his disciples' feet?

If I had been there in the garden at Gethsemane, seeing Jesus in agony, would I have stayed awake with him? Would I have been able to console him, encourage him, let him know I had his back no matter what happened, knowing the consequences that likely awaited me?

If I had been there when Jesus was on trial, would I have stood up for him among the crowds, knowing the authorities could arrest me, sealing for myself the same fate as Jesus?

If I had been there while Jesus struggled toward Calvary's hill, would I have volunteered to carry the cross, interrupted the procession, and offered him water, risking being put to death?

If I had been there when they nailed Jesus to the cross, what would I have done? What would I have said? Would I even be able to look at him? How could I have suffered with him? With compassion?

If I had been there when Jesus was raised from the dead and heard the claims of others that it was true, would I have believed, or would I have doubted like others? Like Thomas?

None of us were there, but we are here now. Opportunities present themselves to us at the oddest of moments. When these moments are at hand, what will we do? Each of us can respond. Each of us can act. Each of us can make a difference in the life of someone who is suffering.

The question is: Will we be there when we are needed?

10

Trust—Use Your Instincts

Trust your instincts and make judgments on what your heart tells you. The heart will not betray you.

—DAVID GEMMELL

"And just like that," he said, pausing to snap his fingers, "my whole life changed instantly."

Dr. Warren Mitchell recited these words about his son at a conference on time management, a topic less critical than the continuing education credits I needed to keep my CPA license active. I didn't know the agenda would go beyond how to structure my days of endless tasks for maximum effectiveness.

Dr. Mitchell earned a PhD and MBA and was an accomplished executive and board member for several high-profile Fortune 500 corporations. He taught graduate-level classes early in his career and, post-career, dabbled in consulting and conducting seminars for high-potential business candidates. His vast degree of experience complemented an eloquent manner of speech that mesmerized me and far surpassed my low expectations entering his summit.

He was also incredibly proud of his son. It would be natural to think of the difficulty one might encounter when attempting to follow in the footsteps of such a highly accomplished individual, much less one's own father. But the stories he shared with us revealed that the opposite was the case. His concluding remarks hit home hard, shedding new light on my view of effectively using time.

Upon completing college, his son ventured out on his own for the first time, accepting employment in a different state. It was a full-time position with a decent salary and benefits package. His son fit in well and enjoyed the fruits of his labor for several years. He frequently contacted his parents, updating them on the business and his progress. The hours were long, and the work was hard, but as part of the management team, he felt a real sense of value and ownership in the company.

Labor issues eventually surfaced, however, and following a contentious negotiating period, the laborers' union went on strike. Along with the management team, Dr. Mitchell's son worked on a thinned production line to manufacture enough products to fulfill crucial customer requirements. It wasn't exciting—just a follow-the-process assembly line—but it proved to be a learning opportunity that supplied salient pointers for operational improvements.

The evening hours were no longer dormant and, instead, were used to complete the regular daytime administrative duties. Along with his colleagues, this became the new norm six days a week. Sunday was a day to rest and refresh for the start of another long week.

His calls home became more frequent as he informed his father of any late-breaking news about the strike. On one occasion, he told his father he planned to use one of those Sundays to catch up with his usual workload, figuring he would have the office to himself without any interruptions. The stress relief from catching up, he also reasoned, would supply enough energy to get him to the following week's day of rest.

Dr. Mitchell hesitated slightly before divulging to the audience that his instincts were sending signals, leading to a heightened concern for his son's safety. But how could he convince this ambitious young man to stand down, cease putting in the extra effort, and stop making an impression on upper management? It's what he would have done in the same situation. He ignored his instincts and remained silent.

The strike lingered for weeks. Eventually, his son decided it was time to tackle the overdue tasks stacking up. He attended Sunday church services, grabbed a fast-food lunch, and headed to the office. Alone at work, he made haste to catch up on his duties.

Meanwhile, in an attempt to break the stalemate in negotiations, union members sought to send an intimidating message to management. They didn't know Dr. Mitchell's son would be in the office that day, nor did his son know some of the union members had planted a bomb to go off that very afternoon. The explosion killed his son instantly.

"And just like that, my whole life changed instantly."

Though I couldn't understand the suffering imposed on his family from this tragic incident, two messages resonated with me: the importance of trusting your instincts and the value of time. We often face situations where both points are front and center. Our head says we should or shouldn't do something. It uses logic, considers facts and figures, processes data, and tells us what to do. It tells us to prepare and starts the fight-or-flight mentality.

Our heart, however, tells us otherwise. It takes us on an emotional roller-coaster ride, bobbing and weaving while steering us in a different direction. Our natural or fickle feelings present a formidable case to reconsider what our head says is logical. Our instincts introduce yet another variable, frequently described as a gut feeling. Reactions stem from a combination of the head and heart, yet our gut instinct usually decides the direction taken on specific issues. Instincts aren't something we can practice, and there are no "seven steps to instinctive thinking" courses. It comes naturally and is the best internal decision-making capability we have.

The best athletes are known for their instinctive capabilities, which is the one trait that separates the great from the good. They constantly make split-second decisions, trusting their instincts and acting upon them. As Maverick instructed Rooster in the film *Top Gun: Maverick*, "Don't think, just do."[98]

In baseball, I grew up hearing the phrase "freeze on a line drive." It was good advice for an anxious tot who was ready to run at the crack of the bat, and its purpose was to avoid the double play. In high school and college baseball, things changed. Coaches taught us to watch the play develop before making a decision, even though we had just milliseconds to react.

Recall the earlier discussion that hesitation in sports will kill you. In football, quarterbacks must decide instantly whether to throw a pass, run with the ball, or take a sack. In basketball, the time frame to pass, shoot, or drive past an opponent is a split second, and any hesitation could waste the opportunity to score. In tennis, players instinctively decide between a forehand or backhand and whether to rush the net or stay back on the court.

Players of all sports train for their sport's basic patterns and tendencies, but the first thought that enters their mind is what they end up doing. It's an automatic instinct, and it comes naturally.

ASIDE FROM A FEW YEARS PLAYING SLOW-PITCH SOFTBALL, IT had been twenty years since my baseball days ended. I was one of twenty-five executives invited to experience a day of baseball at Coors Field, home of the Colorado Rockies baseball organization. Most participants hadn't played baseball since Little League, and some never played the game.

Nonetheless, we trotted on the field, fully decked out in a Rockies baseball uniform with our names embroidered on our jerseys. We fielded ground balls, pitched in the bullpen, and took a few swings during batting practice. I figured half of the executives would die of a heart attack or kill themselves trying to catch fly balls.

At the end of the session, they held a contest, with each player getting three pitches to hit. The one hitting the furthest ball would be the winner. It sounded attractive to everyone—until Hall-of-Famer Goose Gossage, decked out in full Rockies garb, walked toward the pitching mound.

Halfway through the lineup, only two batters had made contact—one on a foul tip, the other a swinging bunt. Dejected hitters would exit the batter's box, giving hitting advice: "Look bad on your first swing and hope Goose will lob an easy pitch for you to hit."

There were two problems with this advice, however. First, these guys didn't have to try to look bad—that came naturally. And second, I planned to swing at anything close.

Not a single ball exited the infield before I came to the plate, one of two remaining participants. When Goose served up the not-so-fast first pitch, I bounced it off the wall in left-center field, 375 feet away. It surprised everyone, including me.

Unfortunately, Mr. Gossage didn't appreciate me stealing his show. His next pitch sailed over the batting cage, drawing laughter, and returning attention to him. Figuring I was lucky the first time, Goose increased the velocity of the second pitch, which, again, I instinctively roped (another "six") to left field. While Coach Polk might have been proud, this didn't sit well with Mr. Gossage, doubly so.

Then, I got my first test at big league pitching. Goose offered me two more pitches instead of the one I had remaining. The first was a cautiously placed (hey, it's a corporate event) inside fastball that brushed me back—generating oohs and aws from the bystanders. After he mischievously smiled and cavalierly apologized, his last pitch headed toward the middle of the plate again—except it moved eight inches right and six inches down. Looking foolish and outmatched, I missed it by a mile.

Later, I thought how intimidating it would be to face him when he was throwing his best stuff. He was one of the greatest; his talent incredible. I left with my instincts intact and prizes—an autographed Goose Gossage jersey and baseball bat.

INSTINCTS PLAYED A SIGNIFICANT ROLE IN BUSINESS EARLY IN my career. Initially, we didn't have robust systems and reporting mechanisms to adequately project the profitability picture for the analysts and investment community. It was quite a predicament, grappling with the unpredictability of sales forecasts while facing the daunting prospect of missing profit estimates due to inaccurate financial forecasts.

Unanticipated product delays, long sales cycles, late-stage competitive price-cutting, the timing of international sales, and even incorrectly dated accounting documents were just a few of the variables that could affect the final results. The thought of two or three of these potential issues occurring in the same quarter led to sleepless nights. Until we integrated proper reporting disciplines, I had to rely on my gut feeling when supplying profitability guidance to the Wall Street analysts.

Billionaire Mark Cuban, an owner of many businesses, said, "Perfection is the enemy of success."[99] Making decisions is a constant. You cannot wait for the perfect solution to a problem; you have to decide what to do and move on. If it turns out the decision was wrong, change it. But don't wait. Time is too important. Rather than falling into the paralysis-by-analysis trap, trusting your instincts is the ticket to moving forward.

Instincts play a prominent role in our lives. We use them as parents raising kids, when choosing a spouse, when deciding between job offers, and when casting our votes. We even use them in our spiritual decisions and how we serve others. Bottom line? We must trust our instincts and listen to the gut feeling of our inner voice.

Diamonds, Deals, and Divine Guidance

You know those weird dreams you sometimes have? The ones that don't make sense, where scenes seem out of sync with characters out of place? Where you wake and, though you scarcely remember the details, except they were bizarre and in a state of disorder, something triggers these dreams—a movie, book, conversation, or ceremony? You remember parts of it vividly but don't recall the rest.

The hippocampus is the region of the brain primarily associated with our memory, located in the inner area of the temporal lobe and part of the limbic system. It's critical in regulating our emotional responses and how we feel and react. It's also involved with how certain body functions work, including what is commonly known as the fight-or-flight response.[100]

The hippocampus helps retrieve distinct types of memory. Explicit or declarative memory helps us remember formulas and facts for a test, items on a grocery list, or lines for a speech. Implicit memory requires no real effort. By swinging a baseball bat hundreds of times every day for years, I developed a procedural memory that allowed it to come naturally long after playing competitive baseball (like with Goose).

Spatial memory is akin to a cognitive map and involves recording information about our environment and orientation. When my daughters went to college, both could pack a car trunk to its brim without a formal plan. Short-term memories convert into long-term memories in the hippocampus, and a range of conditions can adversely affect the hippocampus, including long-term exposure to elevated stress levels.[101]

Thomas Andrillon, a neuroscientist at Monash University in Australia, said, "We have a tendency to immediately forget dreams, and it's likely that people who rarely report dreams are just forgetting them more easily. It might be hard to believe that you had a dream if you don't remember anything, but studies consistently show that even people who haven't recalled a single dream in decades or even their lifetime, do, in fact, recall them if they are awakened at the right moment."[102]

He added, "But dreams that are more vivid, emotional, and coherent seem to be better remembered; perhaps because they trigger more awakening, and their organized narrative makes them easier to store."[103]

I've had memories of some of those wacky dreams that come out of nowhere. Familiar thoughts of past failures that seemed distant suddenly returned, and I was left mystified. One such flashback was set off by a simple conversation.

Lindy and I were returning with Jamie, who had flown in from Colorado. She hoped Florida's warmth and its waters' peace would refresh her mind in the midst of "test cramming" before taking the national nursing NCLEX examination. Her weightlifting disciplines were proving handy as she toted only a carry-on bag with marine-grade, polyester boat-rope handles, holding the fifty pounds of books she would review over the next week. I recalled the similar doorstop-worthy study books I carried when I slugged through the CPA examinations.

Jamie seemed confident, had been tutored for months, and had completed a thorough review course to aid in the test-taking. In addition to the diverse content of the examination, she learned how to break down questions and decipher all the medical and pharmacology terminology, most of which would likely be forgotten soon after passing the test.

She aimed to pass the exam on her first attempt. Jesting, I assured her she would do much better than I had done in my prior testing attempts.

That evening, my slumber was anything but peaceful as I struggled with an uncanny dream fed by that simple discussion in the car earlier. Memories I believed to be archived had now reappeared. The books and nursing exam brought me back to my three-time struggle with the CPA exam. Combined with my writing difficulty, familiar thoughts plagued my mind: *Maybe I am not good enough to do this.*

Making matters worse, the hesitation I had experienced with the Chicago White Sox's contract offer resurfaced. There were replays of conversations I had over the years. One was with an accomplished executive who grew up in an environment designed to convince him his accomplishments were insufficient. Another was with a well-known doctor who adopted the opinions of his parents, who quipped he wasn't good enough.

Many others, in various stages of life and with vast sets of circumstances and professions, shared similar inadequate feelings. I took comfort in knowing I wasn't alone.

As I tried to shake off the effects of this nightmarish snooze, the fear of failure needled at me. But my instincts told me I was in a much better place now and needed to trust them. Trusting instincts involves something incredibly significant—it requires taking a leap of faith.

We often enjoy looking at optical illusions because they trick the brain into seeing something that may not be there and into perceiving reality in different ways. The brain is a processor and thinks in simple terms. When our eyes perceive a visual stimulus in one way, the brain forms a different view based on images it has seen before. No two people experience illusions in the same way, and in some cases, the visual effects aren't seen at all.

Putting optical illusions aside, how can you get clarity regarding something you can't see or don't understand? How can you believe and trust what you cannot see? Scenarios like these are active in our lives at home, school, work, social gatherings, and as part of our worship services.

The apostle Thomas faced the challenge of believing and trusting in something he hadn't seen. Nobody wants to be known for lacking faith, yet most of us have this tendency, especially during tough times. I had times when my faith came into question, so the biblical rendition of this doubting Thomas presented new insight. When I studied it further, it prompted me to question if the story of Thomas was really about Thomas. It took me back to the burial site and the resurrection of Jesus.

Grayish skies preceded the day's dawning. Crunching gravel interrupted the early morning stillness as Mary Magdalene and a few other women headed toward Jesus's tomb. They carried spices used to anoint the body and minimize odors of decay. They were surprised to see the stone rolled away and the body of Jesus gone. They were even more surprised when two men in bright clothes suddenly appeared. And if it were possible, they must have been further startled when the men told them Jesus had arisen from the dead. When the gravesite strangers quoted Jesus, it kindled the women's memory of his having said he would need to be crucified and then be resurrected.

The women returned and told the apostles of the morning's events. The apostles, on the whole, didn't believe their nonsensical story, but it did pique Peter's curiosity. Luke's account said Peter ran to the tomb to check it out. He leaned in, saw the linen strips, noticed the missing body, and left the scene, wondering what had happened.

Later in the day, Cleopas and another follower of Jesus set out for Emmaus, a small village close to Jerusalem. They were rehearsing the events like detectives, unaware when Jesus joined them on the trail and inquired about their discussions. They delivered a Cliff's Notes version of what recently happened but remained unaware Jesus was in their presence. Jesus poked at their sluggishness to believe what the prophets had spoken and responded with a full explanation of the scriptures. As they approached the village, Jesus indicated he would continue his journey. Intrigued by the depth of Jesus's knowledge, they urged him to stay the night.

Dinner was a replay of the Last Supper. Jesus took the bread, blessed and broke it, then handed it to them. They recognized him immediately. Before they could say "Oh my Lord," Jesus vanished. They sat in shock, wondering. *What just happened? Why didn't this register with us on the trail? Why didn't our instincts kick in?*

That same evening, the disciples hid behind closed doors, fearful of arrest. Suddenly, Jesus appeared and stood among them, and when they saw Jesus, his pierced hands, and punctured side, they became convinced he was alive. They were understandably ecstatic.

But our leading man Thomas was absent from this miraculous reappearance. We're not sure where he was, but soon the disciples rejoiced in telling Thomas they had seen Jesus. In the flesh. For real. In fact, they told him repeatedly. But Thomas wouldn't believe them. He wanted the same proof they proclaimed to have, to see the wounds on his hands and side. Without the evidence, he wouldn't budge. He was the same as they were, unbelieving until given proof.

A little over a week later, the disciples congregated at the same place behind closed doors. Jesus appeared again, and this time Thomas was present. His reaction to seeing Jesus was the same as the disciples' first viewing. He saw Jesus, touched him, and with unambiguous evidence, he believed. Jesus said, "Thomas, because you have seen Me, you have believed. Blessed are those who have not seen and yet have believed."[104]

Why Thomas? Why does he get the bad rap for being an unbeliever? Why has he been tagged with the seemingly eternal label of "biggest doubter of all time?" Why not Mary Magdalene, who first noticed the body of Jesus missing? Why not Peter, who was at the tomb and saw the body missing and the linens neatly folded? Why not the two disciples on the road to Emmaus, who didn't believe until they saw Jesus breaking bread at dinner that night? Why not the other disciples who were told Jesus had risen but were fortunate to be in the room when Jesus showed up offering peace?

Why weren't any of these people singled out with their own story as "the one who doubted?" All of them were hesitant, doubtful, afraid to believe, and needed to see to believe. Sheesh! Why pick on Thomas?

Trust may start with dipping our toe in the water, but eventually, it requires a full plunge into the pool, bearing the consequences of the risks associated with our choices.

Early in life, we were trained to listen and listen often. Teachers taught us concepts and subjects. Parents imparted to us behavior modification skills ("Stop acting like your father"), stamina ("You'll sit there until you finish all that spinach"), irony ("Keep crying and I'll give you something to cry about"), and logic ("Because I said so, that's why").

They also taught us traits like honesty, love, and discipline (through chores). Ministers cited scriptures on how to treat and serve others. We absorbed the information and learned from people we thought were trustworthy or respected because of their position of authority.

Yet, after many years of instruction, we came out of our school-age years not knowing who we were or who we wanted to become. Various surveys show that over 50 percent—and in some cases up to 80 percent—of college students change their major at least once, and students change their majors an average of two to three times before they decide on a career.

Trust is bilateral. On one side, we view trust from our perspective. Whom do we trust? Why do we trust? How do we trust? On the flip side, we should view trust through the lens of others looking to place their trust in us. The spectrum is broad. Some have very little or no trust. Others have a tremendous amount of trust and require minimum stipulations. Most are in the middle, leaning slightly in one direction.

Think of a conversation you were engaged in about someone who isn't present. Comments made and opinions given put the absent person in unfavorable terms. I have always tried to stand up for the missing individual—not to be argumentative with those in the discussion but to stand up and give a defense for the absent person to ensure those involved in the conversation hear both sides of the story. It's what I would hope for if I wasn't present. The reactions of the accusers who have been unexpectedly challenged are fascinating to watch. Either the topic changes, (which is good), or the conversation ceases (even better).

Trust works the same way when looking through the lens of both sides—why you trust someone and why that person trusts you. Recognize a need for trust from the outset, whether it's a person, a decision, or a circumstance. Look for ways in which some sign of trust is already in place. Know it is doubtful any single person can satisfy all your requirements. Few can. Be patient. Because trust grows over time, look for those who seem to be or have proven to be trustworthy.

I use the five principles we previously covered when looking at those I need to be able to trust, assuming they will view me in a like manner. These are true for teammates, friends, business colleagues, teachers, doctors, politicians, parents, family members, in-laws, and spiritual people. It is how we cultivate trust.

1. **Identification.** Who does the person say they are, and have they consistently shown they live by their word? Do they stick to their principles, even when it is difficult to do so?

2. **Motivation.** What motivates them? How do they spend their time? Are their motives in line with your needs? Or will they contradict the direction you are taking?

3. **Preparation.** Do they have a decent work ethic at work or home, in school, playing sports, or other activities? Their historical accomplishments are a good indicator of their willingness to work hard.

4. **Accountability**. How does the individual respond when they make mistakes? Do they hold themselves accountable for their actions? Do they make excuses or place blame? Do they respect the boundaries of others?

5. **Compassion**. Do they care for and treat people compassionately, especially those suffering, disadvantaged, or culturally different?

All of these lead to trust.

I became more confident trusting someone who had these traits, as I knew they would have similar expectations of me. It wasn't a perfect process, though. I misread some individuals primarily because of their secret self-centered motives. Some closest to me used me to their advantage.

In other cases, the most loyal and trustworthy people around me were those I spent little time with. People assured me they would be there for me when demanding times surfaced but ended up as no-shows. Others made promises, only to break them, leaving their commitments unfulfilled and me needing answers. Using these five principles helped me identify and minimize exceptions, such as those mentioned.

KNOW YOU CAN TRUST GOD IN YOUR TIME OF NEED. ABRAHAM was willing to trust God when he set out to sacrifice his son Isaac. Joseph trusted God when sold by his brothers and later imprisoned. Moses trusted God when cornered at the banks of the Red Sea, David when facing Goliath, Jonah when in the belly of the great fish, and Daniel when thrown in the lions' den. That wasn't just then, however; it's now. Our world has become one of distrust, but it doesn't have to be that way.

We will face thousands of questions throughout our lives. Our task is trying to find the right answers. The questions will be daunting, and for some, there will be no explanation. We will strive to solve an issue and clear the air, but we mustn't be so misguided as to think our drawn-out efforts will be sufficient to help us figure things out.

Our first step must be to turn to God before all our human reasoning is exhausted—not after. Hope and security come in knowing the problem-resolution skills we deploy are unnecessary to attain peace, but that will happen only when we put our trust in God. Because we don't need all the answers, it is best that we heed the words of Proverbs: "Trust in the Lord with all your heart; and lean not on your own understanding. In all your ways submit to him, and he will make your paths straight."[105]

On some level, we will always wonder if, when, or how things will work. We might say or do something that touches a person's heart, but its impact won't emerge until after we are gone. Despite our lack of knowing this has occurred, our legacy will extend beyond our mortal lives. Jesus walked this world thousands of years ago, yet his lasting influence is compelling and continues to change lives. Hopefully, ours will too.

JOHN KAVANAUGH'S STORY EPITOMIZES THE TRUE MEANING OF trust. He worked at a place in Calcutta referred to as "the house of the dying." This facility, established by Mother Teresa, provided free hospice care to people experiencing poverty, and Kavanaugh was there looking for answers about his future direction.

On his first visit with Mother Teresa, she asked him, "What can I do for you?"

He asked, "Pray that I have clarity."

Mother Teresa said firmly, "No. I will not do that." He was surprised and asked her why. She explained, "Clarity is the last thing you are clinging to and must let go of."

Taken aback, he said, "But you seem to have clarity from God."

Mother Teresa laughed. "I have never had clarity; what I have always had is trust. So, I will pray that you trust God."[106]

Aren't most of us like John Kavanaugh?

I'm at the top of the list, always wanting and praying for clarity. I've prayed to see God's word revealed in my life and for opportunities to serve others, even if it's uncomfortable for me. I want clarity on how to handle hardship, temptation, and relationships. I want to see power proven through prayer. I want to see precise ways to show kindness and comfort to the downtrodden. I pray for clarity on how I can be the example of goodness, the light in the lives of those lost and searching.

But as Mother Teresa taught, clarity is something to which we cannot cling, and, instead, we must trust. We need the strength and wisdom to trust God's way is best for our lives.

When Thomas saw Jesus alive, he responded like his brothers had done, by rejoicing and believing. But as for the rest of the story, he still goes down as the weak guy with little faith and no trust. Even after sitting with this story for a while, I still didn't have an answer as to why he was that guy. So, I did a background check to see if I could find anything peculiar.

Thomas was chosen to be one of the twelve apostles of Jesus Christ. He was loyal and courageous, willing to go with Jesus to see the deceased Lazarus. He seemed honest, saying the disciples didn't understand why Jesus was the way to God. And, of course, he was human. When the disciples claimed to have seen Jesus, he may not have been in the right frame of mind. What little we know about Thomas in the scriptures points to him being a pretty good guy. My research resulted in a dead end.

Or did it?

Where is the story of this doubting Thomas in the book of Matthew? It's not there. How about in the book of Mark? Nope, not there either. What about the book of Luke? No siree. So why is the story of Thomas only in the book of John? What do we know about John, and does it have anything to do with Thomas? Is there a message we can take from the story of Thomas being solely in the book of John?

We know that, at some of the most critical times in the life of Jesus, John was with him. He was with him at the transfiguration, in the garden of Gethsemane, at the Last Supper, when Jesus hung on the cross, and when the risen Jesus restored Peter. We also know John was known as the "one whom Jesus loved."[107]

Remember when Mary Magdalene saw the empty tomb and scurried back to tell the disciples? Luke's account of the scene indicated that everyone went incognito except Peter, who immediately ran to the grave, saw the empty linens, and left perplexed. It's only in John's book that we learn he was also at the scene. Mary Magdalene went to Peter and John to tell them of the missing body. When Peter dashed back to the tomb site, John went with him and actually arrived first.

When John arrived, "he stooped down and looked in, he saw the linen cloths lying there, but he did not go in."[108] What John first "saw" becomes clear, knowing the Greek word used in this verse is *blepo*, which means to have sight or glance[109] at something. He didn't enter but merely peeked inside. He noticed something was different, but it didn't quite register.

When Peter finally arrived, "He went into the tomb; and he saw the linen cloths lying there, and the handkerchief that had been around his head, not lying with the linen cloths, but folded together in a place by itself."[110] What Peter "saw," translated from the Greek word *thereo*, was a careful perusal of the details of an object.[111]

Peter is likened to a CSI detective, looking at the specific evidence from a crime scene. He saw the handkerchief separated from the other linens as though Jesus sat on the stone, folding it before he placed it down. Peter was mentally trying to assemble the sequence of events based on the facts at the scene.

Then John, "who came to the tomb first, went in also, and he saw and believed."[112] When John entered the tomb, he saw something different. What he saw this time is translated from the Greek word *eidon,* which means he knew and understood the significance of the situation. John grasped the importance of undisturbed clothes and knew Jesus had risen from death.[113] John, the one whom Jesus loved, believed without seeing Jesus. It was unquestionable and clear. His faith and trust in Jesus were both confirmed.

There is more to the story of Thomas than his doubts and unbelief. The inclusion of John brings forth a more profound message, a lesson about clarity. Often enough, we don't see things clearly. We may only see things partially or not see things at all. Like when we fail, disappointments surface, losses mount, hardships repeat, and our sense of self-worth dissipates. In those times, we may have to rely on our instincts, instincts that come naturally to us because of what we have experienced, trusted, and believed.

We weren't there when Jesus rose from the dead. Most of us, if not all, would have been like Thomas and the others, needing to see before believing. But we are here now, having not seen, with the opportunity to believe—just as Jesus explained to Thomas. Whom we trust and how we trust is paramount to securing any peace in our lives.

Instincts are often overlooked in the story of Thomas. Frequently, his label as "Doubting Thomas" comes without considering the significance of his actions during those tumultuous times. When many of Christ's followers fled, Thomas chose to stay. Were his instincts telling him something that others missed? Doubt, often misunderstood, doesn't signify a disavowal of faith. In fact, Thomas's journey is a testament to the complex interplay between doubt and belief.

Thomas's instincts, which compelled him to stay with the disciples, reveal a remarkable determination to seek the truth and strengthen his faith. He dared to ask the difficult questions, to confront his doubts head-on, and to grapple with the mysteries of faith. In this sense, Thomas represents not just a momentary hesitation but a courageous exploration of faith, which should be an inspiration to all of us.

As we navigate our own spiritual journeys, we can draw a valuable lesson from Thomas. We mustn't be content with superficial or unquestioning faith. Instead, we should trust our instincts to guide us in our quest for a deeper understanding of God's love for us. Doubt can be a stepping stone to an unwavering faith, and our instincts, if followed with an open heart, can lead us to a place of profound spiritual growth and peace.

11

Speech – Speak Softly and Embrace Silence

Everyone should be quick to listen, slow to speak, and slow to become angry.

—JAMES 1:19

If you have watched a Little League baseball game, undoubtedly you have seen this play out. Astonishingly, it also occurs in the major leagues. The batter hits a pop-up, and two players run to catch it. With heads tilted toward the sky and eyes focused on the ball, they close in on each other, hearing footsteps and sensing a collision. Both shout, "I've got it." They collide, and the bobbled ball drops to the ground. Or they both stop, and the ball drops between them. They glare at one another while the batter stands safely on base.

I have used this example when speaking to students, asking for a show of hands if they believe these two players were communicating. Most students raise their hands, a few don't, and the remainder stay focused on their iPhones. At this time, I remind them communication is more than simply about giving and receiving information. It requires a connection between the two.

George Bernard Shaw once said, "The single biggest problem in communication is the illusion that it has taken place."[114] In the pop-fly scenario, coaches teach priority schemes so when one player shouts, "I've got it," the other acknowledges by saying, "Take it." That connection between the two players completes communication and provides a clear pathway to better results, like catching the fly ball.

Many of us were likely taught at an early age the old saying that "sticks and stones may break my bones, but words will never hurt me." This statement may be true, physically speaking, but words can inflict damage in other ways. One familiar example is sarcasm. Its original meaning was "to tear flesh" and this is why the Proverb writer said, "The words of the reckless pierce like swords."[115] Harsh words, unwarranted criticism, name-calling, and false accusations are like swords. They can deeply cut into the spirit of the heart.

In a world brimming with diverse means of communication and often frenetic technological distractions, the art of effective communication is paramount. It's not merely about the exchange of words, but the cultivation of connections and relationships that withstand the test of time. To be successful, we must grasp the significance of prioritizing genuine interactions over virtual distractions. We must appreciate the subtle nuances of different forms of communication, whether it's the spoken word, the written message, or the unspoken cues of body language. These connections are the lifeblood of our relationships, be they with family, friends, or colleagues. Understanding and mastering the various modes of communication will not only enrich our personal and professional lives but also allow us to navigate our human connections with empathy, authenticity, and a deep sense of purpose.

There are many mediums to choose from when communicating verbally. We watch YouTube, hold Zoom calls, and listen to music and podcasts—many times from the very cell phones we use. Occasionally, we have actual conversations with each other, but in many ways, technology has impeded open communications. Restaurants are inundated with patrons addicted to their cell phones or glued to table video games, taking away what used to be time for family dinner conversations. The same patterns and distractions occur at home, where we minimize the importance of discussions about school activities, work, the upcoming weekend, or a quickly approaching vacation.

We claim there's not enough time. In a survey of one thousand Christians, 42 percent cited a "lack of priority and time" as the main reasons for not reading the Bible.[116] Since we choose to prioritize how we use our time, we can only point the finger at ourselves.

Written communications have evolved from markings, symbols, and alphabets to emails, texts, and tweets. Social media is a global phenomenon, with Facebook approaching three billion users[117] and their industry sidekick formerly known as Twitter (now simply known by the vague title "X") having 186 million daily active users sending five hundred million tweets daily.[118] It is no surprise to parents when they can't get their children to answer a phone call but can get a near-immediate response when they send a text.

The significance of nonverbal communication also deserves attention. Facial expressions disclose one's demeanor, and bodily gestures can indicate anything from elation to discouragement. The variations are limitless, and the reactions plentiful.

Early on in my career, I learned the importance of body language, especially when the time approached to release our quarterly earnings report to the Wall Street investors. I prepared for these updates in a glass-lined office where anyone walking by could see me. They formed opinions based on how I sat, my facial expressions, and the demeanor I used with those who were assisting me. Employees told me later they could sense if our company results would be favorable or not from my body language. I quickly learned the need to maintain the same body language regardless of good or bad news.

One of my favorite body-language learning experiences came at a Goldman Sachs investor symposium in Palm Springs, California. The keynote speaker for this event was the CEO of the industry-leading company in the markets where we competed.

There was an unwritten law that executives shouldn't attend the specific company sessions of their competitors. But this was a general session, and I was interested in hearing his thoughts on the future of our industry.

Casually late, I arrived as the introductions started, greeted by coffee tables loaded with various calorie-laden treats. I indulged in a few that weren't messy, avoiding the need to use my tie as a napkin. Thousands of investors were seated, with many squinting for an open seat to avoid standing the entire one-hour presentation. A movable wall served as a leaning post, and I noticed a dozen or so sell-side analysts and day traders in the back row, with online PCs on their laps and a cell phone in hand.

Sell-side analysts research a group of companies, create financial models to establish price targets, and make "buy" or "sell" recommendations to investors. Day traders take advantage of intraday market fluctuations and try to maximize profits, buying and selling stocks within hours, sometimes within seconds. Some day traders claim their average hold time for certain stocks is less than ten seconds. So much for creating value for your portfolio over the long term! The traders at this conference were ready to buy or sell stocks should new market-moving information be divulged in the presentation or if a speaker's body language hinted at an upspoken direction.

The CEO started with his customary salutations. Minutes into his pitch, I surmised something was awry. I had seen him several times and watched him handle investors with poise. This day was different. He was perspiring, appeared downcast, occasionally winced, and walked gingerly. Some of the back-row traders also noticed his body language. I was close enough to hear whispers.

"Something is wrong."

"He looks stressed."

"He's about to deliver bad news."

"I'm selling the second I hear anything weird."

They were locked and loaded, ready to pull the trigger on their "sell" orders.

A brief time later, the CEO was noticeably uncomfortable. When he paused his speech, the silence was deafening. Many thought it was time for him to break the bad news about his company's upcoming financial results. Instead, he told the audience he had emergency surgery the day before. He had flown coast to coast, acknowledged he was physically struggling, and had forgotten his pain medications. Sensing angst from those in the room, he assured them his company was doing well. With a refilled prescription on the way, he would feel much better soon.

I watched the day traders frantically cancel and change "sell" orders to "buy" orders.

NONVERBAL COMMUNICATION IS AS OLD AS HUMANITY. Adam and Eve didn't need to admit they had eaten from the forbidden tree; their guilt was evident when they sewed fig leaves to cover their nakedness. When God looked with favor on Abel and his offering, Cain's downcast face showed his disdain. The rich man seeking eternal life told Jesus he had obeyed all the commandments since his youth. But when Jesus told him he was missing one thing—that he needed to sell everything he owned and give it to people in need—the rich man's face fell, and he walked away, demonstrating that his wealth was more important than doing what Jesus asked of him.

The nonverbal communication involving Peter's denial are straightforward. We previously mentioned Peter assuring Jesus of his loyalty. He committed to die for Jesus, vowing never to disown him, regardless of the circumstances. After the authorities took Jesus into custody, several people approached Peter and identified him as a follower of Christ. Each time he failed miserably, claiming he didn't know Jesus. After his final denial, he remembered Jesus telling him this would happen.

Jesus turned and simply looked at him, and at this, Peter walked outside and wept. Jesus didn't show any anger toward Peter, only sorrow. Some might've expected Peter to be scolded for his lack of courage, but instead, he saw Jesus. Silent. Disappointed. Burdened with grief. Looking through Peter's eyes and into his heart. Peter didn't have to face the wrath of Jesus, he only needed to see the heartbreak in his eyes. That was sufficient punishment. Without a single word spoken, there was clear communication between them.

A TIME-TESTED PRINCIPLE FOR COMMUNICATION CONNECTION comes from the book of James. "Everyone should be quick to listen, slow to speak, and slow to anger."[119] This advice has saved me more times than I can count. In today's educational curricula, there is a greater emphasis on offering speech classes than teaching the art of listening. It may be why people talk more than they listen. I've always believed God gave us two ears and one mouth for a reason, and there is more value in listening than speaking.

And so, we are clear: listening is different from hearing.

Hearing is simple. It collects data, like perceiving sounds and making sense of varying noises or tones. Listening is more involved because it requires understanding spoken words, speakers' tones, and emotional undertones or overtones. It helps one process non-verbal cues in order to reason and remember. The listener pays attention, doesn't interrupt during a conversation and looks to gain an understanding before responding.

With hearing, you say, "I hear it."

With listening, you can say, "I get it."

We see this in debates on television or while listening to radio talk shows when individuals give opinions before they have gathered sufficient facts. Interruptions are frequent, and both parties talk simultaneously, getting louder with each sentence to a point where nobody can understand anything being said. Listening is essential when trying to influence others.

Answering or responding without listening can be troublesome. Most of us have seen or been part of a simple disagreement that quickly escalated to a boiling point, fanning the flames and starting a fire. James's caution to be slow to speak is wise advice, suggesting it's best to let cooler heads prevail.

Early in my career, when I allowed someone to amp me up verbally or in writing, I resorted to my "wait a day" rule. I found it was better to let time pass before responding because, in the heat of the moment, I realized I might say something I would regret. Time heals, but it also helps us calmly collect our emotions.

Counselors suggest you take the time to write a letter to the person aggravating you to the point of frustration. Write out everything you want to say and be straightforward. But when done, read it and then destroy it. I like this idea because I write what I want to say, then feel relief when I'm done. It works for me.

The Proverb writer compliments James's advice, saying, "A soft answer turns away wrath, but a harsh word stirs up anger."[120] Always maintain self-control because the communication connection becomes impossible without it. Minimize the emotional aspects of communication. This powerful verse of scripture can become a great asset if you can master it.

THE YEAR WE MISSED THE CONSENSUS EARNINGS ESTIMATES multiple times, we were inundated with shareholder calls demanding answers and accountability. I quickly learned how important money was to people, especially to angry investors. Responding with harsh words and a defiant tone would have only made matters worse. I was more effective with investors when I deployed this simple advice—listen and respond slowly and calmly. Admitting our shortfalls and offering plans to recover from our failures lent credence, and it allowed the dialogue to be meaningful and the connection plausible.

When engaging in meaningful communication, three questions from a common philosophy are worth considering.

1. *Is what you are saying true?* Never say anything you know to be false against anyone. If you don't know, don't assume or guess. Speak clearly and be respectful. Refrain from filling in moments of silence with comments that don't move the conversation forward correctly. Appreciate the person whom you are speaking with and apologize for anything said in error. Honesty is the best starting point in any collaboration.

2. *Is what you are saying kind?* Too often, sarcasm enters conversations when there is a disagreement or confrontation. "Kill them with kindness" is a mantra for dealing with difficult people. But unfortunately, the opposite often occurs, and kindness and care are in short supply for undeserving people. Acknowledge the feelings and emotions in conversation and look for common ground if there is a difference of opinion. Feel free to ask questions to understand where the other person is coming from. Kindness is remarkably potent and can generate a sensible response when exchanged genuinely.

3. *Is what you are saying necessary?* If it isn't needed, ZIP IT! Plain and simple. Does anyone come to mind who drifts off-topic and starts rambling without thinking? Many of us have done this. To keep a conversation moving, we search for things to say that have nothing to do with solving a dispute or making a salient point. Silence is golden and immensely powerful, especially when your words are irrefutable.

Our words can be inspiring and influential, but they also have the power to be dangerously harmful.

Working through this took me a while—a challenging task for someone who regularly spoke to people worldwide. Groups included friends and foes, suppliers who tried to help us win and competitors who looked for ways to beat us down, investors who were pleased with their returns and others who were enraged with their losses, employees and teammates who worked for the good of the team and others who looked out for themselves. Connecting with people with different or unknown motives is very tricky. Our best efforts to communicate with others require us to be aware of the snares of speech and the traps that can make a conversation futile instead of fruitful.

Anger is a snare. Nobody can make us angry because it is our choice. It is merely an emotional reaction to an event we engage in with others. Steer clear of starting a conversation if you are infuriated or frustrated.

Self-righteousness is another snare. I believe the scriptures are God's words to us, and it is helpful for us to read and study them as often as possible because they give us wisdom concerning the treatment of others.

However, one of the reasons churchgoers sometimes don't connect when communicating is that they continually use "book, chapter, and verse" to prove nonconformance and render guilt but neglect to consider the need for building a grace-filled relationship. Our interpretations of scripture are fallible, but the message from Jesus is perfect and straightforward. He modeled how we should live and treat one another. He wants us to know his truth but wants something other than our memory bank of scriptures—he wants our hearts and a loving relationship. Wouldn't it be more straightforward if we were known by how closely our lives were like that of Jesus?

Is it possible to master the complete list of snares, including boasting, exaggeration, mocking or nagging, abusive language, or adult temper tantrums? Can we even remember them all? Not a chance. James didn't intend to discourage anyone with his warning nor convince us to throw in the towel and be speechless. His caution was to make us aware of ineffective communication methods when speaking with others. We must elevate others to help them. Our influence grows when we adopt a less prominent role and speak sparingly.

What we fill our minds with day-to-day influences our ability to communicate, whether we are supportive or discouraging. Surveys vary on exact numbers, but the conclusions are consistent: the average person watches hours of television daily, equivalent to years over a lifetime. Streaming methods draw us in with more choices, and commercials challenge our self-control, enticing us with promises of youth, fame, and fortune. Video games and phone apps addict us, consuming precious time on mindless activities.

We need to engage in meaningful, enriching content that nurtures our minds. Trade the mindless scrolling through social media or playing video games (at least some of it) for productive and purposeful activities that stimulate personal growth and connection. By making conscious choices in our consumption of information, we empower ourselves to become better communicators, fostering a more positive and supportive environment for ourselves and those around us.

What we listen to can influence our outlook as well. It's like a father who gave his two sons very different messages in their youth. He told one he would grow up to be a doctor and told the other he would end up in prison. He was right on both accounts. His words influenced them both at an early age and became their reality later in life. It's better to fill ourselves—and others—with hope, joy, and peace because the words that come from within will influence others.

PAY ATTENTION TO A SELDOM-USED BUT POWERFUL FORM OF communication. *Silence.* When used correctly, silence is highly effective and beneficial in connecting with people.

The prophet Isaiah prophesied seven hundred years before the time Jesus would suffer. He explained how Jesus would be crushed for our sins, beaten, oppressed, treated harshly, and led like a lamb to the slaughter.[121] He also predicted Jesus would use silence to thwart the power of those with authority who were trying to eradicate him. We can trace these prophecies to the time of Jesus and see the specific patterns of when he spoke and when he was silent.

Jesus faced the chief priests and council, both of whom searched for ways to justify putting him to death. They claimed he was a radical and that his teachings were false. Many witnesses came forward, but their testimonies were inconsistent. The evidence they sought to convict Jesus was inconclusive, and they had no case. Frustrated, the high priest stood and asked for answers from Jesus. His petition came from a position of strength much more significant than Jesus's earthly position. The high priest used his authority to bully and demand answers.

But Jesus kept silent. He didn't take the bait. He held his peace, giving no credence to the frivolous claims against him. Why respond to nonsense?

The high priest, however, wouldn't let it go. Like a prosecuting attorney, he circled the wagons and approached the interrogation from a different angle. He pushed forward, knowing he was forbidden to ask questions if the witnesses would be implicated by his answer. He tried to lure Jesus with a question that would supply him with the evidence he sought. He asked Jesus if he was the Son of God. Those around sat silently, waiting for the answer to a point-blank question.

Unafraid, Jesus broke his silence. Why? Because he was sure of his identity. At that moment, his courage didn't wane even though his answer would result in him effectively being given a death sentence. Jesus had prepared for this throughout his life, knowing the events now unfolding had been inevitable. Knowing his Father had guaranteed his eventual victory, his confidence didn't fade. He responded firmly, yes! He affirmed that he was the Son of God and boldly said they would see him sitting at his Father's side.

At that point, the high priest turned into a drama king. He tore his clothes to pieces. He highlighted the alleged blasphemy, believing it was enough to condemn Jesus. No more witnesses were required. They considered Jesus guilty, and the horrendous treatment of their prisoner began. They had everything they needed except the power to lay down a sentence. Only the Roman governor had such power, so they went to Pontius Pilate to get the conviction and punishment ratified.

Pilate asked Jesus, "Are you the King of the Jews?"

Jesus didn't refute the facts. "It is as you say."[122]

The chief priests continued with their false accusations, but Jesus said nothing.

Pilate reiterated the high priests' false testimony against Jesus. Again, Jesus said nothing.

Pilate marveled at Jesus's silence but was perplexed that he didn't ask for help. Both knew Pilate could get Jesus out of this pickle. All Jesus had to do was ask.

But Jesus didn't need help because, by the will of his Father, he could do whatever he wanted. The two remained at a standstill.

Pilate was shaken and started looking for an escape from this dilemma. It came when he heard Jesus was a Galilean, so he then sent him to the head of that jurisdiction. To Herod.

Herod was aware of Jesus and wanted to meet him, but Jesus was unimportant to him really, merely a spectacle, a short-term phenomenon. Herod wanted to see Jesus perform some of the miracles that were the talk of the town.

But Jesus would have no part in it.

As the chief priests violently accused Jesus, Herod took his turn to interrogate him about the accusations. Again, Jesus remained silent. Herod mocked and ridiculed Jesus but still made no progress. He finally got bored and sent him back to Pilate.

Pilate, of course, still wanted nothing to do with Jesus either. To appease the accusers and put this whole scene to bed, he had Jesus whipped. When the rulers wanted more, Pilate pitted Jesus against a convicted criminal, certain this would get Jesus released. But the unruly crowds clamored for the rebel Barabbas. Running out of options, Pilate returned to Jesus and struck up a conversation. "Where are you from?"

Jesus said nothing.

"Do you refuse to speak to me?" Jesus remained silent.

He asked again, "Don't you realize I have the power to free or crucify you?"

Jesus responded. He had listened, waited patiently to speak, and did so without anger. "You have no power over me if it were not given to you from above."[123]

Pilate didn't have a substantive response, so he tried again to get Jesus released. Eventually, he gave in and gave up.

There is a significant point to understand when rehearsing this scene. When anybody presented hearsay, false accusations, or unfounded reports, Jesus remained silent. But when they challenged Jesus as the Son of God, he responded with the facts and spoke the truth. Our human emotions would make us wonder if, deep down, Jesus was thinking, *Don't you dare challenge my Father, or me.* We can communicate more effectively by patterning our responses to facts and hearsay as Jesus did.

WE OFTEN READ ABOUT PEOPLE WHO BREAK THEIR SILENCE. Athletes apologize for their off-the-field behavior; business leaders confess after being caught cooking the books; gangsters admit their crimes and politicians their marital affairs; companies divulge product problems, and community officials discuss hometown scandals. People break their silence when they have done something wrong and their secrets get exposed.

This was not the case with Jesus. When the high priest questioned him as though he was withholding information, Jesus responded, "I have spoken openly to the world. I always taught in synagogues or at the temple, where all the Jews come together. I said nothing in secret."[124] It's intriguing to see the poise and power he showed, using silence in his communications but a no-holding-back approach when confronted about his mission. In the tensest moments, Jesus was in control of his speech. We must practice learning similar skills so we can perform as admirably as Jesus did when we encounter dire circumstances.

ALL OF US HAVE SECRETS, BE IT SOMETHING WE HAVE DONE wrong, something we have or don't have, or something we covet. Sometimes I used my executive position to give the impression that I was more knowledgeable about our business than I was. Unfortunately, this almost came back to bite me once in a meeting with our number one shareholder.

I was the company spokesperson when dealing with Wall Street analysts, and every other month I would speak at some investor conference. I would tell our story and build relationships with current and prospective analysts who monitored our company, hoping to attract new investors. These firms were always looking for ways to invest their clients' fortunes, and this outreach was a terrific way to assess any interest they might have in buying shares of our stock. Most of the analysts attending the conferences had simple backgrounds, which was right up my alley. I could speak in generic terms about our go-to-market strategies and expand on the business and financial specifics.

What I disliked were the technology conferences because the audiences were highly technical. We would usually send a specialist to these events. I avoided them, and for good reason—I didn't want to embarrass myself or our company because of my limited technical knowledge.

Once, however, I was alone at a technology conference in Boston after our technical expert dropped out unexpectedly. I prepared, studied, and memorized as many technical terms as possible. My strategy was to speak until the last minute, leaving little time for random questions at the end. It was a discreet approach, but I knew I had little chance of fielding technical questions successfully.

I was petrified walking on stage, and my knees shook for the entire twenty minutes. I pulled off my plan without a hitch, and when finished, I ran from the stage, having averted an investor relations debacle. My buzzwords were impressive, and I appeared to be a technology expert to the audience. My Boston-to-San Francisco flight and a couple of Bailey's on the rocks provided ample time to release the adrenaline.

By morning, it was as though my world had changed. I woke up energized, believing I had mastered the technology presentation the day before. I mutated overnight, now thinking I was the next Elon Musk. With an unfounded cockiness, I turned into a risk-taker. I was ready to impress our largest shareholder with my new technological ingenuity. The plan was to meet with the lead analyst for the firm, Kevin Taft. He had been through the thick and thin of our financial problems but was still a huge supporter, and my courtesy drop-in would provide a brief update.

That changed when I entered a conference room, greeted by the whole firm. Over a dozen people encircled an empty seat designated for me. I knew none of them, but they all knew me, including the dreaded technical people. The tone of the meeting was different from what I expected. They were long-term investors and expected a full-blown company presentation, including a comprehensive view of future technologies. The only set of slides on my flash drive was the technical pitch I made the day before, which was generic and intended for a twenty-minute overview. They gave me the luxury of a two-hour window to go through a detailed presentation, which meant I had to wing it.

I briefly considered Norman Vincent Peale's book, *The Power of Positive Thinking* (Prentice Hall, 1952), but only had time to remember the title. The daredevil I woke up pretending to be was either hiding behind his pitchfork or had left the building. While the technical folks prepared the visual equipment, I recalled a magazine article I had read on my flight the night before. The article mentioned the average life expectancy of a CFO in any company is three years. I was in my fourth year, so getting fired would likely soon come. But it incentivized me to push ahead with my reckless precociousness and minimal technical forte.

I began babbling technical terms such as micro-electrical and mechanical systems, probe memory, and holographic storage. I rambled on about exabytes, yottabytes, and zettabytes. I mentioned reading how a drop of synthetic DNA could store all the data created since the world began. They were superfluous comments, and I didn't know what I was talking about, but judging by their faces, they didn't either. Gaining momentum, I dared to go on. They were mesmerized, and though I was out of my league, I was cruising along like I was Einstein.

The meeting neared its end, and judging by their reactions, I believed I had the sale. Having convinced them of our technology strategy, they hinted at the likelihood of increasing their investment in our company. All I had to do was seal the deal and get out of Dodge.

By this time, the top management members gathered their notes and prepared to leave. But I was on a roll, remembered a cool technology term I heard, and figured I would impress the shareholders one last time. As I stuffed documents into my briefcase, I mentioned we were investigating a longer-term, game-breaking technology related to the "superparamagnetic" effect. I would brief them about it the next time we met.

A young intern in the back of the room stopped everyone, including me, in our tracks. "What is the superparamagnetic effect?"

Everyone in the room stopped and turned toward me, interested in my response.

I was busted. I had no idea what it was. So, I did the only thing that made sense: I answered logically. I told him I didn't have enough time to explain it because I had to catch a flight.

My secret, pretending to be someone I wasn't, had been exposed. I stretched the truth about my flight to keep my secret hidden. Thank goodness I never had to explain it later.

Nicodemus held dual occupations. He was a member of the Sanhedrin (the Supreme Court of the Jews, responsible for the regulations of the land), and he was a Pharisee (a religious leader dedicated to keeping the law). He was inquisitive and diligently searched for truth, even if his view contradicted the legalism of the Pharisees. He is mentioned briefly in scripture, but his story is quite moving.

We first hear of him coming to Jesus in the dark of night. He acknowledged that the teachings and miracles he saw proved Jesus came from God. It is unclear if he was confused, lacked something, or was searching for answers when his curiosity moved him to seek the truth at night when disturbances would be infrequent. The likely reason for his late-night visit was to remain anonymous, and he could keep his visit with Jesus a secret from those in his echelon. When he finished his Q&A session with Jesus, he left further intrigued but void of complete understanding.

I can relate to this coming by dark. After a teenage date night with Lindy, I pulled up curbside in front of her house, hoping to converse privately before walking her to the front door. Immediately after turning off the engine, the front porch light flashed on and off like Fourth of July fireworks. Her father did not like the idea of his daughter being in a dark car with me.

I figured I could outsmart the old farm boy on our next date. As we approached Lindy's home, I gained enough speed to cut off the engine, place the car in neutral, and coast to the same spot silently and secretly with excellent precision. It was a great plan. My future father-in-law took fifteen seconds to begin his porchlight display.

There would be no third attempt. As we returned from our next date at ten o'clock, her father greeted us on the street. With a broom in hand, he was sweeping the curb at the exact spot where we previously parked. The old guy thwarted my attempts to silently and secretly park, and his use of silence, broom in hand, was highly effective.

JESUS DIDN'T TEACH SECRETLY. HE KNEW THE JEWS PLANNED to kill him as he headed toward Judea and the Feast of the Tabernacles. When his brothers suggested the moment he should go, Jesus said the time wasn't right. Time is often described as a specific instant, hour, or season. But in this case, it's expressed as a time of opportunity. Jesus wasn't punctually early or casually late. He showed up at the most opportunistic time when everyone was settled in and ready for him to teach.

As was often the case, Jesus created a stir. The Jews marveled at his teachings—so much so that the Pharisees sent temple guards to arrest him. But the guards were also amazed and returned without a prisoner. Their empty return struck a nerve with the Pharisees, who responded disparagingly about Jesus and cursed those who believed in him.

Nicodemus, who was also present, responded timidly to defend Jesus and cited several legal rules as his basis. His heart was ready to defend Jesus because of his belief, but his head said, "Don't you dare do it." Now was the time for Nicodemus to go full throttle, to be courageous about his conviction and support of Jesus. The Pharisees were ready to break the law and convict Jesus, and this was an excellent opportunity for Nicodemus to break his silence. But when they finished their arguments and the case was closed for the day, Nicodemus revealed his not-so-bold response. Everyone, including Nicodemus, went home.

Most of us have encountered similar situations. I certainly have. We face circumstances that directly contradict what we know and believe to be correct. If we stand up to them, we will be unpopular. We won't fit in with worldly norms. Our hearts tell us to be strong. But our heads tell us that if we stand up for what is right, we risk facing further hardship, mockery, and ridicule. We could defend our spiritual beliefs but bow to the pressure and respond with half-hearted defenses instead. We are embarrassed and leave, ashamed and silent.

Other rulers who believed in Jesus joined Nicodemus in their silence. They weren't willing to admit it publicly, fearful as they were of losing their jobs and being thrown out of the synagogues. The praise of men outweighed the glorification of God, and so Nicodemus continued to live a lie. He was among those looking to do the impossible, trying to be a secret disciple. There was just too much to lose. He was unwilling to dare to take the risk by supporting and openly following Jesus.

Jesus had no secrets, however. He was able to bring to light the hidden secrets of darkness and expose the motives of the heart. If only Nicodemus could understand.

Earlier, we discussed how Thomas got—and still gets—a bad rap as the doubter. We also learned he wasn't the only one who wouldn't believe until he saw Jesus alive.

Nicodemus wasn't the only one being a secret disciple of Jesus.

A rich man from Arimathea named Joseph also lived a secret life as a disciple of Jesus. He feared the Jews just as Nicodemus did. He was a prominent council member, a virtuous and upright man who stood by the divine laws. But something changed in Joseph because, after the crucifixion, he boldly went to Pilate and asked for the body of Jesus. This boldness meant he went fearlessly and daringly. He must have made quite an impression because Pilate permitted him to take the body.

When Joseph took the body, he wasn't alone. Someone like himself accompanied him. Nicodemus. Both were disciples of Jesus, and both had lived secret lives out of fear. And now, both were preparing the body of Jesus following Jewish burial customs. They did so in the open for everyone to see. There was no more silence about their belief in Jesus. No more secrets about their confession of faith. No more fear of anyone because of their love for Jesus. On this day, they broke their silence.

If we haven't done so, the time will come when we must decide if we will break our silence. We must be free from secret sins, stop being secret disciples, and begin openly communicating our love for God. Then, our connection with others needing help and searching for hope will be more fruitful.

THE ART OF SPEAKING SUBTLETY IS THE CORNERSTONE OF LASTing relationships. It's not merely a skill to be mastered but an understanding of the myriad ways we can convey our thoughts, emotions, and intentions. Search the sacred texts and delve into the virtue of speaking softly. Embrace the gentleness and nuance of your words to cultivate bonds that can withstand the test of time. Our words, spoken softly and thoughtfully, possess the power to transform not only the world around us but also the hearts of those with whom we share them.

The moments of silence we occasionally choose to embrace aren't empty voids but fertile grounds for understanding and connection. Silence is a tool in our communication arsenal, allowing us to listen with intention and speak when our words bear the greatest impact. It is through these deliberate choices that we forge relationships with purpose. These tools can create a legacy of profound connections that enrich our lives and the lives of others.

THE FINISH

12

Influencing and Encouraging Others

The meaning of life is to find your gift.
The purpose of life is to give it away.
—Pablo Picasso

I wish I could have fully understood these values earlier in my life rather than letting them gradually unfold over time and through experiencing layers upon layers of difficulties. But the truth is some people only learn the hard way through disappointments. We get knocked down by a failure but pick ourselves up and give it another shot. Understanding what is important to us and those we love takes time.

Once athletes reach their peak, they begin a downward trend as age takes its toll. Their bodies don't allow them to play at the same level as in their prime. They struggle, wanting to continue playing a game they love, but oftentimes they have difficulty deciding when to call it quits.

Business executives have successful careers using their skills, sharp wit, and leadership to achieve prominent positions. Their rewards are financial success and a distinguished status. Eventually, however, they also lose their energy and drive. Highly motivated and talented newcomers stand ready to steer companies with new, innovative ideas.

Parents put their heart and soul into their children, experiencing the highs and lows of raising them in a world stacked with opportunity, promise, and excitement, yet tainted with brokenness. They are cautiously optimistic, having equipped their children as they leave home to embark on their journey in life.

The common thread in these scenarios is that, regardless of our accomplishments, career length, or teaching efforts, the time will come to move on and pass the baton to the next person. Our experiences produce wisdom, and we can take pride in our accomplishments, but our successes likely required collaboration and cooperation with many individuals—we certainly didn't do it alone. The people who participated in our journey were loyal supporters who provided encouragement and constructive feedback, especially when obstacles surfaced. They identified areas for improvement and helped refine our skills. Many opened doors to opportunities we would never have recognized. They were with us every step of the way—in times of prosperity and destitution. Together, we shared objectives and trust. We were connected and understood we needed each other. Nature teaches us this very idea of connection.

I spent nearly half my life in Florida, where the average palm tree grows to fifty feet, and yet its roots penetrate only the top twelve-to-thirty-six inches of soil. There is no tap root, and they prefer sandy soil that makes them easy to uproot. They mature independently, isolated from their nearby counterparts.

The other half of my life was in Colorado, where I learned the secret to healthy aspen trees. The leafy aspens grow in clusters, never alone, and multiply from their roots. I planted a few in our backyard and watched the shoots take over my yard within a few years. They were meant to flourish in the Colorado Rockies, where I could enjoy the majestic fall season filled with multicolored aspen groves connected by their roots. New saplings can be thirty-to-forty yards away from their parent tree, yet they are part of the same system or the same family.

The most prominent trees are the California redwoods, which grow up to 350 feet high. They are wide enough for automobiles to navigate through their chiseled trunks. Common sense tells us trees this size require a deep root system to anchor their heights from nature's forces. But the redwoods have shallow roots, roughly six feet deep. They spread hundreds of feet from the tree trunk in search of surface water and intertwine with the roots of multiple redwood trees, locking themselves together and supporting each other. This root structure supplies tremendous strength to battle high winds and raging floods.

Unlike palm trees, aspens and redwoods never stand alone. They are rooted together, connected, and need each other to survive.

WE, TOO, HAVE A SYSTEM OF ROOTS. HEALTHY FAMILY CONNECtions provide nurturing closeness, guidance, and generational traditions. Our relationships with friends, teammates, and colleagues give us personal satisfaction through the involvement and enjoyment we share. Spiritual connections with those sharing a similar belief provide support and encouragement, a togetherness that holds us up when life pushes us down. We are connected, firmly planted, strengthened, and established like the roots of the redwoods and aspens.

Sounds good, right? But there is one exception—one colossal roadblock to this need for one another.

We love our independence!

The United States of America was founded with the Declaration of Independence, which gives us certain rights, including life, liberty, and the pursuit of happiness. We are all created equal and have a duty to defend these rights for ourselves and others. Young people need guidance on how to care for themselves, be confident, collaborate with people in developing relationships, and choose their friends wisely. But they also want to experience new things, make decisions, and independently unravel who they are and what they want to do. We often hear them say, "I've got to be me," or "I want to do it my way," and even "I don't need anybody to tell me what to do." How do we reconcile this need for one another with the desire to go it alone? Do we really need each other, and if so, why?

The answer is simple: relationships!

People are relational. If we are to love God and love people, it starts with relationships. Developing relationships and learning from each other is essential to mutual respect, and both are contagious and build on each other. A spirit of cooperation to solve problems is more effective than the one-person approach. Sound relationships allow us to trust and be trusted, creating a willingness to forgive and a safe place for those who feel discouraged and alone. Building an environment of serving one another leads to common hope and abundant love, and the compounding effect creates a healthy (not an isolation-inducing) level of space and supports independence.

Encouragement is the means to build healthy relationships by showing support and instilling hope. It goes beyond the athlete's pat on the back, high-five, or chest-bumping to acknowledge a great play. It surpasses encouraging the patient rehabilitating, the person trying to lose weight, the student who failed an examination, the parent dealing with child behavioral issues, and the couple struggling with marital problems.

Its meaning in Latin is "to put into the heart." To encourage, we need to authentically connect and create a bond that accepts others as they are. We boost confidence by emboldening others to take on challenges, giving them a sense of purpose, and inspiring them to stay committed and to persevere through setbacks. By fostering a sense of optimism and resilience, we tap into their full potential, empowering their personal growth and development. Strengthening these relationships deepens our connection with others and builds further trust. It creates a ripple effect that extends a source of inspiration to others.

When we encourage each other, we grow together. Helping others is more than an obligation or duty. It is a yearning that comes from within our hearts that allows us to share suffering, pain, and recovery. We do this because we see the need for each other and desire to put our relationship into their heart. Like the farmer who shared his seed corn, encouraging our neighbors to get better will enable us to be better.

ENCOURAGEMENT IS A PREREQUISITE FOR OUR ABILITY TO positively influence others. But it can also simply be a precursor because although the two are similar, they aren't always connected. I can encourage somebody to complete an overdue task but cannot influence them to change their approach to ensure the tardiness doesn't persist. I can encourage a child to do well on an examination but can never influence them to study more diligently in the future. I can encourage someone to stay clear of an addiction but neglect to influence them to seek alternative plans to free them from their vices.

Influence causes a change in someone. Encouragement reinforces it.

Author John Steimle said, "A life without influence is a life without meaning."[125] The ability to impact the beliefs or actions of others is possible through the power of influence, and effective influence goes beyond changing behaviors—it changes one's mindset. Our willingness to help others is the fuse to spark this movement.

A tomato seed germinates two weeks after being placed in the soil and bears fruit within three to four months. The orchid seed takes a month to sprout and nearly eighteen months before it fully blooms. The Chinese bamboo tree seed needs five years of cultivating, watering, and fertilizing before it breaks the soil. But within six weeks of first sunlight, it can grow up to ninety feet tall. From start to finish, these life cycles illustrate the different timing and maturation effects of our influence on others.

Some people can be influenced in short order, if not at once. People kindly react when they feel appreciated. Some hear or see something repeatedly and are off and running, taking steps to fulfill their internal desires. Television commercials are a classic example of influencing people to react quickly. Car salespeople and real estate brokers often use the idea of lost opportunity for those who wait to sign the bottom line. They sprinkle in a few kind words, and with a bit of nudging, a sale is completed.

In other instances, the seeds of influence take time to sink in. People need to process what they have heard or seen. They must convince or, at a minimum, justify their potential direction. Influential points bolster their thought process aimed at behavioral change. Eventually, it feels good or sounds good and, for various reasons, seems to make sense. Their mindset matures and changes, and so they are free to choose their pathway without hesitation.

Some people receive advice and counsel for years, even decades. They receive words of encouragement unsparingly. Never-ending efforts to steer them in the right direction often get ignored. There is no sign they are listening to, much less absorbing, the attempts by some to help. Time passes without any acknowledgment, and our efforts to influence appear fruitless.

Lindy and I had countless discussions about our influence when raising our daughters. We wondered if they were listening. We questioned whether they understood the lessons we taught. We fretted over the advice we had given about safety when they dated, traveled with a friend, or went off to college. We prayed they would be kind and helpful to others. Some years later, they informed us they had heeded our counsel by choosing ways that were in line with what we had taught them. Many of our daughters' characteristics were developed undercover, unseen. Hopefully, our influence had something to do with it. We believe it did.

Diamonds, Deals, and Divine Guidance

Consider those who have encouraged or influenced you. Was it somebody with a prominent position, a fancy title, or working at a large organization? Someone famous, the best in their profession, a manager of many people, or educated enough to be considered an expert?

Jesus didn't have any of these things. Instead, he was content to teach and lead by example. He encouraged people with his message, not his popularity. He influenced people by the way he lived, and his message and life are still impacting millions of people today.

How is this possible? Why was he so successful? Because he was truthful and credible. Though his miracles were remarkable, Jesus didn't try to impress. But he did try to encourage and influence people to do what is right, to love God and love people.

Jesus's influence is evident in the life of his apostle Paul, whose accomplishments were plentiful and his legacy iconic. Paul's story traces back to a young man named Stephen when Christianity was experiencing enormous growth, and more leaders were needed to help with the simplest tasks. Stephen had a stellar reputation and was asked to support this robust interest in Christianity. He helped spread the good news, delivered inspiring messages, and did many good things for the people. He made news because he was the news.

Certain groups challenged Stephen's teaching, but they were always outmatched and couldn't contend with him. Stung by losing their debates with him, they persuaded others to declare Stephen's words profane. They incited a group of people, seized him, and brought him to the authorities to have him stopped or killed.

Everyone in attendance glared at Stephen as he stood before the council. They noticed his face was different, like the face of an angel. As peculiar as this was, it remained unexplained.

While Stephen stood before the council, Saul (later to be renamed Paul) prowled in the background. Nothing fazed Stephen. As Supreme Court Justice Amy Coney Barrett did in her Supreme

Court hearings, he pleaded his case without notes. From Abraham and Joseph to Moses and Joshua, he weaved through the history of the Israelites' delivery from Egyptian bondage and their defiance against God, moving through a pattern of behavior that eventually led to the rejection of Jesus. He was relentless in his conviction and captivated the audience. There were no interruptions because nobody could disprove his testimony.

Stephen's chastisement to those listening was genuine but also deadly. His candid claims of their disobedience infuriated the crowds, who convicted him of blasphemy. Legal protocols to convict him were disregarded. They dragged him out of the city and stoned him to death without delay. Jesus's influence on Stephen was apparent. Before dying, he asked for them to be forgiven. After the stoning, witnesses placed their clothes at Saul's feet, who watched from a distance. Saul consented to Stephen's death and delighted in watching this out-of-control mob.

This is where the two stories connect: Saul and Stephen, linked together, forever. Yet there is no distinct influence on or from either one. If Stephen had any impact on Saul, it wasn't evident. If it were even possible, it would take time. When Stephen died, any chance of influencing Saul seemed unlikely.

IT WOULD BE SAD IF THIS STORY ENDED HERE BECAUSE THE circumstances are similar to those we often face. We say things to encourage and help people. We go out of our way to do good. We are patient, kind, and caring. Our efforts often get little reaction. We put in a lot of time and energy but impart little value. We think our efforts have failed and wonder what we could have done differently. We question our ability to influence.

We run through our checklist of ways to influence others. We established a good relationship, have experience with the matter, and have a good reputation for working on similar issues. We are committed to helping and are confident we can do so. We have sound reasoning and a well-thought-out plan. Our intentions are good and honest. We live by the same principles we espouse, and we lead by example.

Why, then, are we unsuccessful in influencing others? Why can't we get a response?

Because influencing people takes time.

Saul's annihilation of the church continued, and his brutality created fear. It ended on his trip to Damascus when he was knocked to the ground and encountered a voice from heaven. His fear of the Lord and a three-day binge of blindness and starvation influenced him and became a turning point in his life. A name change from Saul to Paul gave him a new identity. It would take years to convince those he terrorized that he was a new man, one like them—a believer.

At first, nobody trusted him, and for good reasons. Only a few allowed him in. Barnabas, known as the "son of encouragement" and an eternal optimist, was one, but then again, Barnabas would support anyone. Barnabas oozed confidence and brought hope to those he met. He was the epitome of someone willing to encourage and influence. His character was unmistakable and his generosity noble. He sold his property when a need existed and then donated the funds. True charity isn't tax-deductible. Barnabas was willing to give—no questions asked, no tax deduction necessary.

Knowing that the people feared Saul for creating havoc and persecuting believers, Barnabas realized they were suspicious of Saul and doubted his sincerity as he spoke of his newfound faith. He figured they assumed his quick change of heart was a gimmick and a way for him to capture and persecute them. Saul had too much baggage, and their reservations were justified. It was doubtful the people would accept Saul, so Barnabas stepped in to alleviate their doubts.

He came to Saul's rescue and sponsored him. His optimism and positive attitude were extraordinary, though likely difficult to grasp considering Saul's malicious past. Most people viewed Saul as an infiltrator, but Barnabas viewed him as genuine. Some looked at Saul and thought the worst; Barnabas looked at him and saw the best. Many viewed Saul and judged him for his past deeds; Barnabas trusted him for his future potential.

Eventually, Paul followed Stephen's footsteps, explaining his conversion openly and honestly. The authorities seized him, and the violent crowds surrounded him, hoping for a repeat of what they did to Stephen. But as the mob shouted for his demise, Paul admitted his greatest mistake—silently approving Stephen's murder.

It took years for Barnabas's encouragement and Stephen's influence to finally emerge in the life of Paul. Barnabas saw the fruits of his labor with Paul, but while Stephen did not, his legacy lived on through Paul.

THIS PROMPTS SOME QUESTIONS. WHAT IS OUR APPROACH TO people today? What thoughts do we harbor when dealing with people, especially those with blemished backgrounds? How do we work with those who have harmed or abandoned us in a critical time of need—those we don't believe deserve a second chance because of their prior mistakes?

As we delve deeper into the stories of individuals who have greatly impacted us, it becomes evident that our approach to people today is intricately connected to the encouragement and influence we have received. These individuals accepted us as we were then, understood our motivations, and genuinely cared for us.

In my case, my wife and children stand out. My parents, siblings, and in-laws contributed. A few preachers and teachers, as well as coaches and bosses, helped. Some close friends and teammates certainly did. All of them said or did something that stirred and shaped me to be the person I am today. They spoke truthfully and kindly, gave honest feedback when critiquing my progress, and held me accountable for my actions and decisions. They trusted me and my instincts. They sponsored me, raised the bar, pushed me to be the best in my profession, and supported me when it was time to step away. Our duty is to pass on the torch of encouragement and influence to others, just as it was done for us.

BARNABAS ASSUMED THE LEAD ROLE IN THE MISSIONARY JOURneys he took with Paul. They went from city to city, teaching vast amounts of people. Barnabas's cousin John Mark joined them as their helper. But midway through their journey, John Mark left to return home, and change was in the winds. This didn't sit well with Paul, who felt John Mark deserted them.

We can only speculate as to why John Mark went home. Maybe he feared the remaining itinerary, fraught with danger and persecution. Perhaps he needed more confidence in teaching people in new nations. He was young, so he may have wanted to be near his mother. It remains a mystery why he left Paul and the others, but one thing is sure: John Mark must have made an impression and impacted those he taught. Otherwise, he wouldn't have been mentioned in the story.

Shortly after John Mark's departure, the leadership role shifted. Paul's ability to teach and to approach this task with tenacity, continually pressing forward with his message, was paying off. When he spoke, the spirit moved in his heart. He knew this was his calling, and he cared for those whose hearts were touched by the word of God. He connected with people in ways most thought unimaginable. And as time went on, likely to the surprise of many, Paul eventually found himself in a prominent role, leading the way.

Barnabas had been Paul's mentor, guiding and protecting his protégé. He encouraged Paul in his direst moments, standing up for him when nobody else would. In the end, after he taught Paul the ropes and influenced his teaching for a while, it was Barnabas who let Paul thrive in a leadership role.

As leaders—be it as captains of our teams, as supervisors of people, as parents, or as friends—we take on the same role: continue to teach, encourage, influence, and provide the resources our mentees need, then get out of the way, and let them flourish. If we persist in teaching and inspiring people, especially children, to think for themselves, there is a higher likelihood they will care about our thoughts and beliefs.

Paul and Barnabas continued to work together. But the two close friends argued over whom to take on their next journey. Barnabas wanted to take his cousin, John Mark. But Paul's anger persisted over his earlier premature departure and unreliability. Their disagreement about John Mark became sharply contentious, and they agreed to part ways. Paul chose Silas as his new partner, and Barnabas took John Mark.

Who was right in this situation?

Did it matter?

And what happened to John Mark after Paul rejected him?

Unfortunately, we don't know the details of John Mark's life. But we do know he was fortunate to have a friend like Barnabas. Just as Barnabas encouraged Paul, he did the same for John Mark.

As Paul neared death, he wrote what many consider to be his last letter, addressed to Timothy. He encouraged Timothy and was proud of his work and sincere faith. He shared memories, delighted in their common purpose and belief, and asked him to visit quickly. As he closed the letter, he told Timothy, "Get John Mark and bring him with you, because he is helpful to me in my ministry."[126] The guy he tossed aside for being a quitter. The unreliable guy he argued about with Barnabas. In Paul's view, John Mark was the comeback kid—another protégé of Barnabas and the beneficiary of his encouragement and influence.

What would have become of Paul without Barnabas? What would have become of John Mark without Barnabas? Barnabas did the same for John Mark as he did for Paul. Their stories are similar. Their mentor was the same. What's most impressive about all of this, however, is that while Barnabas didn't ask to be in a leadership role, he was a natural leader. He was willing to step away, let go, and move on, letting the one he mentored assume the lead role.

WE HAVE THE OPPORTUNITY AND RESPONSIBILITY TO ENCOURage one another, but encouragement is more than being friendly and polite to people we know and trust. We will surely meet people who will rise or fall to the level of others' expectations. We will encounter individuals who have baggage, soured relationships, and tainted backgrounds. The encouragement we give can help mold and shape their lives, so we must look for the potential in people that isn't always seen. Be willing to forgive them for their past shortcomings and failures. When we elevate people to surpass expectations and reach new levels, we enable them to become leaders their way. We had our turn, and now it is theirs. It's their time to impact the future.

Likewise, we can influence others by passing along our knowledge and skills to them. We can share our experiences, both good and bad. We can reveal the lessons we learned from our mistakes and convey the wisdom gained from our successes and disappointments.

Author John Maxwell wrote, "To make an impact on your people, you must be a river, not a reservoir."[127] His message is clear: Don't let the goodness within you be dormant. Let it flow to others for their benefit.

Use your influence to build people up. Your words hold power. As a leader, friend, coworker, husband, or wife, find ways to encourage those around you with words of affirmation, whether by a simple note, text, email, or voice mail. Be the light that often shines in dark places. Let your light shine as you lift the spirits of those around you. You never know—your kindness may just end up helping ease the pain of hopelessness deep inside the hearts of others.

The values I learned through my disappointments made me a better person, and I wouldn't have understood their importance if I hadn't endured them. By working with others I realized the significance of these impacts on me and how their lessons helped me. I discovered that encouraging others provided mutual benefit. Together, we provided support during challenging times, alleviated each other's burdens, and shared a sense of comfort. We created bonds of trust and reliance that jointly became a source of inspiration. Living with these values positively impacted my life, so transferring them to encourage and influence others became my game plan.

There are two critical questions for you to consider as you share your heart with others. Ask yourself: Who is your Barnabas? Then ask: Who are you a Barnabas to?

13

The Finish Line

*Winning does not always mean coming in first...
real victory is in arriving at the finish line with
no regrets because you know you've gone all out.*
—Anton Apolo Ohno

Plans prepare us for the future and its ending.
    I thought I had all the plans necessary to succeed. When one didn't work, I would go to plan B. Then plan C. It's what many of us do. We plan continuously—a lifetime ritual.

I went from thinking I could be a professional baseball player to believing if I prepared long and hard enough, I could pass any test and excel in any role I chose. But I needed to do more than just think or believe I could achieve something substantial. I needed a new perspective that comes only from persevering through life's battles. I needed to endure the trials associated with success and failure, reaching goals or not, living a dream, or having one shattered. I needed to face disappointment and loss on multiple fronts and participate in all its highs and lows. If I could weather those storms without necessarily winning or succeeding, I would know I was good enough to make something significant happen.

Fortunately, I had teachers, coaches, and bosses along the way who pushed me to excel. They moved me in a higher direction when they asked for extraordinary efforts, better focus, and higher standards. My teammates, employees, and friends encouraged me tremendously and conveyed their belief that I could impact their lives. Amid all the obstacles, my family's unending love and support brought calm to my heart, hope to my mind, and peace to my soul. I hope I contributed some benefit to everyone who participated in my journey. Their impact on me was remarkable, and I am forever grateful.

I eventually learned God had plans for me—as he does for you—that serve a different purpose. His plans are unique for each of us. They are for our benefit, and they will prevail, but that doesn't mean we should stop making plans. Nor should we be discouraged if they don't work out. The good news is whatever God has planned for us will be much better than anything we ever imagined.

God doesn't look at our outward appearance or accomplishments as we navigate our internal and external battles. Instead, he looks at our hearts. He sees our motives while we experience conflicts and disappointments. Author John Maxwell once said, "Experience is not the best teacher; evaluated experience is the best teacher."[128] We must evaluate our experiences—be they good or bad, successful or not—to learn how to move forward with our lives regardless of what happens at any given time.

For many years and through countless dreams, I viewed greatness as being the best at whatever I was doing at the time, whether that was an all-star baseball player, a budding business owner, or a prominent executive for a large global corporation. I also tried to be a loving husband and good parent in a world that doesn't often give proper credit or attention to those roles.

If I wasn't successful, though, how could I be considered the best? And if I wasn't the best, how could I convince myself I was good enough? I was taught to win, lured by a society that emphasized winning mattered and anything short of coming in first place meant failure.

It took seven years to right the ship at StorageTek. We fixed or changed every inefficient and broken process, and we were relentless at improving every weakness. We rebuilt relationships internally with employees and externally with every constituent involved. As mentors, we pushed people to excel to gain their buy-in and convinced them they could make this recovery happen.

Our mindset changed. We no longer looked down on ourselves as failures, and we stopped listening to the naysayers who said we couldn't survive. Instead, we cleared a new pathway by unleashing profitability hidden under burdensome bureaucracies, and as a result, we marched forth as leaders in our industry.

Something more substantial than results moved us, however, motivating us to do more than we had ever imagined. We were on a roll and could feel it—we were loose, creative, confident, and more productive—and knew great things would happen because we worked under a new mantra with a higher purpose. We engaged in a directional change and relished fighting for it, no longer fearing the drudgery of working through complex issues. The winds of success carried us with every improvement, fix, or creation. We knew our future would be different and successful.

Before Sun Microsystems acquired our company for over $4 billion, a few of us celebrated at a restaurant close to the New York Stock Exchange. Robust profits returned to our business, and we became darlings with shareholders who watched their investment in our stock soar to new heights, along with an additional premium from the acquisition. The following day, I would watch the opening bell on the trading floor of Wall Street—an event I missed earlier when our business floundered.

Unlike other parts of New York City, the evening hours around Wall Street are subdued. Adding to that, a long day preceded our late dinner, with only a few restaurant patrons remaining. I always enjoyed the delicacy of a shrimp cocktail but noticed the selection was absent from the menu. I inquired about the offering and told the waiter we were celebrating that evening. He nodded and left curiously.

Thirty minutes and a near-empty bottle of wine later, the sweaty waiter returned and apologized for the delay, presenting a trio of fresh shrimp resting on ice surrounding a crystal dish filled with cocktail sauce. We learned he ran six blocks to find shrimp for the appetizer. It was as though he knew our success story and wanted to join the celebration. I knew then that what we accomplished was remarkable.

As dinner concluded, the bill included a $90 charge for the shrimp. I guessed the waiter wanted a piece of our success too! Still a CFO at heart, I considered the moment and our circumstances and decided I was okay with letting the premium price slide. It was the best $90 I ever spent on three shrimp.

Our business turnaround didn't happen overnight or come without suffering and loss. The results were exceptional and financially lucrative. Lehman Brothers research analyst Harry Blount, who knew of my baseball background, told me, "Welcome to the Big Leagues of Business. You're an all-star." Shareholders said, "You all finally fixed it." If Dave Weiss had accepted my resignation, I wouldn't have been a part of this dramatic about-face for the company. I'm grateful he didn't.

WITH THE ACQUISITION COMPLETE AND HAVING HAD TIME TO reflect, I couldn't pinpoint any single incident that occurred on my journey that was the turning point in my life. Rather, I realized it was the accumulation of a lot of events, both good and bad, and the meaningful impacts I learned from those events that did. Experiencing all of them, the joys and successes along with the misery and disappointments, is what got me past the finish line in my race to conquer self-doubt.

I wrestled for decades with the idea of not being good enough, thanks to a vanishing baseball dream, personal setbacks, and dismal business results. But rather than engaging in a deep self-reflection in each of those moments, I allowed external sources and opinions to shape my individuality. This lack of self-awareness prevented me from fully understanding my authenticity.

My family, friends, and community influenced my beliefs, values, and expectations early on, while later, such influence came from my network of highly intellectual and very driven colleagues. In many cases, I personalized their views, and their expectations became my objectives. It wasn't a matter of them being wrong or a bad influence on me in the end because they likely assumed their views were what I desired. Eventually, life's harsh lessons nudged me through this uncertainty, pinpointed anything contradictory to my principles, and helped me embrace my true identity.

The fear of failure was a powerful motivator in athletics and business and fueled my resiliency. I was uncomfortable with the unknown and gravitated toward activities where things were certain. I did the things I knew I could control, particularly engaging in my out-of-balance work habits. Eventually, I discovered many things I feared ultimately became blessings in disguise. Setbacks became catalysts for new growth, learning experiences, and an open door for new opportunities.

This story of a captured soldier epitomized the relevancy of my fears, the same concerns many struggle to overcome.

Caught behind enemy lines, a soldier's fate was at stake. His captors placed him in front of a firing squad, and after this, the captain of the guard approached him with a proposal. He offered the soldier one of two options. He could face the firing squad with the certainty of instant death. Or he could face the uncertainty of walking through a nearby door marked "Unknown Horrors."

The soldier thought for a few seconds. He didn't look at the knob, which would have opened the door to uncertainty with a simple turn. Instead, his eyes fixated on the title above the door's frame as if it were his only option. He chose the firing squad, and he was killed instantly.

After removing the body, one of the guards asked the captain, "Sir, what is behind the door marked 'Unknown Horrors?'"

The captain turned toward the door and responded, "Freedom!"

Too often, we face demanding situations, struggle under harsh circumstances, and fail miserably in our quest for greatness. Unfortunately, we admit defeat, choosing the firing squad as the resolution to end our suffering and disappointment. We surrender to the uncertainty of what life might bring next, fearful of what we do not know, cringing at what may or may not happen.

We navigate our lives away from the difficult path, unaware that freedom is on the other side, along with success, prosperity, and peace. We miss the greatness that lies within us—not dead, just dormant. We neglect to ascertain that personal sacrifice is necessary to finish what we started professionally, personally, and spiritually. We fear the unknown.

After decades of learning, I'll take my chances with the door marked "Unknown Horrors."

At the onset of this book, when my spiritual interests were still incubating, I mentioned Joshua's inspirational story and his incredible faith when he faced the walls of Jericho. But another story, an earlier one about Joshua and his sidekick Caleb, continues to encourage me forty years later.

The Israelites had been released from Egyptian bondage. With Moses as their leader, they saw plagues unleashed, witnessed the parting of a body of water that gave them safe passage, and were an honored group of people. When they approached the land of

Canaan, God instructed Moses to send a dozen leaders to check things out, to see if the land was good or bad and whether the people living there were strong or weak, many or few.

Were the towns open for entry or secured with walls? Was the soil fertile or poor, the grounds loaded with trees or barren? And since the early grapes were on the vines, Moses recommended they bring back some of the land's fruit to show the people. When their exploration concluded, the leaders returned to Moses and the Israelite community carrying a cluster of grapes, pomegranates, and figs, proving the land flowed with milk and honey.

Then came the dreadful word—but—a term often connected to one's degree of faith and willpower. The leaders laid out all the difficulties and risks, saying the people were powerful and the cities large and heavily armored. Dangerous and intimidating people were everywhere—in the hills, near the sea, and along the river. The odds of success were minimal.

Caleb, however, understood the potential they had with God on their side. He silenced the naysayers and said, "Let us go up at once and take possession, for we are well able to overcome it."[129]

But the others on the reconnaissance team were fearful and spread a bad report about the land they explored. They claimed giants roamed the land, and that the land devoured anyone living in it. They would be outmatched and appear like grasshoppers in their adversaries' eyes. Their convincing report scared the whole community, who wept aloud all night and grumbled against Moses. They commiserated about having been brought to die in this land and considered it better to return to Egypt to live in bondage. Disheartened, they seemed destined to give up rather than face their current challenges and experience new opportunities. They chose to panic rather than face the unknown with God at their side.

Joshua and Caleb weren't happy campers. They were the only two leaders who trusted God would be with them in their battle. They were convinced the land was good and the opportunity to win even better. With God's protection, there was no need to fear any giants in the land.

We all have giants in our lives—financial challenges, health issues, or relationship difficulties, for example. Our unconquered giant might be a lack of direction and purpose or discipline and prioritization. Our giant might be an inability to cope with losing a loved one and the emotional grief that mentally drains us. It could be the giant of insecurity and self-doubt creating a fear of failure that hinders growth and prevents the pursuit of dreams. Whatever giants we have, they seem huge.

My giants, especially fearing failure, made me feel small. My inner critic kept pushing the idea that they were insurmountable and that I didn't have what it took to conquer them. That is until I put my trust in God and his ways rather than relying on my abilities, efforts, and plans. Then, the battle changed, and the giants started falling. I didn't eliminate them because a new one often seemed to come around the corner. But they no longer controlled me or my purpose in life.

IF I PREPARED DILIGENTLY, I FELT MORE IN CONTROL AND LESS overwhelmed in stressful situations. It helped ease my anxiety and boosted my confidence, especially when facing critical decision-making scenarios with significant financial implications. It helped me temper the fears of the unknown and encouraged an expansion of viewpoints. It put me in a position to seize the moment—and win.

Accountability fostered a high-performance culture and built credibility and trust with those contributing to my success. Others would follow suit, striving to exceed expectations rather than simply meeting them. When I placed myself in the position of others and understood their deepest needs, it reminded me compassion is a way of living and not a reaction to a single event.

It highlighted awareness of influential internal characteristics—patience, forgiveness, and gratitude—all promoting hope for those desperately searching for help. Serving others was fruitful for them but also for me.

Instincts provide an automatic response to a situation, while intuition gives us the insight to see beyond what is obvious. The two are closely linked, unique to each of us, and help us assess the people we associate with and the situations we encounter. Our inner voice guides us toward unlimited and unknown possibilities and aligns our aspirations, even if they defy logic and appear overwhelming. I made healthier progress when relying on my instincts rather than others' opinions or academic prowess.

It's a good thing to trust your instincts, especially in dire circumstances. It's infinitely greater to "Trust in the Lord with all your heart and lean not on your own understanding."[130]

Combining an inner fighting spirit with soft speech encouraged others to listen and became a highly influential practice. It helped defuse tense situations, minimized escalating conflicts, and increased the chances of finding common ground. It gave me a sense of control, projected composure, and tempered emotional responses. A calm nature created a cooperative environment and helped break down barriers of disagreement.

But the underlying reason for any success I had, beyond my skills, experiences, and personal relationships, was a growing spirituality and trust in God. Within the depths of my struggles—that is where I found strength. It was my beacon of hope, constantly reminding me I wasn't alone on my journey. It helped channel my energy toward personal growth connected to eternal life rather than earthly life.

I realized the challenges I endured weren't meant to break me down but to build me up, to shape me into a better person with a more vital purpose. The failures I embraced became stepping stones that gradually shifted my perspective on the valuable things in life. Difficulties were no longer as overwhelming as before because I could draw strength from within to face current and future challenges that came my way. Trusting God gave my life new meaning, allowed me to manage my giants more effectively, and provided strength to overcome adversity and self-doubt.

I WAS FORTUNATE TO RETIRE FOR THE FIRST TIME AT FORTY-EIGHT. It didn't last long. I took my chances helping a start-up company that didn't end well, selling it for pennies on the dollar. Then I joined a second start-up company, which introduced new and different issues with business and people that I never imagined could happen. Yet they did. The impacts outlined in this book were tested to the highest levels, but they stood firm, as did I. But that's another story for another day.

The lasting impacts of the values that helped me earlier tested my resolve again. It reminded me of everything I had been through, what I learned, and how I grew and helped me understand I could survive and thrive during difficult times. I no longer feared being unvalued. God helped me see the value he placed in me, and I relied on him rather than myself.

BEFORE WE CONCLUDE, LET'S REHEARSE WHY WE PURSUE greatness. Let's understand why we seek approval from other sources. Why do we compare ourselves to somebody we deem prominent? Why do we search for validation in unfamiliar places and uncertain circumstances?

Russell Conwell was a man on a mission. His idea to build a reasonably priced university was admirable. Unfortunately, he had no financial means to do so. But that didn't stop him. He uniquely raised money as an orator delivering the same speech thousands of times. His "Acres of Diamonds" lesson inspired people searching for help in their lives, including their pursuit of greatness. Its inspirational message continues today.

In his story, an African farmer heard tales of others making millions discovering diamonds. Excited over the potential for wealth, he sold his farm, raising enough cash to prospect for valuable gems. He spent the rest of his life wandering the wilderness, searching pointlessly. Having depleted his funds, he wore himself out. Discouraged and disheartened, he opted for suicide and drowned himself in a river.

Back at the ranch, the new owner enjoyed the peaceful sights and sounds of a small stream flowing on the property. A bright flash in the calm waters caught his attention, and he picked up a sizable stone unique enough to display on the fireplace mantle. Weeks later, a visitor noticed it and nearly fainted.

"Do you know what you have found?" he asked the owner.

"I thought it was a pretty piece of crystal," he replied.

The visitor told him the stone was among the largest diamonds ever unearthed. The property owner quivered, uncertain of the magnitude of his discovery. He said the stream was full of similar stones cast across the creek's bottom. They discovered the most productive diamond mine on the African continent.

The first farmer, who went searching for treasure in a distant land, unknowingly owned free and clear acres of diamonds. The whole time, it was right in his backyard.

This story typifies our search for greatness. Often, approval and value validation come through external sources. We idolize iconic figures. We seek what they have, thinking it is what we want. We work hard and win a few battles along the way, enough to believe we are getting closer to our destiny.

At times, we enjoy small successes and feel good about ourselves and our situation. We bask in the recognition we receive, then search for more of the same. We keep thinking greatness is right around the corner, that it will come with the next at-bat, the next business proposition, the next promotion, or the next award. We spend significant effort searching for the next high-profile, highly recognized position or the opportunity of a lifetime that portrays significance, notoriety, authority, or greatness.

Yet all along, we don't recognize the acres of diamonds already scattered abundantly throughout our lives.

THE BIBLICAL PARABLE OF THE RICH FOOL WARNS US OF THE missteps that often come with success. This man produced years of bumper crops, so much so that he didn't know what to do with all that he had accumulated. He came up with a plan: expansion! He would tear down his scant barns and build bigger ones to stockpile his grain surplus and continue his accumulation of wealth. Then, he figured he could take life easy—eat, drink, and be merry.

We often hear this parable and think there is no personal application. By doing so, however, we make a couple of mistakes. The first mistake is assuming we aren't rich, and that this parable applies only to millionaires and billionaires. Our perspective is flawed because we lack an understanding of what it means to be poor when compared to our view of being wealthy. If we have food on the table, clothes, live in an apartment or home, and have an automobile, we are among the world's wealthy.

Not long ago, an adult with as little as $3,000 was among the wealthiest half of the world.[131] We often consider the elites, Hollywood actors, business executives, or professional athletes as the only ones who are rich. The reality is—we are too!

The second blunder is thinking we aren't fools. Are we any different than the rich? Rather than share, do we enjoy our wealth, keeping it to ourselves as we store it for the good times we seek in the future? Are the barns we have any different from those who have more than us? Do our barns get filled with each check we deposit?

We face this same dilemma. We work hard to get ahead, plan, prepare for the future, and provide a good life for our family. Our efforts (hopefully) get rewarded, and we save for a rainy day. All of this is right and good. But as our fortune grows, so do the requirements to use our resources for good purposes.

This story isn't simply about money. It's about using our time and abilities, being steadfast in our efforts to help others, and balancing our rewards between personal use and sharing with less fortunate people. This parable challenges us to close this chasm altogether.

How often have we heard someone say to finish strong? Parents tell their children to finish the school year strong. Coaches push their athletes to gut it out and make a final push to the end. Play until the clock reads 0:00. Every game and every story has an end.

The world puts much emphasis on coming in first place, whether it is being the top student, the winner of *The Voice*, the MVP of the Super Bowl, the Olympic gold medal winner, or the executive of the year. We view winning as the ultimate achievement and strive hard to achieve the prize. It's an admirable goal, and our efforts to reach that dream provide benefits beyond any institutional education or training we undertake.

But what happens when we don't win, reach our highest expectations, or achieve our dream? How do parents communicate with their children when they don't win the spelling bee, become the star athlete or top singer, or achieve baccalaureate honors? How do we explain a championship game loss affected by a referee's incorrect call that changed the outcome? How do we process the repeated failures in our attempts to secure financial security through our chosen career path?

We don't have to finish first in any of life's challenges. There is no need to fret if we don't win our race or reach our desired pinnacle. We don't need to panic or despair when things don't go our way. We don't need to experience those feelings of "I'm not good enough" when we don't achieve our goals.

But we do need to keep fighting, push forward, and do our best. It's not about finishing in first place; it's about finishing strong and becoming a better person after we have gone through a challenge. After the failure. After the disappointment. After the hardship. Commit to finishing the race, regardless of its difficulty.

I don't believe God cares about, nor is he interested in, what we have accumulated or own. But he does care what owns us. Ultimately, it won't matter if we have trophies, accolades, or plaques hanging on the wall. He won't measure us by our worldly accomplishments or conquests. He doesn't look at us with the idea that we aren't good enough when we don't accomplish our goals or surpass the competition. What he cares about is that we do our absolute best. When we do, he sees the value we bring to the world that we don't see in ourselves.

Our victory comes from trusting in God and fighting to the end, doing God's will to our very last breath, and finishing the race—that will be our victory. A successful life does not require coming in first, second, or third place, or placing at all, for that matter. Don't run life's race to place; instead, run life's race to finish. Finish what you started to the best of your ability—to the very end.

GOD HAD A DIFFERENT PLAN FOR ME. I COULD HAVE HAD A PLAN for every letter of the alphabet, and none of them would have been better than his plan for me. It took decades of time and debacles for me to understand this, to embrace it, and to realize that God was looking out for my best interest behind the scenes. I am so grateful he gave me the time to learn through life's difficulties, to understand what matters most, and to share his message with others.

He has a plan for you too, and he's working on it right now as you read, consider, react, and change. Some of you carry depression and wounds from hurt. Some live in broken marriages and damaged relationships. Others battle addictions or diseases and have mental or physical scars. A lot of you have leathered skin from life's blistering consequences. Many struggle with a weak or often lost faith.

Look for those things of value that will help you understand you are good enough. There is value rooted deeply within every one of you—a uniqueness, something special that makes you who you are—that can be used to develop, mold, and stir you to be the person you wish to become and that creates more value with every battle you face. It took me a while to understand my self-worth wasn't tied to batting averages or business profits. Instead, my self-worth was connected to faith, family, and friends. Only you can determine yours.

Know who you are and where you came from. Decide what you stand for. Discover the spirit within you that moves you in a heavenly direction. Work hard to prepare yourself for the opportunities and challenges ahead of you.

If things don't go as planned, own it. Be accountable for what has happened and how you will change. Don't go at it alone. Many people can help you. Accept their generosity and return it with compassion to others in need.

Care for people constantly. Trust your instincts because nobody knows better about the circumstances you face. Be kind to others. Speak gently and softly as you influence them in their lives. Share your experience and wisdom, inspiring people never to give up. Lead them to a better pathway, with a view of heaven, setting your minds on things above instead of those in this world.

Doing this will provide *lasting impacts* to you and for those you serve—far beyond what you could imagine. They will help you cross your finish line.

Acknowledgments

In crafting this manuscript, I am deeply humbled and grateful for the extraordinary people who have been my guiding lights, compass points, and sources of inspiration in my life.

First and foremost, my wife Lindy, the cornerstone of my life, has been with me through all my endeavors, including this remarkable writing journey. Her unwavering love and steadfast support have been uplifting, making every challenge seem conquerable.

To my daughters, Brooke and Jamie, who fill my life with endless joy and who have unknowingly been my greatest teachers, thank you for the love and light you bring into my life.

My beloved parents and in-laws who instilled in me a blend of wisdom, faith, and love, which grounds me each day. My siblings, my companions in laughter and tears, and my lifelong allies.

The preachers, who shared their spiritual wisdom and planted the seeds of faith within my soul, and the teachers, who nurtured my mind with knowledge on the path of understanding.

To the coaches and bosses who saw potential in me, even when I doubted myself, your belief in my abilities was the catalyst for my growth and success. Your guidance, mentorship, and unrelenting push for excellence have shaped the person I am today.

To my close friends and teammates, who have shared in my victories and defeats, you have been an inspiration throughout my journey, and your camaraderie has been priceless.

I would like to express my heartfelt gratitude to the dedicated team at Luminare Press for their invaluable feedback in making this book a reality for me.

All of you have said or done something that stirred my spirit and shaped me into the person I am today. Thank you for being the guiding stars in my life.

Acknowledgments

As I reflect on this incredible support system, I am reminded of the profound responsibility we bear—passing the torch of encouragement and influence to others, in the same way it was extended to us. May this book, born from the depths of our collective experiences, be a beacon of light for those seeking inspiration and spiritual guidance, just as it was for me.

Together, we can inspire those who follow in our footsteps. Together, we can make lasting impacts on their lives.

About the Author

BOBBY KOCOL has a comprehensive business background as a former CEO, CFO, and CPA, dealing in multibillion-dollar transactions. He has an MBA, served on the board of directors for numerous companies, held an advisory role in college programs to assist business students, and taught graduate-level courses. He has guided companies, employees, students, and athletes in mastering the essential disciplines for successful careers while enriching their personal lives. His passion to excel has been a driving force in his life.

Bobby has been a keynote speaker, delivering corporate messages across the globe through myriad conferences, sales meetings, Wall Street financial institutions, Fortune 500 corporations, and media outlets. He was recognized by *Colorado Business Magazine* (*Colorado Biz*) as an outstanding business leader, published with the Juran Institute, and has been a featured corporate speaker on Sky Radio with United and American Airlines.

He was drafted three times to play professional baseball, and at Mississippi State, he was an Academic All-American in baseball, a team captain, and the Most Valuable Player of his nationally ranked team who participated in the prestigious College World Series.

Bobby is an avid student of the Bible and the interpretations of Greek language. He enjoys delivering spiritual lessons with practical applications using his experiences and faith journey to captivate his listeners. In *Diamonds, Deals, and Divine Guidance*, he offers tools to help readers choose a path of passion, ambition, and unwavering faith that can help conquer self-doubt, unlock boundless peace and fulfillment, and create lasting impacts in the lives of others. For more about the author and updates on his book, visit **www.bobbykocol.com**.

Endnotes

1. Joe Falls, "Lolich a Lollapaluza," *The Detroit Free Press,* April 9, 1964, https://www.newspapers.com/clip/38738913/joe_falls_lolich_a_lollapaluza/.
2. Jerry Green, "Workhorse Lolich could always be counted on to finish what he started," *The Detroit News.* Originally printed March 31, 1997.
3. Dick Gordon, "White Sox Persist In Trying To Sign Titan Centerfielder," *The Florida Today,* January, 1977.
4. W.E. Vine, *Vine's Complete Expository Dictionary* (Thomas Nelson Publishers), 581.
5. Robert Young, *Young's Analytical Concordance to the Bible* (Hendrickson Publishers), 902.
6. Jeremiah 29:11, 13.
7. Andrew Luttrell (Ph.D.), "Why Persuasion Is Personal: The Neuroscience of Influence," *Psychology Today,* June 20, 2020, https://www.psychologytoday.com/us/blog/difference-opinion/202006/why-persuasion-is-personal-the-neuroscience-influence.
8. Bronnie Ware, *The Top Five Regrets of the Dying,* Hay House Inc., 2019.
9. William M. Bulkeley, "Storage Technology Faces Harsh Critics Amid Missteps," *The Wall Street Journal,* May 11, 1999.
10. Ibid.
11. Stephen Keating, "Iridian Gripes Publicly," *The Wall Street Journal,* September 21, 1999.
12. Kris Hudson, "StorageTek Sees Low Earnings," *Boulder Daily Camera,* October 14, 1999.
13. Joseph Pereira, "Storage Technology to Consider Sale of Company," *The Wall Street Journal,* October 18, 1999.
14. Ibid.
15. Proverbs 3:5-6 (NASB).
16. 2 Samuel 14:14a (NLT).
17. 2 Samuel 14:14b (NLT).

18. John Accola, "StorageTek takes beating in trading," *Denver Rocky Mountain News*, February 4, 2000.
19. Andrew Backover, "StorageTek to jettison 1 in 5 jobs," *The Denver Post*, October 29, 1999.
20. 1 Corinthians 10:13.
21. W.E. Vine, *Vine's Complete Expository Dictionary* (Thomas Nelson Publishers), 206.
22. Kris Hudson, "StorageTek on a profitable role," *Denver Rocky Mountain News*, August 1, 2000.
23. Ibid.
24. Andy Vuong, "StorageTek rises above 1999 woes," *The Denver Post*, October 14, 2001.
25. Luke 17:30-32.
26. Genesis 19:26.
27. Luke 22:61.
28. William Barclay, *The Daily Study Bible Series, Gospel of John Volume 2 Revised Edition* (Westminster John Knox Press), 271.
29. Federal Trade Commission, "New Data Shows FTC Received 2.8 Million Fraud Reports from Consumers in 2021," February 22, 2022, https://www.ftc.gov/news-events/news/press-releases/2022/02/new-data-shows-ftc-received-28-million-fraud-reports-consumers-2021-0.
30. Eugene Bekker, "What Are Your Odds of Getting Your Identity Stolen?," *Identity and Privacy*, April 15, 2021, https://www.identityforce.com/blog/identity-theft-odds-identity-theft-statistics.
31. Goodreads, "*Stephen R. Covey Quotable Quote*," https://www.goodreads.com/quotes/591733-we-hear-a-lot-about-identity-theft-when-someone-takes (accessed October, 2023).
32. Augustine, "Quote by Augustine," *Bible Portal*, https://bibleportal.com/bible-quote/in-order-to-discover-the-character-of-people-we-have-only-to-observe-what-they-love.
33. Exodus 3:11.
34. Exodus 3:14.
35. 1 Corinthians 15:8-9.
36. Biblesoft, Inc., *THAYER'S GREEK LEXICON*, Electronic Database, 2011, https://biblehub.com/greek/1626.htm#:~:text=ektroma.

37. John 6:48.
38. John 8:12.
39. John 11:25.
40. John 14:6.
41. John 15:5.
42. John 19:22.
43. Hebrews 13:8.
44. Leading Motivational Speakers, "How Much Do Celebrity Speakers Cost?" March 6, 2020, https://leadingmotivationalspeakers.com/celebrity-speakers-cost.
45. Joe Walsh, "Yellen Earned $7.2 Million In Speaking Fees Over Last Two Years," *Forbes,* January 1, 2021, forbes.com/sites/joewalsh/2021/01/01/yellen-earned-72-million-in-speaking-fees-over-last-two-years/?sh=6b11cca626f9.
46. Proverbs 16:2 (NAS).
47. Robert Young, *Young's Analytical Concordance to the Bible* (Hendrickson Publishers), 925.
48. Ibid.
49. Psalms 51:10 (ASV).
50. William Barclay, *The Daily Study Bible Series, Gospel of Matthew* (Westminster John Knox Press), 107.
51. 1 Corinthians 4:5 (NAS).
52. W.E. Vine, *Vine's Complete Expository Dictionary* (Thomas Nelson Publishers), 297.
53. Acts 17:26.
54. Matthew 5:6.
55. Hebrews 11:7 (NKJV).
56. W.E. Vine, *Vine's Complete Expository Dictionary* (Thomas Nelson Publishers), 230.
57. William Barclay, *The Daily Study Bible Series, Gospel of Luke Revised Edition* (Westminster John Knox Press), 165.
58. 2 Corinthians 5:14 (NAS).
59. W.E. Vine, *Vine's Complete Expository Dictionary* (Thomas Nelson Publishers), 124.

Endnotes

60. AZ Quotes, *"Fundamental Quotes,"* https://www.azquotes.com/quotes/topics/fundamentals.html (accessed October, 2023).
61. Quote Fancy, *"Lou Holtz Quotes,"* https://quotefancy.com/quote/854275/Lou-Holtz-Build-your-empire-on-the-firm-foundation-of-the-fundamentals (accessed October, 2023).
62. AZ Quotes, *"Fundamental Quotes,"* https://www.azquotes.com/quotes/topics/fundamentals.html (accessed October, 2023).
63. Little League Baseball, Incorporated, "2022 Little League Competitors," Wikipedia, https://en.wikipedia.org/wiki/Little_League_Baseball.
64. Helen Armitage, *"American Idol's* Current Age Limit for Contestants," *Screenrant,* May 13, 2021, https://screenrant.com/american-idol-show-age-limit/.
65. Macrotrends, "IBM: Number of Employees 2010-2023," https://macrotrends.net/stocks/charts/ibm/ibm/number-of-employees.
66. Amos 4:12.
67. Matthew 3:3.
68. 2 Timothy 2:21.
69. Salynn Boyles, "Want to Sleep Better? Make Your Bed," *CNY homepage,* Updated January 25, 2012, https://www.cnyhomepage.com/news/want-to-sleep-better-make-your-bed/.
70. James 1:2-3 (NAS).
71. W.E. Vine, *Vine's Complete Expository Dictionary* (Thomas Nelson Publishers), 512.
72. Romans 3:23.
73. W.E. Vine, *Vine's Complete Expository Dictionary* (Thomas Nelson Publishers), 83.
74. Dr. Henry Cloud & Dr. John Townsend, *Boundaries* (Zondervan), 30.
75. W.E. Vine, *Vine's Complete Expository Dictionary* (Thomas Nelson Publishers), 83.
76. Dr. Henry Cloud & Dr. John Townsend, *Boundaries* (Zondervan), 31.
77. Ibid.
78. W.E. Vine, *Vine's Complete Expository Dictionary* (Thomas Nelson Publishers), 530.
79. 2 Corinthians 5:10.
80. Luke 17:10 (NKJV).

81. J.E. Bates, *The Good Corn and Other Stories* (Longman).
82. *Star Trek II: The Wrath of Khan,* (directed by Nicholas Meyer), Paramount Pictures, 1982.
83. Matthew 20:30.
84. Robert Young, *Young's Analytical Concordance to the Bible* (Hendrickson Publishers), 655.
85. Matthew 20:34.
86. W.E. Vine, *Vine's Complete Expository Dictionary* (Thomas Nelson Publishers), 116.
87. Brainy Quote, *Glennon Doyle Melton Quotes,* https://www.brainyquote.com/quotes/glennon_doyle_melton_899011#:~:text=Compassion%20does%20not%20just%20happen.%20Pity%20does%2C%20but,love%20is%20more%20important%20than%20comfort%20or%20convenience (accessed October, 2023).
88. William Miller, "Death of a Genius," *Time Life Magazine,* May 2, 1955, 64, https://books.google.com/books?id=dlYEAAAAMBAJ&q=%22man+of+value%22#v=snippet&q=%22man%20of%20value%22&f=false.
89. Philippians 2:3-4.
90. W.E. Vine, *Vine's Complete Expository Dictionary* (Thomas Nelson Publishers), 64.
91. Deuteronomy 34:3.
92. Deuteronomy 21:17.
93. Parade, "55 of Dr. Martin Luther King, Jr.'s Most Inspiring Motivational Quotes," https://parade.com/252644/viannguyen/15-of-martin-luther-king-jr-s-most-inspiring-motivational-quotes/, May, 22, 2023.
94. W.E. Vine, *Vine's Complete Expository Dictionary* (Thomas Nelson Publishers), 382.
95. Ibid.
96. John 21:15-19.
97. John 15:13.
98. *Top Gun: Maverick,* (directed by Joseph Kosinski), Paramount Pictures, 2022.
99. Michale Roub, "Mark Cuban was right – "Perfection is the enemy of success," *Inflection 360,* September 3, 2018, https://inflection360.

ENDNOTES

com/mark-cuban-was-right-perfection-is-the-enemy-of-success/.

100. Rachael Ajmera, MS, RD (Medically reviewed by Nancy Hammond, M.D.), "What is the Hippocampus?," *Medical News Today,* Updated February 17, 2023, https://www.medicalnewstoday.com/articles/313295.

101. Ibid.

102. Bahar Gholipour, "Why Can't We Remember Our Dreams?," *Live Science,* May 31, 2018, https://www.livescience.com/62703-why-we-forget-dreams-quickly.html.

103. Ibid.

104. John 20:29.

105. Proverbs 3:5-6.

106. Sue Miley, "Trust: Mother Teresa's Prayer for the Clinger," *Crossroads Professional Counseling,* May 18, 2010, https://crossroadcounselor.com/christian-living/trust-mother-teresas-prayer-for-the-clinger/.

107. John 13:23.

108. John 20:5.

109. W.E. Vine, *Vine's Complete Expository Dictionary* (Thomas Nelson Publishers), 556-557.

110. John 20:6-7 (NKJV).

111. W.E. Vine, *Vine's Complete Expository Dictionary* (Thomas Nelson Publishers), 557.

112. John 20:8 (NKJV).

113. W.E. Vine, *Vine's Complete Expository Dictionary* (Thomas Nelson Publishers), 557.

114. Goodreads, *"George Bernard Shaw Quotable Quote,"* https://www.goodreads.com/quotes/178425-the-single-biggest-problem-in-communication-is-the-illusion-that (accessed October, 2023).

115. Proverbs 12:18.

116. Joseph Hartropp, "Christians aren't reading the Bible. Why not, and what can we do about it?" *Christian Today,* April 27, 2017, https://www.christiantoday.com/article/christians-arent-reading-the-bible-why-not-and-what-can-we-do-about-it/108024.htm.

117. Salman Aslam, "80+ Facebook Statistics You Need to Know in 2023," *Omnicore,* March 3, 2023, https://www.omnicoreagency.com/Facebook-statistics/.

118. Margot Whitney, "39 Twitter Statistics Marketers Need to Know in 2022,"*(Wordstream,* Updated August 11, 2023, https://www.wordstream.com/blog/ws/2020/04/14/twitter-statistics.
119. James 1:19.
120. Proverbs 15:1.
121. Isaiah 53:3-11.
122. Luke 23:3 (NKJV).
123. John 19:8-11 (NKJV).
124. John 18:20.
125. Kites and Roses, *31+ Influence Quotes about Persuasion and Leadership,* https://kitesandroses.com/influence-quotes/ (accessed October, 2023).
126. 2 Timothy 4:11.
127. John C. Maxwell, *The 21 Most Powerful Minutes in a Leader's Day,* (Nashville: Thomas Nelson Publishers, 2000), 155.
128. The John Maxwell Company, *Borrowing Experience,* October 6, 2011, https://www.johnmaxwell.com/blog/borrowing-experience/.
129. Numbers 13:30 (NKJV).
130. Proverbs 3:5-6.
131. Ana Swanson, "You might be among the world's richest people and not realize it," *The Washington Post,* January 21, 2016, https://www.washingtonpost.com/news/wonk/wp/2016/01/21/you-might-be-among-the-richest-people-in-the-world-and-not-realize-it/.

www.ingramcontent.com/pod-product-compliance
Lightning Source LLC
LaVergne TN
LVHW010157070526
838199LV00062B/4393